W9-ASJ-683

A12900 764725

ILLINOIS CENTRAL COLLEGE
P94.5.A372U578 1994
STACKS
Ceramic uncles & celluloid mammies

A12900 764725

WITHDRAWN

Ceramic
Uncles &
Celluloid
Mammies

.

Black Images and Their Influence on Culture

Patricia A. Turner

Ceramic Uncles & Celluloid Mammies

Patricia A. Turner

ANCHOR BOOKS
New York London Toronto
Sydney Auckland

I.C.C. LIBRARY

Ceramic Uncles & Celluloid Mammies

*Black Images and Their
Influence on Culture*

85280

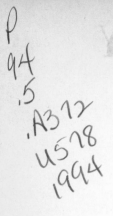

P
94
.5
.A372
U578
1994

AN ANCHOR BOOK
PUBLISHED BY DOUBLEDAY
a division of Bantam Doubleday Dell Publishing Group, Inc.
1540 Broadway, New York, New York 10036

ANCHOR BOOKS, DOUBLEDAY, and the portrayal of an anchor
are trademarks of Doubleday, a division of
Bantam Doubleday Dell Publishing Group, Inc.

Book Design by Gretchen Achilles

Library of Congress Cataloging-in-Publication Data

Turner, Patricia A.
    Ceramic uncles & celluloid mammies : black images and their
influence on culture / Patricia A. Turner.
        p.   cm.
    Includes index.
    1. Afro-Americans in mass media—United States. 2. Popular
culture—United States—History.   I. Title.   II. Title: Ceramic
uncles and celluloid mammies.
P94.5.A372U578   1994
302.23′089′96073—dc20   93-38542
                                                              CIP

ISBN 0-385-46784-2
Copyright © 1994 by Patricia A. Turner
All Rights Reserved
Printed in the United States of America
September 1994

First Edition

10 9 8 7 6 5 4 3 2 1

To Kevin and Daniel

Contents

Acknowledgments

I am grateful for the financial support I received for early phases of this research from the Trotter Institute for the Study of Black Culture at the University of Massachusetts—Boston. A U.C. Davis Faculty Development Award granted by the Office of the Provost under the direction of Carol Tomlinson-Keasey enabled me to finish the manuscript. I would also like to thank the U.C. Davis Illustrations Services staff, in particular photographer Steve Stevenson, for doing such a wonderful job with the photographs.

I would like to thank the many archivists who have worked in the U.C. Berkeley Folklore Archive during the past two decades. The Archive's founder, Alan Dundes, first began needling me to write this book in 1981. Throughout the years he has offered much support and enthusiasm.

I am indebted to dozens of students, colleagues, and friends who shared artifacts and insights with me. I am particularly grateful to Janette Faulkner and Marlon Riggs whose comments helped me sharpen my theories about contemptible collectibles.

Lively discussions with my friend and colleague Mary Helen Washington also contributed to the shape of several of the essays in this book. She also introduced me to literary agent Carol Mann who helped me find my way to Anchor Books and the capable editorial hands of Charlie Conrad and his assistant, Jon Furay.

Carol Beck, Aklil Bekele, Gladys Bell, Eva Hendricks and Linda Kluz performed sundry clerical tasks with efficiency and good humor.

Finally, I would like to thank my husband, Kevin Smith, and our young son, Daniel Turner Smith, for knowing when I needed to be left alone and when I needed to take a break.

Preliminary research on Chapter 1, originally titled "Safety in Stereotypes: A Study of Antiblack Material Blason Populaire," appeared in *International Folklore Review* 5 (1987): 28–34 © 1987 New Abbey Publications; an earlier version of Chapter 2 "Alligator Bait" appeared in *International Folklore Review* 7 (1989): 75–79 © 1989 New Abbey Publications; a briefer version of Chapter 6 "Everything Is *Not* Satisfactual" appeared in the *Trotter Institute Review* (Winter 1987): 16–17; a different version of Chapter 8 under the title "Blacks in Disguise" appeared in the *Trotter Institute Review* (Summer 1987): 19–20; a different version of Chapter 9 under the title "The Good Old Days" appeared in the *Trotter Institute Review* (Fall 1987): 21–22; Chapter 10 combines "Tainted Glory: Truth and Fiction in Contemporary Hollywood" *Trotter Institute Review* (Spring 1990): 5–9 and "A Kinder, Gentler FBI" *Trotter Institute Review* (Spring 1990): 19–20; a different version of Chapter 12 appeared as "From Homer to Hoke: A Small Step for African-American Mankind" in the *Journal of Negro Education* 60 (Summer Yearbook 1991): 342–353 © 1991 Howard University.

Introduction

Did I ever tell you the one . . . the "nigger ain't worth shit" story? Thousands know it—it was all over black Washington, D.C. Well, let's see. There was this show . . . *Pick Temple's Ranch,* a children's show that came on about five o'clock. Oh, I remember everyone callin' around. This was the early sixties and you never saw a black face on television, not one that wasn't cleanin' up or lookin' after the whites or something. This is early integration—you know, extremely cautious. It was the usual procedure—introduce a few here and there. Now Pick Temple had had a few on by this time. Anyway, there was this little boy . . . must have been four. He was a confident, precocious little boy. My God, I'll die with this story in my mind. It's so right and cruel at the same time. It really gets the black psyche or something. Anyway, the . . . you know I was going to say "the white man, the man." Pick Temple asks this boy, "What do you want to be when you grow up?" So this little boy looks up at him all confident and everything. Well, he speaks up and says, "A <u>WHITE MAN</u>"—you know, as if he'd given it a lot of thought, as if a white man was an occupation like a fireman. If I were writing down this story I would write down <u>WHITE MAN</u> underlined, capitalized. So Pick Temple thinks there for a minute and finally says, "Why a white man?" He should have stopped right there . . . you know, quit while he was ahead. Well, the boy speaks up in a tone as if nothing's unusual. " 'Cause my momma says a nigger ain't worth shit." The TV went black right then and there and phones rang all over black Washington. I think the whites were shocked, though about the profanity, not the insight. Y'all·weren't too bright in those days. I was just thinking that boy must be grown now . . . I wonder what he's like? Someone should track him down.

Textured Recollections

The above text is filed in the Afro-American Legend folder in the U.C. Berkeley Folklore Archive. The Archive contains over a million individual folklore texts—proverbs, riddles, folktales, jokes, songs, myths, etc.—collected and critiqued by students enrolled in the folklore courses that have been offered on the campus for several decades. For folklorists, the steel-gray filing cabinets are like the wooden trunks of fabric from which quilters ferret out the sundry pieces with which to make a quilt. Sometimes a quilter's hands and eyes will settle on a particularly rich, resilient bolt of fabric. At once strong and lovely, the bolt will inspire the design of the quilt and feed the core fabric around which complementary scraps are embellished. When I found the text above, I knew my hands and eyes had discovered just such a bolt. The student-collector had taken care to capture his informant's voice. He squashed any impulse to edit out the asides and interruptions—what folklorists call oral literary criticism—and let the speaker comment on the story as it unfolded. As a result, we feel as though we can hear the narrator as he ponders the ramifications of his recollection.

The story itself—part legend, part personal experience narrative —reveals much about the relationship between African Americans and popular culture. The narrator's assessment of the absence of blacks on television in the 1960s rings true to all of us who recall that era. It is not an idle, idiosyncratic impression. In television, as well as other vehicles of popular culture, images of African Americans have been limited and are often one-dimensional. As the informant points out, television presented blacks in relation to whites, "cleanin' up or lookin' after them." To the narrator and, if his recollection is accurate, the rest of black Washington, the sight of a black four-year-old boy on *Pick Temple's Ranch* was a special occasion. It wouldn't surprise me if the phones were ringing *before* the boy made his startling revelation. In those days, African-American faces on television were so rare that we were all anxious that our friends and relatives not miss an opportunity to see one of us on the screen.

There is much to ponder from the inferred dialogue between the little boy and his mother. What forces moved her to the conviction that "niggers ain't worth shit"? How did she come to internalize the contempt that so many members of the dominant culture had at that time? How often and in how many ways did she share this notion with her son? The narrator tells us that the little boy was "confident" and "precocious." The intrepid youngster obviously experienced no stage fright. He very matter-of-factly shared his unorthodox ambition with Pick Temple. At the age of four or thereabouts, he had resolved to shed his skin and to distance himself from his family and friends. He had decided that when he grew up, he wanted to look like Pick Temple.

I should note here that I have made no attempt to confirm the "facts" of this story. In fact, it bears a striking resemblance to one that is often told about *The Art Linkletter Show.* What is important is that a man has fashioned the story this way; it has imposed itself into this individual's thoughts in this form. Because it is "right and cruel," the narrator tells us that he'll "die with this story in my mind." To me, these are the stories worth contemplating and documenting. Frankly, I don't think too many people will die with a short story by Ralph Ellison or a novel by Toni Morrison on their minds. Rather, the stories that speak to us, that become a part of us, that shape the way we work and play in the world are those that embody the personal truths of our lives.

Personal truths frequently translate into collective truths that echo the sentiments of a whole community. In 1992 I appeared as a commentator in *Color Adjustment,* a documentary about the images of African Americans in prime-time television. Reflecting back on my childhood in the 1950s and 1960s, I said semifacetiously that while my mother loathed making long distance phone calls, even when there was a death in the family, she would call long distance to share news that a "Negro" was scheduled to appear on a television program. African Americans who have seen *Color Adjustment* are forever saying to me that my comments corroborate their personal recollections of the first decade of television. Our images were few and far between, and we hungered for more of them. My parents never told me "a nigger ain't worth shit." But in subtle ways they did communicate a sense of fractured possibility and a near resignation to second-class citizenship. These anecdotes and recollections really can "get at the black psyche or something."

Subtle shifts in the modes of black/white communications are embedded in the text of the Pick Temple anecdote. The narrator catches himself before he indulges in the African-American tendency to reduce all whites into one monolithic, imagined "white man." Poor Pick Temple almost becomes every(white)man. But the host's decision to follow up on the boy's statement demonstrates his ignorance of black attitudes about whites. On a deeper level, the storytelling session itself suggests that black/white communications have improved. After all, the black narrator seems quite willing to share the story with the white folklore collector. The "y'all weren't too bright in those days" certainly indicates that a jocular warmth and familiarity has developed between the African-American informant and the white collector.

From Scraps to Quilts

One of my favorite quilts was made by a group of Southern African-American women. They used over a dozen different fabrics. The unmistakable red, white, and blue scraps of a cotton Confederate flag appear in various spaces on the quilt. Scraps of a blue polyester fabric inscribed with chain-linklike images nestle against it in adjacent spaces. I often fantasize about these black women, sitting together cutting up the flag that symbolized the goals of their oppressors and piecing it together with fabric taken from their daughters' nightgowns, their husbands' pants, their discarded pillowcases. And then someone from the quilting bee must have taken it home and slept under it. From the numerous stains and frazzled threads, it seems likely that people have done more than keep warm under it. They made love on, gave birth on, and vomited on a quilt containing a desecrated Confederate flag. To my mind, no one has ever made better use of the stars and bars.

For the most part, the raw material of this book is not *black* folklore or *black* popular culture. The material objects, verbal folklore, and media portrayals are the products of the white imagination. The ceramic uncle cookie jars, cast-iron jolly nigger piggy banks, ethnic slurs, caricatured performances, and one-dimensional media portrayals discussed in the chapters that follow are comparable to the Confederate flag carved up by the good black ladies of the South. Exemplifying the ill will, oppression, and domination of blacks by whites, the merchants of popular culture have used these icons to shackle our psyches as deftly as enslavers once used real chains to shackle our bodies.

My research suggests that at least since the seventeenth century— since contact between sub-Saharan Africans and Englishmen was regularized—the images of blacks have been distorted in mainstream popular culture, but this book focuses on only the past 150 years. Since the creation of Uncle Tom, an ominous ideology has been passed from one generation to the next. Most of the prior research in this topic has focused on the fairly obvious kinds of caricatures that are now discernible to any "politically correct" viewer. Few individuals would debate the racist vision implicit in D. W. Griffith's controversial masterpiece *The Birth of a Nation*. What may be more dangerous, however, than blatant caricatures are the subtle distortions that have emerged and continue to dominate all genres of popular culture. Most of the chapters in this book will focus on examples not normally identified as antiblack ones.

Each chapter is informed by my contemplations of some aspect of the "Niggers Ain't Worth Shit" story. I lean on it the way a quilter relies on a multihued, intricately textured, and tightly woven bolt of fabric to connect ostensibly disparate scraps of material. I discovered it early in my career as a folklorist and it, along with a hundred other discoveries, convinced me, then and now, that the most illuminating understandings of an individual's or a community's worldview come from an understanding of the traditional lore they share.

In addition to foraging through the Folklore Archives, I have spent a great deal of my time during the past dozen or so years perusing antique and collectibles fairs, prowling the card tables of garage sales, going to the movies, reading popular magazines, and watching television. Since I teach classes on folk and popular culture, these are not leisure-time activities for me. They enable me to incorporate ostensibly mundane and ordinary mass-produced culture into the academic arena. Because I have been focusing on such an eclectic range of media, the theoretical underpinnings of my arguments are similarly diverse. I found Freudian-based analysis a provocative tool for putting together a theory to explain why I kept finding openmouthed alligators pursuing blacks in a wide range of collectibles. Elsewhere, I compare the fundamental narrative structures of two movies in order to posit a hypothesis about the tenacity of antiblack stereotypes.

The following chapters link my contemplations of cookie jars, political jokes, movies, and the like with the larger social and political trends that influence overall attitudes about blacks. Those who maintain that ours is a color-blind society have had to confront several disturbing images in the past couple of years. The initial success with which white retailer Charles Stuart convinced the nation that a black assailant had brutally killed his wife and the infant she was carrying in her womb—the potency that the Willie Horton image developed during the 1988 presidential campaign—the brutal beating of Rodney King by Los Angeles policemen—the Milwaukee police department's refusal to take seriously the complaints of white serial killer Jeffrey Dahmer's black neighbors. These and other recent confrontations reflect the tenacity of negative stereotypes about black men and women. Using the images of blacks prevalent in popular culture, I establish possible connections between the finite and often distorted range of depictions of blacks in popular culture to the very real treatment that they receive in contemporary society. Why didn't the Boston police investigate the possibility that Charles Stuart had killed his wife? What did the L.A. policemen see as they slammed their batons into Rodney King's body? Why did the image of Willie Horton turn voters away from Michael Dukakis? Why did the Milwaukee policemen discredit the allegations voiced by Dahmer's black neighbors? When confronted with blacks in the real world do whites rely upon expectations generated by the reel world? If so, then the racial tension that continues to mark the American landscape will persist.

1

Insidious
Iconography

Four times a year the San Mateo County Expo in northern California is taken over by a mammoth antique and collectibles fair. Thousands of square feet become transformed into an antique lover's mecca. A walk through this or any of the other hundreds of antique and collectibles extravaganzas held each year from coast to coast guarantees nostalgia buffs a stroll down the memory lane of his or her choice. From 150-year-old Shaker furniture to two-year-old Happy Meals memorabilia, the two-day event attended by 800 dealers has something old or not so old for every taste and price range. Fully restored, shiny, polished antique vehicles grace the halls. Multicolored jukeboxes already programmed with 1940s, 1950s, or 1960s music serenade the potential buyers. Any dish that has ever been used in any kitchen at any time is bound to be found among the crystal, porcelain, melmac, and stoneware place settings that are artfully arranged on perfectly appointed tables throughout. The success of the San Mateo Antique and Collectors Fair and like events stands as proof of a fascination and near obsession that many Americans have with the physical artifacts of our past.

Since at least 1979 (the first year I attended the fair), dealers have included on their tables a wide assortment of objects that are inscribed with a black face and/or body. Peeping from amid a cookie jar dealer's collection of colorful, plump, ceramic animals or brightly glazed quaint structures will be a toothsome, overweight mammy or a neatly uniformed pappy cookie jar. Yellowed pages of once-popular rags such as "Old Nigger Joe" or "My Dark Virginny Gal" are crammed into the countless cardboard boxes of sheet music. Golliwogs, pickaninnies, and the occasional ebony-toned bisque doll-baby are posed on the shelves of the doll collectors.

The visual impact of these black-faced objects tends to be fairly mild. Surrounded by dozens of other colorful quaint salt-and-pepper shakers, the pairs of bright-eyed, round-faced mammy and pappy shakers are unlikely to evoke more than bemused curiosity. However, in the last fifteen years more and more vendors have begun to specialize in any and all artifacts that reflect a black image. Thus it is possible to find booths that are taken over by all sorts of black objects. In spite of their many formal differences, cast-iron banks, tin cars, tablecloths, and cereal advertisements are clustered together because of their content, because they are inscribed with blackness. The same pair of black-faced salt-and-pepper shakers that seemed like harmless curios within the context of other condiment containers assumes an entirely different meaning when surrounded by a battalion of other physical objects all inhabited by smiling black faces.

In San Mateo and in other places, vendors who specialize in these items have had to confront angry passersby who are disturbed by the mostly caricatured black images contained in such displays. The black-faced carriage boy hitching posts that stand as sentinels in front of a posh boutique in Marin County's lily-white community of Tiburon have provoked a series of encounters dating back at least to 1984. After visiting the community, a black woman wrote to the mayor to complain about the statues, saying "The townspeople of Tiburon delivered a message to me by their use of racism—the black tourist in Tiburon is not welcome there. . . . Please consider removing these atrocities or paint the faces white [a practice known as double-dipping]. . . . The joke or quaintness of these black models of an idyllic lifestyle is an insult to me."[1] The whole controversy was played out in *The Ark*, a weekly Tiburon newspaper. According to *The Ark*'s editor, the ensuing controversy was the most notable in the newspaper's history up until that point. One letter writer dismissed the African-American woman's complaint by asserting "Through our benevolence, her race has come a long way, baby, in our white society, but don't push it." The store owner stuck to his guns, and to his statues, and refused to remove them. After the controversy subsided, the statues were eventually painted white.

Several years later, in 1991, an even more pernicious display and exchange of letters in a small-town newspaper rattled tempers on the other side of the continent in New Hampshire. Instead of featuring lawn-boy statues outside of his store, proprietor Thomas Breen crowded his store window with assorted artifacts containing images of blacks. Although tourists, residents, town officials, and even a local minister have asked Breen to remove his racially charged window display, the fifty-three-year-old New Hampshire native has stead-fastly refused to do so. Breen claims to recognize the negativity im-plicit in this merchandise, but defends his windows by saying "I don't put it there to hurt anybody. . . . it's part of history. What if we had a book burning and destroyed all this stuff? No one would know it existed."[2] Nonetheless, Breen's commitment to displaying these po-tentially volatile artifacts stems much more from a capitalistic incli-nation to make money than from a desire to expose the racism of the past. He told a reporter for the *Boston Globe*, "The bottom line is that I make money off black Americana. Everything black sells."[3] Breen willingly acknowledged that in his basement workshop he took newly made reproductions of racist artifacts and "aged" them in order to increase the price at which he could sell them. With no apparent shame, he boasted about making his own black-faced wood carvings and cast-iron door stops.

Breen dates the emergence of a demand for what he refers to as black Americana to approximately 1981. This date matches those cited by others who chart the rise and fall of popularity of certain kinds of antiques and collectibles. Many experts agree that it was the publicity surrounding the large collection of African-American social worker Janette Faulkner that catapulted these kinds of objects from boxes in the back of junk stores to the windows of antique stores. Faulkner's fascination began in the 1960s when she began to visit antique stores with friends. The image of a sloppily dressed, poorly groomed, toothless black man inspired her to seek out other tangible artifacts of American racism. By the late 1970s she had amassed thousands of items. Although not an educator by profession, Faulkner was convinced that if handled correctly, these artifacts and informa-tion surrounding their creation would prove to be an invaluable tool with which teachers could demonstrate the enormous impact of racism in American history. After she displayed a sampling of her collection on NBC's *Today* show, interest in the icons spread. Sensing that more people would show an interest in these materials, antique and collectibles dealers actively sought the items and prices quickly escalated. Yet the academic community did not immediately share the commercial world's enthusiasm. Faulkner encountered roadblock after roadblock as she tried to get a publishing house interested in a book about her collection and a museum interested in displaying it. Finally, in 1982, the Berkeley Art Center raised the funds necessary to underwrite a display of several hundred items from Faulkner's collection. Eager to put the items in their proper context, the center worked with faculty and graduate students from the nearby University of California at Berkeley campus to ensure that the exhibition would be informative rather than exploitative.

Just as seeing several of the artifacts grouped together in a collectible case can trigger an enormous range of emotional responses, so did the month-long exhibit at the Berkeley Art Center. One visitor who could not get the images out of his mind was a fledgling young African-American independent filmmaker, Marlon Riggs. Riggs shared Faulkner's conviction that there was much to be learned from an intelligent look at the historical circumstances that generated these objects in the first place. Riggs decided to make a sixty-minute documentary film on the objects and other media that embodied similarly racist stereotypes. After surmounting numerous problems regarding funding and support for the project, in 1987 Riggs completed *Ethnic Notions*, a multi–award-winning documentary. As *Ethnic Notions* has become one of the most frequently purchased and rented educational films in America, Faulkner's dream to use these charged artifacts as tools with which we increase our understanding of the nature and evolution of racism has been partially realized.

Like any good documentary, *Ethnic Notions* raises at least as many questions as it answers. First of all, how precisely can these items be defined, and what nomenclature appropriately describes them? Who made them and why? Who sells them and why? Who buys them and why? Why is the demand for the objects great enough to support cottage industries devoted to their reproduction? What clues do their popularity offer to past and present race relations in this country and elsewhere in the world? How are these items different from authentic black folk art and genuine black fine art?

The first three chapters of this book tackle these questions. They focus on physical, tangible artifacts that embody a derogatory image of blacks. During the past two hundred years conspicuously racist images of blacks have adorned a wide range of print and three-dimensional objects. From cookie jars to oyster cans, from restaurant signs to greeting cards, black faces and bodies have been rendered in physical form in material culture.

History and classification are the goals of Chapter 1. Here I attempt to locate "contemptible collectibles" within the context of other material culture artifacts. Using the overall appearance of the black image contained in the objects, I assign them to categories. In particular, this chapter examines the ways in which the clothing worn by the blacks depicted in these artifacts establishes an insidious pattern—a pattern that reinforces a limited range of social and political possibilities for blacks. Gender, status, and occupational roles are clearly established by the finery ascribed to the black characters. Finally, Chapter 1 compares the depiction of blacks in material culture to their depiction in other genres of folk and fine art.

After identifying the categories that link the clothes worn by the blacks depicted, I move beyond the bodies themselves to the items frequently positioned with the characters. Several images recur frequently. Blacks are depicted eating the same foods over and over again. According to these images, blacks have an insatiable appetite for fried chicken and watermelon. When their hands are not wrapped around a juicy food, they are often confronted by alligators. Supposedly alligators possess an insatiable appetite for African Americans. Chapter 2 probes these appetites—those that are allegedly possessed *by* blacks and those that are attributed to other beings *for* blacks. Alligators play a prominent role in both black- and white-generated folklore in tales, legends, and jokes. By comparing and contrasting these two types of alligator lore, we can perhaps explain this seemingly morbid fascination with alligator/African-American couplings.

"Thank God those days are over and nobody makes those things anymore." This is a comment I have heard more times than I can recall. And unfortunately, I am forced to correct those who naively assume that these contemptible collectibles are vestiges of the past, unfortunate reminders of long-gone eras that preceded the post–civil rights era. Chapter 3 examines the current production or reproduction of these items by contemporary manufacturers. The most commonly rendered reproductions are those that feature African-American women. What does this fascination with overweight, jovial images of black women and sloppily attired pickaninnies happily ensconced in kitchens suggest about contemporary views of African Americans? What does the demand for reproductions of essentially racist material reveal about the contemporary state of relations between black and white Americans?

After more than a dozen years of collecting, classifying, analyzing, and teaching about contemptible collectibles. I sometimes forget that many people are unsettled and disturbed by them, particularly the first time they are exposed to a cluster of grinning ceramic black faces en masse. After my editor sent the first version of the book cover, I shared it with a number of friends and colleagues who urged me to coax him into commissioning something tamer and more innocuous. But any reader repulsed by the cover will be undone by material explored in the first three chapters. With this in mind, I forewarn the reader that the coarseness and crudeness of images and jokes may be unnerving. But as troubling as many of these images are, I think they must be confronted. Contemptible collectibles need to be added to the raw material from which we mine our studies of the complexities of race relations in America.

1

Contemptible Collectibles

Ann Landers's syndicated advice column frequently functions as a somewhat unsettling barometer of mainstream American folk belief and concern. In late 1982 Landers and her readers engaged in a heated debate about black-boy cast-iron lawn ornaments. Reader number one wanted to know if she should tell her neighbor how offensive she found the grinning little groom. Reader number two chastised Landers for not telling reader number one about George Washington's faithful eight-year-old slave, who froze to death while holding the general's horse's reins.[1] Defending her own family's possession of a similar statue, reader number three concluded her letter by asserting that "The black people who object to it (as they pass by in their Cadillacs) should be grateful for the progress they have made in this country." A decorative object, a heartwarming (albeit false) nugget of folk history, and an antiblack slur constitute the fodder for this exchange of letters containing a full range of clues about the dos and don'ts of racial stereotyping in the United States after the civil rights movement. This chapter focuses on objects like the seemingly innocuous three-dimensional icon that triggered the first letter. But as the subsequent letters so clearly reveal, the ways in which individuals interpret and find meaning in these objects is greatly influenced by standards established and perpetuated through other channels. As I

define, classify, and analyze the family of material objects from which
the lawn boy was born, I shall examine folklore and other modes of
discourse that project at times similar and at times very different
images of blacks.

The "faithful groom" is physically one of the largest and most
easily recognized artifacts within a range of underinvestigated, tangible objects that we can use to expand our understanding of the tenacity of racist stereotypes. These artifacts are the kitchenwares, advertising memorabilia, toys, and other material objects that include any
partial or complete picture of a black person. It is not surprising that
a faithful groom statue prompted the letter exchange because it is one
of the few items that lends itself to external display. Your neighbors
are much more likely to know if you have a black-boy hitching post
than if you have a mammy cookie jar. Determining the most accurate
nomenclature for this category of materials is problematic. Unfortunately, writers and collectors have contributed to this confusion about
the proper name for these objects. Antique dealer Dawn Reno entitled
her 1986 book on this subject *Collecting Black Americana*. The first
chapter is titled "Advertising," and it offers an overview of the companies that have crafted black images as their corporate trademarks;
for example, Aunt Jemima pancakes, Cream of Wheat cereal, and
Gold Dust washing powder. The second chapter of her book is titled
"Art," and it features paintings by renowned black painters such as
Henry Ossawa Tanner and Edward Mitchell Bannister. Douglas
Congdon-Martin's 1990 book is titled *Images in Black: 150 Years of
Black Collectibles.* On the cover of his book he juxtaposes an exquisite
oil painting of an attractive black woman above a picture of a smiling
broad-lipped Aunt Jemima–style condiment container. This capri-
cious grouping suggests that images painted, sculpted, or photographed by African-American fine artists can be deposited in the
same bank with distorted caricatures of blacks mass-produced by
white-owned companies. By using the terms black Americana and
black collectibles in their titles, Reno and Congdon-Martin are coding
blackness to mean both images *of* blacks and images *by* blacks. These
authors are not alone in their refusal to distinguish art blacks can be
proud of from the mass-produced schlock that distorts and degrades
us. Auctioneers, gallery owners, and museum curators regularly cluster together ironwork skillfully crafted by Louisianan artisans with
tobacco cans depicting toothless, sloppily attired black men.

The first three chapters of this book are about the schlock—the thick-lipped faces on cereal boxes, the sloppily dressed figures on sheet music, the half-naked children on postcards. They are about the ways in which even after the institution of slavery was over, American consumers found acceptable ways of buying and selling the souls of black folk. Writers, dealers, and other authorities who persist in calling these toys, ephemeral objects, kitchenware, and related items *black* cultural artifacts are wrong. With few exceptions, these items were made by and for white people. When the Milton Bradley Company manufactured and marketed the Jolly Darkie Target Game in 1890, they were counting on white consumers to purchase the game, the object of which was to score "bull's-eyes" by throwing a ball into the gaping mouth of a black male figure. Including the word black in any label for these items contributes to the erroneous impression that blacks were integral to the production or distribution process. Manufacturers eager to capitalize on the racism that has long permeated our society exploited distorted representations of blacks.

Like the other artifacts to be examined in these chapters, the faithful groom and the Jolly Darkie game are symbolically potent. Their superficial features (color, size, shape) are disparate; three-dimensional hitching posts and flat, cardboard games aren't ordinarily classified together. But the cast-iron statue, the cardboard game, and the myriad of other objects are linked by the range of messages they send. When reader number one saw the groom outside of her neighbor's home, she "read" potential trouble in it. Speculating that passersby would believe the groom's owners were racists, she may have been concerned about the potential contagious effect of the statue's proximity to her home. In other words, she didn't want to be considered a racist herself. These artifacts can all be identified in terms of what they symbolize—a recognizable racist or, more specifically, an antiblack component rooted in their unswerving depiction of distasteful characteristics. Although terms such as racist collectibles or antiblack artifacts would certainly be preferable to black memorabilia or black collectibles, they don't resonate in the way that a term I first heard in the early 1980s does. Ever since I heard someone refer to them as contemptible collectibles, that is the label that comes to my mind whenever I see them. They represent one of the most deplorable and least well documented impulses in American consumer history.

And as we shall see, this impulse is not as dormant as we would like to think.

Contemptible collectibles have not received the attention and scrutiny they deserve for several reasons. The civil rights movement increased the general population's awareness of African Americans' status as second-class citizens and resulted in a change in the common definitions of "racist." Whereas prior to the 1960s, many people didn't associate the possession of a faithful groom hitching post with racism, during and after the 1960s the underlying prejudice reflected in the ownership and production of such statues became apparent to a larger segment of the American population. Of course, the response was by no means universal. Some people put their faithful grooms in the back of the garage around the same time they stopped telling racist jokes. Others merely painted their grooms white. Then, of course, people like Ann Landers's reader number three still proudly display their grooms and probably shamelessly tell jokes such as:

Question: What do nine out of ten Cadillac owners say?
Answer: Dem sho' is fine cars.[2]

Along with the impetus to sequester any tangible symbol of racism, the academic study of contemptible collectibles was delayed by the fact that the scholarly analysis of mass-produced physical objects is a new and not completely accepted academic pursuit. Only a small portion of these items qualify as authentic African-American folk art (traditional art made by and for African Americans); most items were produced in bulk and sold in stores. Studying genuine folk art and fine arts traditions has always been a more acceptable enterprise. Post–civil rights movement interest in contemptible collectibles has been stimulated by an unlikely source: antique collectors. The publicity Janette Faulkner and other collectors have received has generated much scholarly interest in these materials.[3]

Contemptible collectibles exhibit only a partial menu of the extant antiblack stereotypes. The most popular icons are those that contain safe, nonthreatening servile depictions of blacks or those that imply that inherent ineptness and imbecility will prevent the race from earning social and political parity. This pattern can be seen by examining the clothes and facial expressions of the men, women, and children as they are rendered in the objects, as well as the objects and products with which they are consistently juxtaposed.

Patched Pickaninnies

> She was one of the blackest of her race; and her round, shining eyes, glittering as glass beads, moved with quick and restless glances over everything in the room. Her mouth half open with astonishment at the wonders of the new Mas'r's parlor, displayed a white and brilliant set of teeth. Her woolly hair was braided in sundry little tails, which stuck out in every direction. The expression of her face was an odd mixture of shrewdness and cunning, over which was oddly drawn, like a veil, an expression of the most doleful gravity and solemnity. She was dressed in a single filthy, ragged garment, made of bagging; and stood with her hands demurely folded in front of her. Altogether, there was something odd and goblin-like about her appearance,—something as Miss Ophelia afterwards said, "so heathenish . . ."[4]

White abolitionist/best-selling author Harriet Beecher Stowe forged the first truly famous pickaninny. In her 1852 antislavery saga *Uncle Tom's Cabin*, she featured a semihumorous/semitragic subplot on the predicaments of Topsy—a slovenly dressed, disreputable, un-cared-for slave girl. Stowe immersed herself in slave narratives, abolitionist tracts, and interviewed whites who had firsthand knowledge of slavery in order to depict Southern life with an appreciable degree of verisimilitude. In these documents and conversations she discovered the neglect faced by so many children born to slave parents. Stowe created the irascible Topsy as a foil to demonstrate that even under the ministrations of the most stalwart, religious individual, a child born to slavery was destined to be an untamable "wild child." Remanded to the care of a New England–born abolitionist, Topsy persists in her slovenly ways in spite of all Miss Ophelia's efforts to educate her. Her character improves somewhat after her young white playmate/mistress preaches to her about salvation. Little Eva, the angelic young white mistress whose premature death prompts changes in all of the major characters, convinces Topsy that Jesus has room in his heart for the likes of her.

Stowe intended audiences to sympathize with the tragic circumstances that resulted in neglected children such as Topsy. She hoped that her readers would use their resources to campaign for the abolition of slavery so that there would be no Topsys in the future. But the preconversion Topsy caught the imagination of the public. Her kinky hair, her filthy clothes, her mischievousness, her barely recognizable patois were the focus of numerous stage shows based on the novel. Stage Topsys and the other pickaninny characters who emerged were happy, mirthful characters who reveled in their misfortune. Their awkward speech, ragamuffin appearance, devilish habits, and butchered English were the sources of humor in the minstrel and Tom shows (discussed in Chapter 4) that remained popular from the early 1850s until well into the twentieth century. Theatrical producers took a character originally intended to generate disgust for slavery and reinvented her as one whose careless actions and carefree attitude suggested that black children could thrive within the confines of the "peculiar institution."

Topsy-like images are evident in all forms of contemptible collectibles. Numerous dolls and other children's toys are inscribed with attributes quite similar to the ones that Stowe enumerated in introducing the character. In fact, one toy that was called a Topsy/Eva or Topsy/Turvy doll featured two dolls who share one body. A pretty, well-dressed, blond-haired white doll when turned upside down becomes a grotesque, thick-lipped, wide-eyed, sloppily dressed black doll. To be sure, even at the end of the nineteenth century some manufacturers made beautiful bisque black dolls without the stereotypical attributes of a pickaninny. But even at the time of their manufacture, they were expensive collectors' items. They weren't the dolls real children played with. When real children played with black dolls, the dolls were made from fabric, not bisque, and had rough woolly hair, thick cherry-red lips, and patched clothing. The 1945 Sears catalog featured a black doll whose outfit was held together by a safety pin. The costume on a 1937 puppet has a prominent patch. If a boy is shown in overalls, they are either too short or one of the shoulder straps droops. The dresses worn by little girls are either torn or too short, or both. Even when a child is wearing a complete, clean outfit, some portion of it is out of place. Sometimes the child fortunate enough to have a complete ensemble has trouble keeping it. The once-popular children's book, *The Story of Little Black Sambo*, highlights the trouble faced by the young hero as he tries to keep his colorful set of clothing. However, these children were lucky to have any clothes at all. In other artifacts inscribed with images of black children, the pattern is the same: The Gold Dust Twins had plenty of gold but no clothes. A wine crate label depicts a naked black infant sitting in the middle of a field, while a souvenir bank consists of a naked black infant sitting on two bananas. Contemptible collectibles rarely depict a clean, well-dressed black child.

In the scenarios, the quasi-human image conveyed by the patched clothes (or lack of them) is often reinforced by other symbols that signal savage or animallike characteristics. Postcards, sheet music, and other print objects that contain full tableaus usually place the children out of doors. Sometimes they are juxtaposed against the crops associated with the South. Plump black babies sit on baskets of cotton or tobacco. Older children are shown crawling on the ground, climbing trees, straddled over logs, or in other ways assuming animal-like postures. Sometimes they are depicted side by side with an animal. The trademark for Two Coons Axle Grease contains an image of a semiclad black child holding a raccoon. The cover of a washable fabric children's book entitled *Pussies and Puppies* contains one image of a puppydog, one image of a pussycat, and one image of a poorly dressed black child.

Black children are never too far from watermelons or alligators. They are shown running toward the former and away from the latter. Postcards, souvenir pencil letter/opener sets, pipes, and cigar box labels are all objects that contain alligator/African-American images. Even more plentiful than such pairings are those in which black children are presented with their mouths stretched open over an obscenely large slice of watermelon. These watermelons convey dual messages. First, they imply that blacks naturally prefer foods that they can eat with their hands. Second, the image of small black child's head peering over an oversized chunk of watermelon suggests that his or her nutritional needs can be supplied by easily accessible crops that grow profusely.

The obvious question raised by all of this is to what extent do these contemptible collectibles mirror a genuine reality of black history. After all, since slave families were rarely given clothing for children before they were old enough to work, wouldn't it be safe to assume that they were poorly dressed, if at all? And since they were sent to work in the fields at a young age, wouldn't it make sense that they were sometimes to be found in baskets of tobacco or cotton? Given the amount of time that they spent out of doors, doesn't it make sense that they would have established a certain rapport with the animals with which they shared their environs?

Harriet Beecher Stowe did her homework. Historical documents offer ample evidence that from the era of slavery to the present, many black children have been underclothed, overworked, underfed, and safer in the company of animals than with some human beings. Contemptible collectibles recast this ugly component of American history into comforting artifacts that suggest that black children have prospered in spite of the abuses that have been inflicted upon them. The red-turbaned female pickaninny trademark for Northrup King and Company seeds is rolling her eyes with delight and puckering her lips with pleasure. Happiness is a seedy slice of watermelon. Picture postcards featuring poorly dressed little black children romping in cotton fields suggest that if they had been given a choice, they would have chosen to spend their days in the field rather than in a schoolroom. Thus consumers can buy products inscribed with images that contradict the harsh and uncomfortable realities.

Even though the image here is of black children, the stereotypes being promoted implicates *all* blacks. Children are not expected to be responsible for keeping themselves clean; rather their parents are expected to keep them tidy. Many twentieth-century consumers may mistakenly assume that antebellum African-American parents possessed full control over the appearance and behavior of their offspring. Convincing themselves that black parents are inherently indifferent to their children's well-being enables whites to justify their treatment of African Americans as second-class citizens. Of course, neither depictions in contemptible collectibles nor similar portrayals in other forms of popular culture acknowledge the white-induced economic factors that might have contributed to the slovenly appearance and substandard education of black children.

Images of black children other than those just described were almost impossible to find until the mid-1960s. For at least one hundred years, the public—black and white—was presented with platoons of plucky pickaninnies as its only image of black children. With characters like Buckwheat and Farina, film and television reinforced the stereotypes rendered in the material forms of popular culture. Buckwheat and Farina were the names of black characters in the Our Gang series of comedy shorts. First produced in 1922, the series ran into the "talkie" era and was sometimes known as "The Little Rascals." By the early 1960s, the derogatory implications of pickaninny images was becoming apparent to larger numbers of people. The television show *Julia*, which debuted in 1968, featured one of the first well-dressed, well-groomed, well-mannered, well-spoken black male children ever presented to the public. But the pickaninny image, while temporarily out of favor in material or celluloid images of blacks, was still evident in verbal lore. The following jokes and riddles circulated in the post–civil rights era:

Version 1
Q: How do you baby-sit black kids?
A: Put Velcro on the ceiling!

Version 2
Q: How do you keep black kids from jumping up and down on the bed?
A: Put Velcro on the ceiling.
Q: How do you get him down?
A: Blindfold a Mexican and tell him there's a piñata in the room.

Q: How do you get a black kid to keep still?
A: Wet his lips and stick him to the wall.

Q: Why don't black babies play in sand boxes?
A: Because cats keep covering them up.

Q: Why do niggers keep their chickens in front yards?
A: To teach their kids how to walk.

The pickaninny packs have had a profound impact on the consciousness of the American population. It is likely that the notion that black children are animallike and savage has influenced public policy. After all, leaders in the 1970s, 1980s, and 1990s grew up and absorbed the images discernible in the popular culture of the 1930s, 1940s, and 1950s. In these decades, access to African-American history as we know it today was limited. It seems safe to assume that in making decisions and forming policies about educational entitlement and support for underprivileged families, some elected and appointed public servants still envision the undeserving raucous, ill-kept black children prominently displayed in advertising copy and picture postcards. The nineteenth-century theatrical entrepreneurs who reinvented Topsy in order to make her a character who would provoke laughs rather than tears established a vile precedent for transforming the conspicuous components of black children's distress into acceptable, palatable (mis)representations.

Invisible Men and Women

After spending their formative years scampering around half naked, black children had only a limited choice for their adult attire. Or at least that is what the narrow range of images discernible in contemptible collectibles would have us believe. Young African-American adults, in particular males, constitute the least-represented age group in these materials. If an alien from a strange planet were to assess the black population based on these items, it would think that those slovenly dressed or naked children almost immediately grew into buxom, boisterous mammies, sheathed from head to toe in colorful garb, or into gray-haired, toothless, Uncle Remus types of men.

Ever since the minstrel era of the early to mid-nineteenth century, popular culture has trained us to anticipate seeing young black men in outlandish, outrageous "leisure" clothes. The antebellum-era white performers who darkened their faces with burnt cork and cosmetically exaggerated the size of their lips chose garish clothes to adorn their bodies as they pranced around on the stage. These figures became known as dancing dandies, zip coons, and sambos. In addition to a pronounced fondness for bright colors and large prints, they also preferred the fast life of the nighttime to the drudgery of day labor. The suits, shirts, hats, gloves, and pants they were shown in were always overdone. If a white lace ruffle around the cuff was the style white men were adopting, the black-faced figures would be depicted with four rows of ruffles, so many that the fabric would fall into their food. Dancing dandies and their descendants would expend the minimum amount of energy required at work in order to save their strength for an evening of dancing, gambling, and womanizing. In his discussion of the dancing man stereotypes as they were exhibited in nineteenth-century minstrel shows, Robert C. Toll argues that white minstrels were echoing the Northern population's distaste for freed Negroes. They made their point by caricaturing upwardly mobile freedmen as ". . . darkie dandies who claimed to be handsome, even though they had the exaggerated physical deformities common to all minstrel blacks."[5] These images from the late nineteenth and early twentieth century are prevalent in artifacts related to the entertainment industry. Sheet music, playbills, and theatrical posters offer a wide array of dancing darky types. Encoded in these artifacts is the message that such men shirk responsibilities in order to live a carefree existence. Consumers need waste no sympathy upon these individuals who think only of instant gratification. Several artifacts give license to the destruction of black men. One popular rag tune was titled "Ten Little Niggers," and it celebrated the gradual disappearance of the characters, "until there was none." At least three different games were manufactured in which the object was to throw a ball or bean bag into the face of a wide-lipped black man. A puzzle featuring a black man in a cape and with a feather in his cap was called Chopped Up Niggers—Puzzles to Put Together.

By the beginning of the twentieth century, some representations of black men show them in attire other than party clothes. Nonmilitary uniforms are everywhere and attest to the limited number of occupational roles accessible to black men. As product trademarks and in print advertising, black men are portrayed in taxicab company uniforms, headwaiter uniforms, butler and chauffeur uniforms. The heel-clicking black spokesman for Charles Denby cigars wore an impeccable red bellhop's uniform. The tailoring is quite detailed: The jacket has nineteen visible buttons, the names CHARLES DENBY is etched on the stiff white collar, and two vertical creases distinguish the pleats in the trousers. In spite of all of the artistic attention to detail, one indispensable part of the uniform is missing: the fly. According to Janette Faulkner, flies are almost never visible in representations of black men's clothing.[6] Most depictions of black males are head shots that highlight big eyes and a wide smile. When full-body shots are presented, the individual is often portrayed with some object or artifice covering the middle section of his body. When the Cream of Wheat man is not standing behind a dining room table, he often has a serving tray containing a piping-hot bowl of the wholesome cereal in front of his midsection. Bottles of whiskey, cans of tobacco, musical instruments, and hats are other objects that frequently function symbolically to castrate black men. These two types of outfits, the uniform and the dancing suit, are the mainstays of the black man's wardrobe from his early adolescence through his old age. Young, thin smiling bellhops grow into old, fat smiling bellhops. Young dancers grow into old dancers.

As seen in contemptible collectibles, the only new clothing option available are the clothes befitting an old "uncle." These "uncle" outfits fall into two categories: the reasonably neat uncles and the sloppy uncles. The neat uncles have crisp uniforms like the ones worn by their younger counterparts, while the sloppy uncles wear ill-fitting garments. As children, black males romp around in shapeless rags; eventually they don a neat uniform of service or overly colorful attire suitable for performance. As old age sets in, the dancing clothes are hung up in favor of tattered old hand-me-downs, not unlike those worn by the black child. The implicit message here is that the black man can look quite dapper when dressed to suit (pun intended) his employer, but when left to his own devices, he is completely inept.

No ominous forces are suggested by the well-fitting uniform of the Cream of Wheat man, the pastel outfit of a faithful groom, or the clothes worn by an old darky. Even in the artifacts that dress the black man in party clothes and locate him in a festive setting, the clothes and stature he assumes are so garish that it becomes obvious that he will appeal only to a black woman with similar bad taste. Conspicuous by its almost total absence from the realm of contemptible collectibles are representations of the stereotypical sex-crazed black man ostensibly devoted to defiling pristine, pedestal-bound white women. The stereotype that infuses so much of the antiblack humor has few physical representations. Visual analogs to the following verbally circulated texts are virtually nonexistent.

Student A: My friend was raped and brutalized by five black men last week. It was disgusting. They brutalized

her and sodomized her and made her do all sorts
of unspeakable acts.

Student B: That's terrible.

Student A: Not really, she outsmarted them. She hid her
money in her shoe.

This is about a Negro who has been accused of raping a white
woman. The Ku Klux Klan got him and cut off all of his sexual
organs. Then they tell him to run like hell or they'll kill him.
Well, he runs like mad until he reaches the top of a high hill.
He turns around and yells back at the Klan: "Ha! ha! ha! You
didn't get this." (He is sticking his tongue out at them.)

Two Negro guys in jail were talking about what they were going
to do when they got out, with the money that they had hidden.
The first fellow said he was going to get himself a white suit,
white hat, white shoes, and a white Cadillac. Then he said he
was going to get himself a white woman and drive to
Mississippi. The second fellow said he was going to get himself
a black suit, black hat, and black shoes, then buy a black
Cadillac and get him a black woman. Then he was going to
Mississippi and ".Watch them white folks hang your black ass."

Q: What's white and twelve inches?
A: Nothing.

There was this guy who frees a leprechaun. The leprechaun
tells him that he can make a wish and it will come true. Later
that night the guy is awakened from his dream by some loud
banging at the door. He answers it and finds a man clothed in
white standing there with a noose in his hand. Then he notices
a group of men, dressed from head to toe in white as well,
standing around a cross burning in the middle of the lawn. The
guy asks the man standing before him, "What the hell's going
on in here?"

"Aren't you the guy that wanted to be well hung like a
nigger?"

As these tenacious jokes suggest, the purported sexual endow-
ment and prowess of black men has remained a viable topic for verbal
speculation, although it is a less acceptable one for material representation. Movies and television have offered black male characters as
dangerous sexual deviants. However, the narrative structure of these
two modes of entertainment allow for retribution. Gus, the black ren-
egade rapist in D. W. Griffith's *Birth of a Nation,* is punished after his
advances result in the death of the innocent white virgin. Static, tangible objects don't lend themselves to such feel-good resolutions. Your
average American is not going to want to take cookies out of a jar
crafted in Gus's likeness. Collector Douglas Congdon-Martin discovered one example of a bisque novelty item in which a shirtless black
male figure is shown peeping through a window at a nude white female figure taking a bath.[7] To my knowledge, this is the only material
object that is likely to aggravate rather than mollify white consumers.
Once again, the pervasive rule governing the depiction of blacks
within contemptible collectibles seems to be: Exploit only those stereotypes that assuage white fears and never those that aggravate
them.

Images of virile black men have been so few and far between in
mainstream popular culture that when real-life black men gain notoriety, the social and political fallout can be staggering. Conservative
supporters for Republican presidential candidate George Bush in
1988, apparently realized how startling and provocative images of
aggressive black men could be. When their candidate's campaign was
at a low point, a new anti-Dukakis political advertisement was released. It contained a picture of Willie Horton, an African-American
male felon who had been released from prison ahead of schedule. The
ad warned voters that Michael Dukakis, the Democratic presidential
candidate, while governor of Massachusetts, had supported a prison
release program that resulted in Horton committing additional violent
crimes. The rest is history. The Dukakis campaign never recovered
from the damage that one picture of one black man had on the voting
public.

Other images of black men were the subject of intense public
scrutiny in the late 1980s and early 1900s. Debates proliferated in
conservative think tanks and congressional meeting rooms about the
kind of art that should and, more significantly, should not be supported by taxpayer money. Financial support for offbeat performance

art, cryptic poetry, and nontraditional dance was challenged. But ask most people what examples of allegedly misused taxpayer dollars were cited, debated, and condemned by the conservatives, and they will respond, "The photographs of white art photographer Robert Mapplethorpe and the films of African-American documentary film-maker Marlon Riggs."

What do Mapplethorpe's photographs and one of Riggs's films have in common? Both contain a number of sexually provocative images of virile black men. Crafted to celebrate the erotic beauty one man can find in another's body, the photographs and the film offered the public representations of African-American maleness unlike any that had been allowed near the mainstream before. The resulting controversy over the public funds that partially supported these projects indicates just how foreign and threatening these representations were to some individuals born and bred on images of dancing darkies and toothless old uncles. When PBS scheduled Riggs's award-winning documentary, *Tongues Untied*, in its summer 1991 schedule, it received more criticism than it had for any single programming decision. Conservative protesters also made their feelings known outside of art galleries exhibiting Mapplethorpe's photographs. In his bid for the Republican presidential nomination in 1992, conservative journalist Patrick Buchanan stole a clip from *Tongues Untied* in order to criticize the Bush administration for allowing such a work to receive public support. Buchanan's attempt to undermine Bush in the same way that Bush had undermined Dukakis didn't quite work. Containing images of white gays, the *Tongues* clip lacked the full potency of the Willie Horton image. In spite of the fact that the $5,000 Riggs was awarded actually came during the Reagan administration, after Buchanan's assault, the director of the National Endowment for the Arts was forced out. Popular culture's tenacious affinity for uniformed, smiling black oldsters and gaudily dressed black youngsters has left many segments of the public ill-prepared for emergence of black men who cannot be pigeonholed into these niches. North Carolina's most famous congressman, Jesse Helms, emerged as one of the most vocal opponents of the Mapplethorpe photographs. Prior to seeing them, Helms's exposure to representations of black men were no doubt limited to Cream of Wheat boxes or those "toothless darkies" that once dominated the Bull Durham smoking tobacco posters of his home state. Accustomed to seeing pictures of black men whose sexuality has been deliberately diffused, Helms was unprepared for photographs that flaunted African-American male virility. The preponderance of these stereotypical images has undermined the efforts of those African-American men whose faces and bodies don't lend themselves to the garments of service occupations or revelry.

Contemptible collectibles also play games with black female sexuality. In these items the African-American woman's image is crafted so as to suggest that any sexual appeal she may have will be evident only to black men and not to white. Like the young black men, the young black women get to wear elaborate party clothes. In sheet music and portrayed in dolls, the black women's alleged preference for fancy finery is always highlighted. The illustrations tend to show black women as infatuated with excessive fanciness—an outfit might consist of a polka-dot shirt covered with a striped vest worn with a checkerboard skirt covering high-heeled two-toned boots and topped off with a multifeathered hat. Their attempts to be fashionplates aren't realized. Presented in this manner, these black women will be physically attractive only to their black male counterparts, who indulge in a similar impulse to overdress. Such images are not intended to capture the interest of white male consumers.

One cluster of black female icons and trademarks highlight their natural "exoticness." Until the 1950s, the trademark for Nigger Hair Smoking Tobacco was a young Negress with obviously African features, including oversized hoops piercing her ears and her nose. Similar earrings and heavy neck chains can be found on young-looking black female dolls, pincushions, appliance covers, and souvenir dinner bells. Whenever these females possess physical attributes that might be perceived as alluring, they are usually in the company of black men. Otherwise no comely features are depicted in conjunction with the exotic ones. Keeping sexy exotics in close proximity to black men allows contemptible collectible creators to control the black woman's physical attractiveness. They were never allowed to entice white men. None of these depictions could be used to substantiate the folk belief that "once you've had black, you never go back."

Mammy/auntie figures constitute the most frequently depicted characters in the realm of contemptible collectibles. Draped in calico from head to toe, Aunt Jemima and her cronies pose no sexual threat to their white mistresses. They want to nourish rather than seduce white men. The artifacts they grace belong almost exclusively to the kitchen. There are mammy memo pads on which a crisp white apron is in fact a pad of paper. The mammy visage is also found on cookie jars, salt shakers, and dinner bells. Mammies model for coffee products, soap powders, and pancake mix. An indispensable component of mammy's equipment is her toothy smile. (Mammies don't have the dental problems of their male counterparts.) She is happy to make your pancakes and wash your clothes. Her culinary skills are evident in her thick waistline. The mammy figures convey the notion that genuine fulfillment for black women comes not from raising their own children or feeding their own man (black families are rarely featured) but from serving in a white family's kitchen. Chapter 3 offers a full analysis of the mammy/auntie motif.

Forged Replicas

Ann Landers and the three readers who pondered the political correctness of lawn jockeys overlooked one possible solution to their problem. Reader number one, who wondered if it was unneighborly to complain about the statue, should have been encouraged to point out to the offending neighbor that similar black-faced lawn ornaments fetch upward of a hundred dollars on the collectibles circuit. The best evidence for the demand for contemptible collectibles stems from the fact that for consumers unable to purchase their very own full-size darky hitching post, a smaller, more affordable reproduction is now available.

To antique and collectibles aficionados, few pronouncements strike more terror than—"reproduction." Nothing could be worse than the discovery that a long-coveted treasure is actually the work of a knock-off artist—that an article purchased as "genuine and authentic" is, in actuality, "phony and fake." But the existence of reproductions signals a given object's obvious popularity and demand. No self-respecting capitalist entrepreneur would go to all of the trouble and effort to manufacture a phony antique or collectible if he or she wasn't convinced that a sizable market for it existed.

Shortly after I became interested in these artifacts, a worldly wise collector took me aside and warned me about reproductions. Not wanting to see me waste any money, she schooled me in the ways of discerning genuine racist collectibles from phony ones. My interest was piqued immediately, not because I did not want to be "taken," but rather because the very existence of fake racist icons stimulated a whole new arena of scholarly inquiry in my mind. Why would anyone want to remake a patently racist object? Who would want to buy one? Were certain items more likely to be reproduced than others? Why? As a result, I became the opposite of most collectors—I actively pursued and purchased the reproductions. I would quickly move past the real stuff and spend my always-meager icon allowance on the fake. Vendors would look at me askance when I voiced my preference for the phony stuff and asked if they could supply any proof that an object was a reproduction before I would buy it.

Based on my collection of contemptible collectible reproductions, I feel quite comfortable making the following generalizations. Artifacts originally cast in plastic or paper are quite popular targets for reproductions. Posters, postcards, advertisements, labels, and other promotional materials lend themselves to reproduction. Cast-iron savings banks and doorstops are also readily available. The banks include the ubiquitous mammy, in the most common model, standing firmly in a red dress, with a white apron and her hands resting on her substantial hips. Also available both as a bank and a doorstop is a three-dimensional scene depicting a sloppily dressed black man heading for or already ensconced in an outhouse. One significant clue to the reproduction puzzle stems from affordability—reproduced racism comes cheap. As I write this in the summer of 1992, mammy banks can be had for under twenty dollars; a Bull Durham smoking tobacco poster retails for about ten dollars; and postcards, such as the Dixie Boy crate label replica, are under one dollar. Products originally intended as advertising trademarks are also quite popular; perhaps more so than products either no longer in existence or no longer dependent on a caricatured trademark. The AAA Sign Company markets a metal sign for Topsy chocolate soda, a beverage no longer available.

With only a few exceptions, most of the reproduced icons are encoded with ostensibly benevolent messages. A sign advertising Topsy Granulated Smoking Tobacco features a parasol-carrying dark-skinned young woman strolling down a path while holding a handsome tin of Topsy tobacco, a product of the Wellman & Dwire Tobacco Company. Although she has the requisite wide smile, her overall appearance is rather nice. San Francisciana Historical Postcard #169 features a smiling young black boy with his hands and mouth wrapped around a juicy section of Florida grapefruit—Dixie Boy brand. However, several items featuring conspicuously hostile images are also available. The AAA Sign Company, the same outfit that manufactures the Topsy sign just described, also sells a United States Fur Company sign. The sign features four men and two animals. Two appropriately dressed white hunters are holding rifles and laughing. Two sloppily dressed black hunters have dropped their weapons as they run from the white hunters, a hunting dog, and a skunk. The slogan at the top of the sign reads, "Send us your Furs" and at the bottom of the sign: "An unwelcome surprise." Clearly the terrified black men are posed as the intended victims of the white hunters on behalf of the fur company.

These items are all standard "reproductions." Manufacturers have duplicated and mass-produced a once-common object. Mammy and pappy salt-and-pepper shakers are replicas of sets that were once in production. The shiny, new Bull Durham poster is a reprint of one once used to pitch the product. At least two other categories of contemporary items are available. The first of these consists of newly made objects clearly intended to evoke feelings of nostalgia but that nonetheless are brand-new items. For example, most craft fairs now feature wooden pickaninny, and sometimes mammy, plaques. They are not replicas in the traditional sense of the word because they are based on the general stereotype of the pickaninny rather than any actual pickaninny toy that once existed. No doubt because of their folksy flavor, pickaninny, mammy, and old darky figures dressed in bright homespun fabric tend to dominate this category.

The final category consists of a whole body of somewhat higher-brow items made, manufactured, and sold by both white and black artisans and craftspeople. Names such as "Heritage Collection" and "Ebony Series" evoke a sense of pride and racial self-awareness. The makers and sellers of these items do not attempt to misrepresent them as old. Instead, they pitch them as symbolically meaningful figurines that introduce white consumers to black history and allow African-

American consumers to feel a positive connection with their past. A category that includes miniatures of activist Frederick Douglass and the well-known Underground Railroad conductor Harriet Tubman probably does not fit within the realm of contemptible collectibles. I suppose these could be labeled "acceptable" collectibles. In most of these objects, a great deal of care is put into rendering a nonstereotypical image. The clothes draped on the figures are clean, well pressed, and appropriate to the figure's station in life. The clothes suggest occupational alternatives to the standard service occupations discernible in the despicable collectibles. The nurse is often depicted, and instrument-wielding musicians constitute a large segment of the figurine population. Warm parent/child juxtapositions, rarely seen in hard-core contemptible collectibles, are plentiful in these acceptable collectibles.

In spite of the positive goals of those who make and market acceptable collectibles, I'm still disconcerted by some aspects of the blossoming cottage industries that are creating and catering to the consumer demand for these icons. Are these figurines substantially different from their reproduced cousins? There is a store in my city that has three black-faced mammy cookie jars. Two are authentic, mass-produced cookie jars from the mid-twentieth century. The third is a contemporary jar designed and sold by a black-owned company. I'm reluctant to classify the first two as contemptible collectibles and the third as an acceptable collectible. The whole phenomena is reminiscent of a pattern that emerged following the Civil War. African Americans, eager to enter the entertainment field, were forced to confront numerous obstacles, not the least of which were those imposed by the extant stage images of blacks. Genuine African-American actors and actresses were put in the awkward position of having to compete with blackface white actresses and actors who had established their careers by mimicking blacks. Consequently, real black performers were judged by standards established by white performers who had distinguished themselves solely on their ability to caricature black folk. Thus breaking into the business meant that blacks had to exaggerate those characteristics audiences associated with blackface white performers. What has this to do with the current collectibles scene? Knowing that mammy cookie jars have become hot items, artisans have crafted kinder and gentler images of maternal-looking black women. Knowing that Frederick Douglass is still often short-changed in history books, sculptors endeavor to capture his likeness in limited edition models.

Beginning in 1619, black human beings were bought and sold in America. Human commodities, they were governed by the laws that protect property, not persons. Even before the slaves were emancipated, entrepreneurs had begun to use images of blacks to sell a distorted picture of Southern life. At the same time that slave traders were making money by selling black men, women, and children in the South, Northern theatrical producers were making equally impressive sums of money by selling the public blackface revues and musical extravaganzas scripted to whitewash the extent of depravity inherent in plantation slavery. In 1863 the selling of real black human beings was at long last over, but the selling of distorted caricatures had just begun.

The impulse to romanticize the conditions of slavery was stronger than it ever had been. Reaping profits from the sense of superiority and comfort these icons offered, generation after generation of entrepreneur packaged and repackaged nonthreatening depictions of blacks. Uncritically accepting the fabricated history lesson entrenched in the iconography, generation after generation of consumers purchased the sweetened formula. After an all-too-brief respite in the 1960s and early 1970s, schools of docile black-faced icons resurfaced in popular culture. The post–civil rights era dealers, vendors, and writers who specialize in contemptible collectibles rarely acknowledge any connection with the entrepreneurs who originally sold these goods. The introduction to *Black Collectables: Mammy and Her Friends* by Jackie Young is particularly revealing. Young begins by admitting that her affection for mammy collectibles dates back to ". . . pleasant times spent in kitchens, including my grandmothers, decorated with the friendly, smiling motherly black mammy image." Eventually she realized "that most of the objects drove home the belittling idea that most black people were only fit for menial jobs like cooks, waiters or servants. Thank goodness the civil rights movement ended this once common portrayal of an entire race and closed that chapter of American culture." She concludes the introduction to her book by advising the reader that "by collecting black memorabilia you can have the dual pleasure of decorating your home and investing in objects that will almost certainly increase in monetary value as time goes by."[8] In antebellum times a capable black female constituted a safe investment for a slave trader; at the turn of the century the success of Aunt Jemima products enhanced the wealth of white merchants; now finding a sufficiently rare mammy cookie jar could make some lucky collector rich. The bottom line is the same. We still live in a world eager to develop new reasons and rationales for commodifying African Americans—past and present.

2

Alligator Bait

In July of 1984, the *New York Times* reported a severe problem faced by the affluent summer population of Hilton Head, South Carolina. It seems that many residents were feeling threatened by the island's increasingly aggressive alligator population. In search of meat, alligators began prowling the beaches and golf courses. This uncharacteristically predatory behavior, which game officials traced to the propensity of tourists to feed the reptiles, alarmed Hilton Head's sunbathers and golfers. Although it was not the only Southern community to report a new aggressive alligator temperament, it is particularly ironic that this island, one of the Georgia Sea Coast islands, should feel threatened by alligators. During the slavery era, this string of small islands served as a sort of centralized landing facility for incoming African captives. As a result, the islands' black population has always retained strong cultural and linguistic links to West Africa. Even today scholars who want to establish connections between African and African-American cultures do much of their fieldwork with Sea Island blacks.[1] White-generated folklore, both verbal and material, suggests that whites have little to fear from alligators but that blacks do. By beginning with nineteenth century white pop culture heroes and African-American folktales and continuing with twentieth-century antiblack material culture as well as urban legends and jokes, we can posit an explanation for the tenacity of the alligator/African-American juxtaposition in American society.

In his 1987 essay "The Alligator," folklorist Jay Mechling acknowledges that his interpretation of alligator symbolism in folklore is "[not] the only culturally formulaic story for interpreting the alligator, only that it is a pervasive one connecting many alligator texts and images."[2] Identifying items from a broad range of verbal, written, and material culture, Mechling posits a convincing thesis about the consistent juxtaposition of blacks and alligators. Using Freudian-based analysis, Mechling concludes that the alligator functions as a mechanism through which the white male can symbolically castrate the black male. Indeed a wealth of alligator lore can be used to substantiate this thesis. However, by examining other examples of alligator lore and employing other modes of analysis as well as the psychoanalytic, we can increase our understanding of the complexity of alligator/African-American juxtapositions.

Dating the first combination of black with alligator in the New World is just as impossible as dating any item of folk culture. We do know that the belief that the alligator was the black's born nemesis persisted in nineteenth-century America. The Davy Crockett chronicled in *Sketches and Eccentricities of Davy Crockett of West Tennessee* (1833) and *Davy Crockett's Almanac* (1837) boasted that he was "half horse, half alligator, a little touched with snapping turtle" and that he was therefore capable of "swallowing a nigger whole if you butter his head and pin his ears back."[3]

In his 1888 text, *Negro Myths From the Georgia Coast*, Charles C. Jones recalls the kind of tale he was told by whites during his childhood.[4] In the tale, a slave named Sawney makes repeated visits to his wife, who is owned by a planter on a neighboring plantation. He brings with him "a bag containing provisions and such choice morsels as he had been able, during the week to accumulate for his better half." Taking a shortcut through the river one Saturday night, he hears what he thinks to be a "sperit." After saying "Tan Back, Masa Sperit, an let me pass," Sawney is attacked by an alligator. Paralyzed with fear, Sawney is unable to escape. His cries alarm slaves in the quarter who come to the swamp and free him by beating the eleven-foot alligator to death. Following a three-month recuperation period, Sawney recovers. Jones delivers this white-generated tale, unlike those he recorded from black informants, in the standard written

English of the late nineteenth century. A sentence from this one reads, "Sawney had so completely lost his wits, was so terrified, and was suffering so much pain, that he neglected to improve the opportunity thus afforded, and betake himself to flight." In this tale and other material shared by whites, the black man is clearly terrified of the alligator. A sample from a black-authored sentence reads, "One time Buh Rabbit, him meet Buh alligator, an eh az um: 'Budder, you take life berry onconsarne.'" This dialect and these characters were made famous to folklorists by Joel Chandler Harris, a contemporary and friend of Jones's.[5] In Harris's and Jones's black-authored tales, Buh (or Brer) alligator possesses no skills that can't be conquered by the indefatigable trickster, usually Buh Rabbit. Like the other animals, the alligator could never get the best of Buh Rabbit. In her indispensable study of the tales in the Uncle Remus corpus, Florence E. Baer traces the analogs and sources of the Uncle Remus tales.[6] Her research suggests that nearly 70 percent of the folktales collected by Harris have African antecedents. Of course the animal in question in these tales is a crocodile, the species from which the American alligator is derived. In neither the African nor the Remus tale type does the alligator/crocodile character outsmart the trickster.

Immediately after the Civil War, conservationist-author John Muir walked from Indiana to the Gulf coast. During his thousand-mile trek he met more than one white Southerner who boasted of his ability to best the scaly enemy. In his journal Muir records, "Alligators are said to be extremely fond of negroes and dogs and naturally the dogs and negroes are afraid of them."[7] However, Muir does not reveal whether he was told this by white or by black Southerners. At least Muir, unlike his Southern associates, was willing to acknowledge his own discomfort in the presence of alligators. He also noted what he perceived as an unfair (to the alligator) tendency on the part of humans to associate reptiles with the devil.

The notion that blacks are inordinately afraid of alligators seems to be limited to the North American continent. African crocodile iconography could easily be the subject of a full-length work. For the purposes of this study it seems important to point out that in many east and west African societies the crocodile represents a source of power, an animal to be feared only when it is treated with disrespect. Robert Farris Thompson has pointed out that the women's associations of the Ejagham—an ethnic group rooted in southwestern Cameroon and southeastern Nigeria—employ the crocodile as a symbol of "powers of oral vengeance and strong government."[8] In her research on African staffs and walking sticks, art historian Ramona Austin comments on the use of crocodiles and other powerful animals in the design of canes.[9] The alligator/crocodile is not the source of any undo fear on the part of blacks in other parts of the New World. Indeed, in her collection of folktales from Jamaica, folklorist Daryl C. Dance includes three tales in which the alligator suffers from the misdeeds of the trickster.[10]

By now it should be clear that when black performers juxtaposed alligators and African Americans, the alligator fared no worse or better than any other animal enemy. When whites pitted the two together, however, the alligator always had the upper hand. At least part of the explanation is somewhat obvious, particularly when we note the observations made by the nineteenth-century collector Charles Jones, whose comments are worth quoting at length:

> Foremost among the reptiles which excited curiosity and aroused the fears of the Georgia colonists, upon their first acquaintance with them, were the alligators. Francis Moore, keeper of the stores, describing them in 1736, says: "They are terrible to look at, stretching open an horrible large mouth big enough to swallow a man with rows of dreadful large sharp teeth, and feet like Draggons, armed with great Claws, and a long Tail with which they throw about with great Strength." To the European newly landed on these shores the alligator was indeed a novelty, repulsive and provocative of dread. Not so with the Negro. His ancestors were well acquainted with the African crocodile, and their [sic] descendants, the habitat of this formidable reptile were from childhood familiar with its roar, and entirely accustomed to its unsightly appearance and habits.[11]

The Southern whites of the slavery era projected their own discomfort with this unfamiliar creature onto the slaves. In the folklore they performed (such as the tale about Sawney), they are transferring their own fears. But in black-created tales such as "Brother Rabbit and the Gizzard Eater," the alligator is just another character susceptible to the omnipotent trickster's guiles.

Indeed I can find no evidence in nineteenth- or twentieth-century African-American–generated folklore to indicate that blacks feared alligators. In *Dust Tracks on the Road,* Zora Neale Hurston recalls that early twentieth-century Floridians treated alligators with the same amount of caution assigned to other sometimes dangerous animals:

> She must have had two or three horrible hours lying there in the edge of the water, hard put to it to keep her face above water, and expecting the attack of an alligator, water moccasin, gar fish, and numerous other creatures which existed only in her terrified mind.[12]

Gospel singer Mahalia Jackson's recollections of her Louisiana childhood include a matter-of-fact account of alligator hunting:

> When I was a little girl growing up in New Orleans we often had baby alligator for breakfast. When you saw one sunning himself in the swamp or on the riverbank, you'd get a stick and creep up real quiet until you got close enough to crack him on the head so hard he never knew what it was that hit him. You ate the tail baked like smothered chicken with onions and garlic and herbs.[13]

Like their nineteenth-century ancestors, twentieth-century blacks who were accustomed to sharing their environment with alligators demonstrated no undue apprehension in the presence of these animals.

Whether the creature in question is an actual alligator has little, if any, effect on the folk's perception. It seems reasonably safe to assume that the layperson lacks precise knowledge about the differences between crocodiles and alligators. In this chapter I consider them as symbolic equivalents. Further, in anthropological terms, alligators and crocodiles are particularly liminal creatures. That is, their symbolic power stems from the fact that they belong to several spheres simultaneously. These creatures can be found in several parts of the world, including Africa and the United States. As reptiles, they are associated with water and land. They are large animals capable of eating people and being eaten by people.

Once again whites have projected their own fears of the alligators on to blacks. Yet this projection analysis, based on the race of the performer or teller of the tale, is only partially satisfying. It doesn't explain Davy Crockett's reveling in his ability to eat the "nigger," nor does it explain the tenacity of this theme into twentieth-century material culture and folklore. For example, a souvenir spoon from Tampa, Florida, dated 1901 depicts an unprotected, barely clad black child's seemingly futile attempt to escape an obviously aggressive alligator. A 1910 cigar box label also pits a hapless as well as clothesless black child against a full-grown alligator. Postcards, probably from the 1930s and '40s, tell the same story. The title of this chapter, "Alligator Bait," comes from an item in the Berkeley Folklore Archives at the University of California. It was submitted by a white student in 1970, who claimed that black children were nicknamed "alligator bait" in his native Louisiana. Perhaps the most shocking feature of these material and verbal items is the fact that the alligator is pursuing a *child*. Yet this kind of representation is in keeping with other depictions of black children. As discussed in Chapter 1, rarely are they depicted with a full set of neat clothing. Physically they are shown on the ground or in trees—in other words, in close proximity to nature. In short, we see black children animalistic and savagelike. Yet this animalistic stereotype seems less severe than the ones in which the child actually is pursued by alligators. In a 1970 article for the *Journal of American Folklore*, Roger D. Abrahams applied the research conducted by Gordon W. Allport and Robin M. Williams, Jr., to African-American expressive folklore.[14] Such stereotypes emerge from generalized preconceptions, such as "Blacks let their children run wild." The inclusion of an alligator in the depiction seems to me to make these items classifiable within Williams and Allport's "intentional-direct" category of stereotype. These items depict more than just the presence of a negative stereotype, they implicitly advocate a form of aggression in eradicating an unwanted people.

Most of the twentieth-century verbal lore merely makes a sexless, ageless black person the victim:

There's LBJ, he's flying down over Louisiana, and they were going to Austin, Texas, and he was in his helicopter. Well, they happened to glance down and in the water there were these two white guys pulling this black guy on skis, so he says, "Land

this helicopter and get those guys over to shore, I want to
commend them for my integration program, they're really
making it, helping it work." And so he lands his helicopter and
calls them over to the bank, says, "Gentlemen, I really do
appreciate you trying to help out in making a better interest of
integrating and having fun with blacks and I'm gonna make
sure that you all get a commendation for this." And so the guys
are sort of baffled, they really don't know what was coming off,
you know, so he gets back in his helicopter and he gets their
names and everything and he takes off. So this one guy says,
"Who in the shit was that?" And the other guy says, "I don't
know, but he don't know a goddam thing about catching
alligators."[15]

There's this guy who walks into a bar. He's got an alligator on
a leash. And the guy says to the bartender, "Do you serve
Negroes here?" The bartender says, "Yeah, we serve anybody
here." The guy says, "Good, give me a scotch on the rocks and
a nigger for my pet alligator."

Q: What do you get when you cross an alligator and a
    roadrunner?
A: A 100-mph nigger-chaser.

A wide-mouth frog goes to the zoo and he hops into the lion's
cage. And he says, "Hello, Mrs. Lion! I'm a wide-mouth frog.
What do you feed your babies?" [Spoken with mouth widely
extended.] Mrs. Lion says, "Go on, get out of here. I don't have
time for you." And so he hops out into the tiger's cage and
says, "Hello, Mrs. Tiger. I'm a wide-mouth frog. What do you
feed your babies?" And Mrs. Tiger says, "Go on, go 'way." So
he hops into the alligator cage and says, "Hello, Mrs. Alligator!
I'm a wide-mouth frog. What do you feed your babies?"
"Wide-mouth frogs." "Oh, really?" [Spoken with tight lips.]

The last joke has been analyzed by Alan Dundes in an article
titled "The Curious Case of the Wide-Mouth Frog."[16] Dundes argues
that the wide-mouth frog, with its large mouth and its inability to
nurture its progeny, is in fact a black male. I believe that further

verification of Dundes's theory can be found in the fact that in most versions of this story, it is the alligator who feeds its babies wide-mouth frogs.

While the verbal lore depicts an ageless, sexless, almost generic "nigger," the material culture tells us more precisely for whom the alligator lurks. A souvenir letter opener/pencil set exemplifies the con-summation of the threat and can be used to pinpoint the alligator's symbolic power. The alligator's exaggerated tail is a letter opener and a black man sans genitals is a pencil who can be stored conveniently in the alligator's jaws. Ostensibly, the item functions as a tool (pun intended) for the white male who has more letters to open and answer than his unfortunate black counterpart. The user of the material item is empowered by it. Neither the alligator nor the black poses any threat to him. The alligator is an accomplice in a dual effort to eradi-cate or, at least, intimidate the black.

An alligator functions well in this capacity for several reasons. Indeed the tenacity of the alligator/African-American juxtaposition can be explained in light of the multiple layers of symbolic meaning implicit in this liminal animal. I think it can be argued that folk perceive the alligator as an exotic, Old World animal. Because popular belief often associates alligators with Africa, we can argue that part of the alligator's appeal to the unconscious stems from the notion that it is another African being that is antagonizing the African American. The black man's suffering is being brought about by one of his own, "natural" enemies.

The shape of the alligator also evokes psychoanalytic interpreta-tion. Jay Mechling argues that the "vagina dentata" is the unifying motif for the alligator's persistence (in juxtapositions with both whites and blacks).[17] Clearly the toothed vagina accounts for part of the alligator's popularity. But the alligator's long body and its reptilian appearance suggests that it, like the snake, could also be a phallic symbol. As any student of white-generated racist jokes can testify, male-to-male penis envy is alive and well and rampant in verbal lore. The alligator represents the white man's desire to overpower the os-tensibly superphallic black man with a white, more potent phallus. The alligator's "whiteness" is discernible in those variants of legends in which alligators that live in sewers supposedly have white bodies, due to the lack of direct sunlight there.[18] The tenacity of the alligator/ African-American juxtaposition can be traced to the multitude of symbolic interpretations implicit in the alligator. The liminal exoticness and the physical characteristics that connote both male and female genitalia contribute to the animal's appeal, making the alligator all things to all people.

Unfortunately, the alligator still bares its teeth for blacks in contemporary popular culture. Certainly one of the most popular television series of the 1980s was NBC's *Miami Vice* (1984–89). The program features the escapades of a "salt-and-pepper" detective team consisting of a hip black former New York policeman and a Southern ex–football-playing detective. The characters' names are Tubbs and Crockett respectively. Crockett the cop, like Davy Crockett the adventurer, is quite comfortable with alligators and lives on a sailboat with his very own pet alligator, Elvis. In the pilot episode, Crockett and Tubbs meet and develop an essentially antagonistic relationship. When the African-American New Yorker goes to confront the white Southerner on his boat, his dismay is evident when he discovers Elvis. In subsequent episodes the two detectives put aside their original hostility, but Tubbs is never as comfortable in Elvis's presence as Crockett is. The subliminal message seems to be that the hip black New Yorker will be allowed to work with the Southern jock if the former remembers his place. If he forgets, the white man has an alligator to keep him in line. This interpretation has obviously been internalized by the sellers and buyers of a popular novelty T-shirt which features a toothy alligator smiling at caricatured depictions of Sonny Crockett (Don Johnson) and Buckwheat.

As stated at the beginning of this chapter, alligators have been prominent in the past decade. Shortly before the Democratic National Convention, a Bay Area newspaper ran a story with the following headline: "Allegations and Alligators Jackson Campaign—A Thriller."[19] It seems that reporters assigned to the Reverend Jesse Jackson, then a contender for the Democratic Party presidential nomination, had adopted an interesting way of chastising the candidate. When he was late for a speaking engagement or changed his itinerary without notifying the press, they would greet him at their next meeting by "squeezing metal alligators [children's toys] so they make an annoying click-clack sound." While "alligator" is the slang name some reporters use for a metal device they wear around their necks to relay messages via the phone to their home office, Jackson's entourage used actual toy alligators. How interesting that the Jackson campaign stimulated this use for them. Jackson's response is interesting too. "I'm sick of allegations," Jackson snapped. "And I'm sick of the alligators." While I don't know whether the Reverend Jesse Jackson would agree with my analysis of the alligator, I think the fact that he began to refer to the white reporters as alligators indicates his awareness that they were out to get him, in more ways than one.

3

Back to the Kitchen

"I saw all of this racist stuff while I was on my vacation [at home, overseas]; I thought of you right away." Since I began my quest for contemptible collectibles in the early 1980s, I have grown accustomed to friends, family members, colleagues, and students returning from near and far and greeting me with comments like this. Once I got used to the idea that racist iconography was going to trigger thoughts of me in the minds of my significant others, I began to have fun by trying to predict exactly what contemptible collectible inspired those thoughts. I've learned to guess that the object in question most probably contains some sort of image of a black woman. Over a decade of collecting experience, I have learned that assorted representations of black women most frequently adorn authentic, reproduced, or retrieved icons. As Chapter 1 notes, black women are depicted in material and print objects as exotic other (as in trademarks for Nigger Hair Smoking Tobacco and Weather Bird Shoes) and precocious pickaninny (as in assorted rag dolls and trademark for Topsy Chocolate Honey Dairy Drink). But my first guess is never pickaninny or exotic other. No image exceeds the popularity and diversity of the smiling, overweight, copiously dressed figure referred to alternately as mammy or auntie.

"You know, before I took your class [heard your lecture, visited

41

your home], I could never remember seeing these objects anywhere, but now I see them all over." Comments like these are the second most common I hear. Most people—black and white—tend to be oblivious to the existence of contemptible collectibles until their presence is pointed out. Once people's eyes have been trained to isolate the smiling black faces and color-coordinated uniforms, they see contemptible collectibles everywhere. But, in particular, they see them in the kitchen. Picture, if you will, the following scenario:

A sleepy homemaker enters her kitchen to make breakfast. After reaching into the pantry for Aunt Jemima pancake flour, she stirs it with her mammy measuring spoons that were nestled in a mammy measuring spoon holder. She rests her mixing spoon on the mammy spoon rest, which sits on her stove adjacent to the auntie salt-and-pepper shakers, the mammy spice rack, and the mammy wooden knife holder. To light the stove, she reaches into the mammy match holder for matches. She brews a pot of Luzianne coffee, handling the hot coffeepot with her mammy potholders. On her mammy table-cloth, she sets the table with mammy dishes, cups, and saucers. After finding the ceramic auntie teapot, she brews a pot of tea in it and puts the mammy creamer and sugar dish and syrup dispenser on the table. For the toast lovers in the family, she removes the mammy electric appliance cover from the toaster and puts in a couple of slices of bread. She slathers butter from the mammy butter dish on the toast. Setting the mammy egg timer, she times the eggs. After washing the breakfast dishes, she replaces the steel wool pad in the mammy scouring pad holder and waters the houseplant sitting in the auntie ceramic planter. She washes her own hands with a bar of soap resting in the mammy soap dish. After emptying dirty clothes from a mammy laundry bag into her washer, she measures in Fun to Wash laundry soap. After checking the mammy wall clock, she realizes it is time to make a grocery list. She reaches for her mammy memo pad and pencil. She consults her mammy recipe box to see what meals she will want to prepare. After checking the mammy cookie jar, auntie cruet set, mammy toothpick holder, and auntie canister set to see if they need replenishing, she makes her shopping list. Before leaving the house she takes her household money from her cast-iron mammy bank.

It may all sound like a kitchen contrived by the writers of the Fox network's popular variety show *In Living Color*, but a sufficiently demented homemaker could equip a real kitchen with all of these

items, without relying on a professional prop master. All of the objects
and products described have been mass-produced at some point during the twentieth century. Many of them are still in production or
have been reproduced in the past fifteen years. This chapter explores
the extraordinary durability of the mammy/auntie image and icons.
When did images of dark-skinned, rotund, benevolent black women
first capture the imagination of the producers of popular culture? To
what extent is the image based on the realities of Southern antebellum
households? How has mammy been made over during the twentieth
century? What does the present fascination with mammy images reveal about contemporary society? What price has been exacted from
the real black women who have been forced to make their way in a
culture that pays homage to a distorted icon?

Birth of a Mammy

In one of the best-known scenes in the film version of Margaret
Mitchell's *Gone With the Wind* (1939), the hapless pickaninny character named Prissie is forced to acknowledge the fibs she has told
about her baby-birthing dexterity. "I don't know nothing about
birthing babies, Miss Scarlet. Mammy and them never let me near
when babies was coming," she screeches to her distraught young mistress. The ability to nurture whites from just after conception to the
point of final expiration is one of the traits consistently associated
with the image of the mammy. But what of mammy herself? Who
presided over her birth? According to historian Catherine Clinton,
"real" antebellum mammies were few and far between:

> This familiar denizen [Mammy] of the Big House is not merely
> a stereotype, but in fact a figment of the combined romantic
> imaginations of the contemporary southern ideologue and the
> modern southern historian. Records do acknowledge the
> presence of female slaves who served as the "right hand" of
> plantation mistresses. Yet documents from the planter class
> during the first fifty years following the American Revolution
> reveal only a handful of such examples. Not until after
> Emancipation did black women run white households or

occupy in any significant number the special positions ascribed
to them in folklore and fiction. The Mammy was created by
white Southerners to redeem the relationship between black
women and white men within slave society in response to the
antislavery attack from the North during the ante-bellum era,
and to embellish it with nostalgia in the post-bellum period. In
the primary records from before the Civil War, hard evidence
for its existence simply does not appear.[1]

Statistics underscore this point. At no time during the pre–Civil
War era did more than 25 percent of the white Southern population
own slaves. Further, most slave owners possessed ten or fewer slaves,
the majority of whom—men and women—were consigned to field
labor. Slaves represented an expensive investment. Only the very
wealthy could afford the luxury of utilizing the women as house servants rather than as field hands. Like the field hands, those black
bondswomen who worked indoors were unlikely to be overweight because their foodstuffs were severely rationed. They were more likely
to be light as dark because household jobs were frequently assigned to
mixed-race women. They were unlikely to be old because nineteenth-
century black women just did not live very long; fewer than 10 percent of black women lived beyond their fiftieth birthday. Thus the
actress who played *Gone With the Wind*'s mammy, Hattie McDaniel,
became the first African American to win an Academy Award for
playing a truly fictional character, a character shaped and molded by
nostalgia merchants eager to create a past that never was.

Although real slaves who fit the mammy niche are few and far
between in the primary sources social historians use to reconstruct the
day-to-day life in the antebellum South, references to such individuals are plentiful in artifacts with which popular culture historians
describe the modes of entertainment that were the most successful in
the early and mid-nineteenth century. Before the Civil War, white
male minstrel entertainers crossed race and gender boundaries by
darkening their faces and wearing women's clothes in order to entertain their audiences with the supposedly authentic music, humor, and
dance ostensibly common on Southern plantations. At the time, pro-
slavery forces and abolitionists were engaged in a heated war of words
over what both sides referred to as the "peculiar institution." Abolitionists used the firsthand accounts of fugitive slaves and freedmen to

support their position that slaves were treated abysmally. Pro-slavery writers countered charges of cruelty by characterizing slave/master relationships as warm familial ones and claiming that lively slave music and ribald humor were rampant on the plantations. The latter view provided excellent fodder for theatrical producers who were determined to lure urban white audiences into theaters. Sheet music, scripts, and posters attest to the popularity of uncle/auntie or pappy/mammy character pairs in the minstrel shows. Spicy humor and musical talent were the most important attributes of minstrel show mammies. They smoked pipes, told stories, and ran the master's house, always singing from dawn to dusk. More important, these minstrel stage characters and the mammy incarnations that followed were innocuous, docile black women who posed no threats to the white families they served. In the words of a popular minstrel song:

> She'd joke wid de old folks and play wid de child
> She'd cry with the sorrowing, laugh wid de gay;
> Tend on the sick bed, and join in de play
> De furst at de funeral, wedding or birth
> De killer of trouble and maker ob mirth
> She spoke her mind freely, was plain as de day
> But never hurt any by what she might say
> If she once made a promise, it neber was broke.[2]

Thus minstrel shows, the most popular form of nineteenth-century entertainment, conveyed a romanticized idyllic South that bore little if any resemblance to reality. The image of the black woman as consummate supermother was born.

Mid-Nineteenth-Century Images

The year 1851 was a watershed in the history of both fictional images of black women and genuine African-American women. The serial newspaper installments (1851) and subsequent publication (1852) of Harriet Beecher Stowe's *Uncle Tom's Cabin* brought into the homes of thousands of Americans a glimpse of a fictionalized black female house servant. Stowe's physical description of Aunt

Chloe, the faithful wife to Uncle Tom and loyal servant to the Shelby family, set the standard for future fictional representations of mammy figures:

> A round, black, shiny face is hers, so glossy as to suggest the idea that she might have been washed over with the whites of eggs, like one of her own tea rusks. Her whole plump countenance beams with satisfaction and contentment from under a well-starched checked turban, bearing on it, however, if we must confess it, a little of that tinge of self-consciousness which becomes the first cook of the neighborhood, as Aunt Chloe was universally held and acknowledged to be.[3]

Stowe conscientiously offers the reader glimpses into Chloe's life as mammy in the "big house" and wife and mother in her own "lowly cabin." Chloe seems completely able to met the needs of her own children as well as the Shelby offspring, registering only minimal tension when her own and her master's children vie for her attention at the same time. When young George Shelby follows her from her post in his parents' kitchen to the cabin where she is trying to feed her own children, she must try to please all:

> . . . Aunt Chloe . . . took her baby on her lap, and begun alternately filling its mouth and her own, and distributing to Mose and Pete, who seemed rather to prefer eating theirs as they rolled about on the floor under the table, tickling each other and occasionally pulling the baby's toes. "Oh, go long, will ye?" said the mother, giving now and then a kick, in a kind of general way under the table, when the movement became too obstreperous. "Can't ye be decent when white folks come to see ye? Stop dat ar, now will ye? Better mind yerselves, or I'll take ye down a button-hole lower, when Mas'r George is gone!"[4]

Stowe's decision to portray Aunt Chloe in a cabin feeding her three children while Uncle Tom and George Shelby looked on did give Aunt Chloe something future mammies often lacked—an implied sex life. The presence of a baby who still needs to be spoon-fed subtly reminds the reader that Chloe is of child-bearing age and that she and Uncle Tom are apparently enjoying some degree of conjugal satisfaction. Young George's presence in the room also reminds the reader that the cabin is assigned to Uncle Tom, not owned by him. Aunt Chloe was not allowed to leave her responsibilities to her master's children behind at the end of the day. Even on their own time, in their own cabin, mammies in the fictive tradition of Aunt Chloe were expected to put the needs of their white charges ahead of those of their own children. Aunt Chloe, like the mammies who would follow, was a white-identified character. She never put her or her family's needs ahead of those of her white charges.

Theatrical producers soon adapted *Uncle Tom's Cabin* to the minstrel show format. Most stage versions lack the novel's melodramatic angst. Playwrights excised those aspects of the plot ill-suited to musical comedy and played up those elements that lent themselves to music and humor. By suggesting that antebellum households had been run by smiling, self-assured, overweight, born-to-nurture black women, fiction writers and journalists began to perpetuate a mythological Southern past that nearly removed all of the heinous dimensions of slavery. Focusing attention on the alleged rapport that developed between these overweight mammies and their white charges deflected attention from the real relationships that evolved between slave and master.

The year 1851 was also when a select group of women's rights activists were addressed by a very real woman who had firsthand knowledge of a black woman's life in slavery. Facing the Women's Rights Convention in Akron, Ohio, former slave Sojourner Truth focused the attention of her audience on her own children and the devastating impact slavery had on her relationship with them:

> Dat man ober dar say dat woman needs to be lifted ober
> ditches, and to have de best place every whar. Nobody eber
> helped me into carriages, or ober mud puddles, or gives me any
> best place and arn't I a woman? Look at me! Look at my arm!
> I have plowed, and I have planted, and gathered into barns and
> no man could head me—and arn't I a woman? I could work as
> much and eat as much as a man (when I could get it), and
> bear de lash well—and arn't I a woman? I have borned thirteen

chilern and seen mos' all sold off into slavery, and when I cried out with a mother's grief, none but Jesus heard—and arn't I a woman?[5]

During the 1850s Sojourner Truth was a stalwart campaigner on the abolitionist and women's rights circuits. She published an autobiographical narrative detailing her life as a bondswoman and her conversion to Christianity. But her story of a genuine slave's experience did not reach anywhere near the audience reached by Stowe's fictional Aunt Chloe. Commonly labeled the world's first best-seller, *Uncle Tom's Cabin* has a permanent place in the history of American popular culture. In the first months following its release, it sold in excess of 10,000 copies per week. In subsequent decades, it remained a best-seller.[6] Stage versions of the play known as Tom shows were equally popular well into the twentieth century. On the other hand, published firsthand accounts of the slave experiences of actual black women such as Sojourner Truth, Harriet Tubman, and Linda Brent were published and sold in the hundreds, not in the hundreds of thousands. They were popular with select antislavery-oriented audiences during the decades immediately prior to the Civil War. After the war they were virtually forgotten until post-1960s African-American historians and literary critics rooted them out of rare book rooms and library special collections and began to mine them for a black woman's point of view of slavery.

Why did the public prefer the fictional Aunt Chloe to the very real Sojourner Truth? Dark-skinned, loyal to her master and mistress, an able cook and housekeeper, plump, asexual, good-humored, Aunt Chloe was one of the first of a long line of fictional black women whose character comforted and assuaged. Abrasive and confrontational, willing to remind her audiences of white male lust, uncompromisingly loyal to her *own* children and her *own* people, Sojourner Truth disturbed and unsettled her audiences. In order to accommodate the needs of Aunt Chloe, the reader need only pursue the elimination of slavery. The only problems with Aunt Chloe's world were that she was unpaid and her owners had the power to sell her family members. Abolish slavery and she would be free to choose to work in the Shelby household. Accommodating the demands of Sojourner Truth required much more substantial social upheaval. Truth was not advocating a more humane structure through which black women would be paid for taking care of white families, she was committed to fostering a world in which black women could shape their own destiny independent of the needs of the white community. Sojourner Truth was fully a black-identified individual; she saw no reason to put the needs of whites ahead of her own. Aunt Chloe allowed the masses to indulge in wishful thinking in a fashion not possible by Sojourner Truth.

Turn-of-the-Century Mammies

Ask most people to name a mammy and they will respond "Aunt Jemima." An advertising trademark for one hundred years, the toothy grin and calico-swathed plump face is synonymous with wholesome, nutritious breakfasts. Aunt Jemima first met the great-grandparents of the consumers who now purchase her line of breakfast foods at the 1893 Columbia Exposition in Chicago (similar to our world's fairs). White entrepreneurs had developed a self-rising pancake flour. In order to convince merchants to plunk down cash for one of the first convenience foods peddled to the American public, journalist and businessman Chris L. Rutt utilized a popular minstrel tune that sang the praises of Aunt Jemima.[7] Rutt's company was eventually purchased by the Davis Milling Company, which opted to demonstrate the convenience of self-rising pancake flour by displaying the product at the Columbia Exposition. The company hired Nancy Green, a black cook, to give the demonstrations and play the part of Aunt Jemima. Green, a former domestic servant for a Chicago judge, was a hit. Her pancake-flipping dexterity and wholesome stories about life in the old South garnered more than 50,000 merchant orders for Aunt Jemima pancake mix.[8]

There are many ironies implicit in the fact that the Columbia Exposition was used to launch Aunt Jemima products. For the duration of the fair, other African-American women, most notably journalist and antilynching advocate Ida B. Wells,* distributed a protest pamphlet entitled "The Reason Why: The Colored American is not in the World's Columbian Exposition." Wells and her supporters wanted

---

* Ida B. Wells married in 1895 and henceforth used the name Wells-Barnett.

the public to know how inadequate they believed the fair's attention to black Americans was. With the support of the elderly abolitionist and activist Frederick Douglass, Wells distributed thousands of these pamphlets throughout the fair's run.[9]

Only recently has Wells begun to receive the academic recognition her late nineteenth- and early twentieth-century accomplishments warrant. In the space of forty years she challenged a separate but equal statute through the court system; campaigned tirelessly on behalf of antilynching legislation; owned and operated several African-American newspapers; investigated the 1917 race riot in East St. Louis; lobbied for the freedom of a dozen or more unfairly incarcerated black Texans; met with President Woodrow Wilson in an effort to dismantle segregation in the federal workplace; and helped organize the National Association for the Advancement of Colored People (NAACP). In spite of Wells's appearance on a commemorative stamp issued by the U.S. Postal Service, her visage is certainly not nearly as well known as the Aunt Jemima countenance that was launched at the Columbia Exposition. Nancy Green's Aunt Jemima appealed to the American public's desire to imagine a harmonious relationship between black women and white families. Entrusted with the most important meal of the day, Aunt Jemima allowed the consumer to construct a nurturing scenario in which gracious black women committed themselves to the care and feeding of white families. This scenario was so compelling that generation after generation of American consumer has embraced it and maintained a steadfast allegiance to Aunt Jemima products.

The role assumed by Ida B. Wells at the Columbia Exposition offered little reassurance. With her pamphlets and her speeches, she implored the American public to assume responsibility for the racial inequities of the day. In her homespun calico garb with a turban around her head, Aunt Jemima comforted the public; in her business-like attire with a fashionable hat on her head, Ida B. Wells vexed the public. Aunt Jemima's was the kind of face people wanted to remember; Ida B. Wells's was the kind they wanted to forget. And that is exactly what happened.

Aunt Jemima Clones

By the turn of the century mammy images had secured a permanent place in American popular culture. Although the selling of real black women had ended with the Civil War, Aunt Jemima was sold. The Davis Milling Company sold the product and its well-known trademark to the Quaker Oats company in 1925. Both companies capitalized on the Aunt Jemima image. Print advertisements urged consumers to buy the products so that they could receive the twin benefits of a wholesome breakfast and the opportunity to redeem package coupons and cash for Aunt Jemima–endorsed products. These included black rag dolls, cookie jars, creamer and sugar dish sets, spice containers, cornmeal and pancake mix cigarette lighters, Halloween masks, recipe cards, cookbooks, and syrup pitchers.

A series of indefatigable mammy figures trooped through the first several decades of twentieth-century literature, film, and popular culture. Like Aunt Jemima and her turn-of-the-century literary counterparts, these mammies were happily ensconced in the households of white employers. Implicit in each rendition was the notion that these thick-waisted black women were happy with their lot, honored to spend their days and nights caring for white benefactors.

Other manufacturers developed their own mammy trademarks. Luzianne coffee, Fun to Wash laundry soap, Aunt Dinah molasses, and Dinah black enamel were all products inscribed with visible mammies on their labels and packages. As mentioned earlier, mammy faces have been imprinted on virtually every possible accessory for the twentieth-century kitchen. In addition to all of the kitchen items already listed, mammy sewing kits, wall sconces, string dispensers, greeting cards, cookbooks, and sheet music have all been produced.

The wholesome mammy image discernible in advertising and kitchen memorabilia was reinforced in film. Audiences cheered when the stalwart mammy in D. W. Griffith's 1915 epic *The Birth of a Nation* (based on Thomas Dixon's popular 1905 novel *The Clansman*) defends her white master's household from the attacks of marauding black and white Union soldiers. She remains loyal to the genteel Camerons throughout and never takes advantage of her freedom. From that point on, few films depicting the "old South" omitted mammy as a stock character. Most resembled the *Birth of a Nation* mammy; they were plump, dark-skinned, abundantly clothed, white-identified black women tenaciously loyal to their masters and mistresses. *The Birth of a Nation* did, however, introduce a new trait into the attribute cluster of the prototypical mammy. In a climactic scene in which black soldiers forcibly enter the Camerons' home, the robust mammy—the role was actually played by a white male actor—physically assaults them. Early twentieth-century mammies did more than just cook for and clean up after white families. If necessary, they would raise their fists against other blacks in order to defend the sanctity of the white household.

Probably the best-known and most well-known movie mammy presided over the mythical plantation Tara in *Gone With the Wind*. In a role that earned her an Academy Award, Hattie McDaniel captivated audiences with her cantankerous portrayal of another mammy whose loyalty to her whites is so strong that she refuses the freedom that comes with the Emancipation Proclamation. Like her counterpart in *The Birth of a Nation*, she physically assaults black soldiers when she perceives a threat to her mistress.

Movie audiences cried when a rare urban auntie proved unequal to the challenges her own child heaps upon her in the 1934 version of *Imitation of Life* based on novel of the same name by Fannie Hurst. Following the pattern first established by Stowe's Aunt Chloe, Aunt Delilah (Louise Beavers) tries to juggle the needs of her own child while taking care of her white employer's. A good-humored, stocky, asexual, dark-skinned black woman, Aunt Delilah unselfishly helps make her white employer rich with her secret pancake recipe (sound familiar?), only to lose the affection of her light-skinned, self-centered daughter who was desperately ashamed of her black bloodline. In some respects, Aunt Delilah is an even more passive, subservient character than Aunt Chloe. At least Aunt Chloe returned to her humble slave cabin at the end of the workday. When Aunt Delilah is offered the financial freedom that would allow her to vacate her downstairs accommodations in her employer's posh New York townhouse and establish her own home, she responds, "My own house. You gonna send me away? Don' do that to me. How I gonna take care of you and Miss Jessie if I'se away?"[10] Just as the mammies in *Birth of a Nation* and *Gone With the Wind* opted to stay with their white masters after the Emancipation Proclamation, Aunt Delilah sees no reason to make her own home. With nearly inexplicable resignation, she makes no effort to profit from the success of her pancake mix recipe or to undo her light-skinned daughter's self-hate complex. Partially because of Aunt Delilah's guidance and care, her white charge, Jessie Pullman, survives a particularly ill-fated romantic attachment. Delilah is less successful at helping her own daughter confront her crisis—a profound self-hate that leads her to run away and begin "passing" for white. Distraught by her daughter's abandonment, Aunt Delilah dies of a broken heart.

Mammy's love for her white employers was not unrequited. Her loyalty was matched by the white public's prolonged love affair with her. During the first several decades of the twentieth century, the Daughters of the American Confederacy (DAC) even petitioned Congress to erect a monument in the likeness of a mammy in Washington.[11] Ironically, at roughly the same time that the DAC was trying permanently to enshrine mammy, the Daughters of the American Revolution (DAR) was trying to prevent renowned African-American opera singer Marian Anderson from performing in Constitution Hall in Washington, D.C. The DAR's decision prompted first lady Eleanor Roosevelt to resign from the prestigious women's organization. Secretary of the Interior Harold Ickes arranged for Anderson to sing on the steps of the Lincoln Memorial. One can only ponder the scenario if the DAC had succeeded in getting the mammy monument approved and constructed. Would the impeccably dressed, conservatively coiffed, vocally sophisticated Anderson have been asked to sing in the shadow of a head-ragged, apron-wearing, grinning mammy statue?

Beginning in the 1950s, the emerging medium of television continued the salute to mammy. Popular from 1950 to 1953, *Beulah* was one of the first shows in which a black character's name was also the series' title. Episodes focused on a suburban household in which a dedicated, loving black housekeeper nurtured a white middle-class family. Following the pattern established by her film and fictional predecessors, she cheerfully dispensed homespun wisdom along with nutritious meals to the white children and their parents.

The Hibernation of Mammy

An invisible line has always divided domestic and professional domains in mainstream American thinking. We still speak of women who stay/work at home and those who work in the "outside" world. Until very recently, work within the home was considered women's work; work outside of the home was men's. This dichotomy has usually been drawn so rigidly that outdoor cooking is still often assigned to the man of the house. The inside/outside split was less applicable to African-American women's history. As many labor historians and sociologists have illustrated, *outside* work for African-American women took place *inside* the homes of white women. Black women left their own kitchens to take care of someone else's.

About two years after *Beulah* went off the air, Rosa Parks and the hundreds of black women who boycotted the Montgomery, Alabama, bus system from late 1955 through most of 1956 may have begun the process that forced mammy into a temporary hibernation. Although Mrs. Parks herself was not a domestic worker, most of the women who participated in the boycott were real-life African-American women who supported their families with the income they earned by running white households. And they bore little resemblance to the smiling, subservient, plump fictional mammies projected in advertising and on film. Jo Ann Gibson Robinson, a boycott leader and eloquent biographer of the women in the movement, succinctly detailed the relations between the black domestic workers and their white female employers:

> Because of the color of her skin and the texture of her hair, almost any white woman at that time could get a job for fifty dollars or more a week, no matter how limited her education was. Jobs for clerks in dimestores, cashiers in markets, telephone operators were numerous, but were not open to black women. A fifty-dollar-a-week worker could employ a black domestic to clean her home, cook the food, wash and iron clothes, and nurse the baby for as little as twenty dollars per week. And, with all house work, baby care, and laundry taken care of there would be thirty dollars clear.[12]

Robinson's observation speaks to several significant issues. First, it debunks the accepted truism that only the wealthy women hired full-time domestic workers. Jim Crow segregation—the codes and practices that enforced the separate but equal doctrine—not only kept black women in the backs of buses, in substandard schools, and in separate public washrooms, it crowded them into one job market. Applying the law of supply and demand, it is easy to see that wages were low because the number of black women who needed jobs exceeded the number of positions. As a result, middle-class white women could easily afford part- or full-time domestic help. But the Montgomery bus boycott and other successful civil rights protests of the late 1950s and the early 1960s liberated black women not only from the backs of buses but also from the white kitchens. Slowly but surely, jobs once considered off limits to black women were available to them.

Rosa Parks, Jo Ann Gibson Robinson, Coretta Scott King, and their sister activists served as flesh-and-blood reminders that the plastic, cast-iron, fabric, ceramic, and celluloid mammies bore little resemblance to real black women. As a result, mammy was granted a brief vacation from her post in white American households. By the 1960s, mammy cookie jars, memo pads, and similar objects were retired into attics and garages. For the most part, manufacturers ceased to market them, and antique and thrift shop proprietors did not display them. Aunt Jemima and her line of breakfast foods was the most noticeable exception to this rule. Long the trademark for pancakes, the parent company refused to retire the treasured symbol of good breakfasts and wholesome living. Instead it opted to recast the image so as to professionalize her look. The Aunt Jemima of the sixties was less rotund and less toothsome than her earlier incarnations. Today's Aunt Jemima has an even trimmer, more professional appearance. Unlike the earlier versions, there is no calico visible anywhere in the likeness on the package.

With the premiere of *Julia* in 1968, television acknowledged some of the new vocational opportunities available to African-American women. Touted as a new and more positive image of the African-American working woman, at least some of Julia's characteristics were reminiscent of those of her predecessors. She was still clad in a uniform; as a registered nurse in a white pediatrician's office, in her role she still nurtured white children. But unlike Beulah and earlier mammy figures, Julia was depicted as putting her own child's well-being squarely ahead of the white children her job required her to nurture. With her job outside of her own or a white woman's home, she represented an important step away from the kitchens to which her ancestors had been confined.

The modern feminist era came on the heels of the civil rights movement. Just as nineteenth-century women became frustrated with attempts to stifle their voices during the antebellum era, women in the 1960s objected to the desire of male antiwar and civil rights activists to limit their contributions to the kitchen and the bedroom. The now-notorious and controversial "great society" programs of the 1960s facilitated the escape of real black women from the kitchens and out of the domestic workplace. The feminist movement did not pave the path away from their own homes for African-American women; rather it, along with the civil rights movement, paved a path away from the homes of white women. Thus just as white women were fighting for rights that would enable them to leave their homes to work, black women were winning rights that would allow them to work outside of white households.

Starting in the late 1950s and through the 1960s and 1970s, a window was broken in the kitchen to which African-American women had been confined. Suddenly they had increased opportunities to seek work outside their own and other people's homes. Educational opportunity grants afforded access to higher education, and employers were eager to display their liberal credentials by hiring African-American employees. Hiring an African-American female satisfied twin requirements of opening doors to minorities and women. Many corporations were careful to place African-American women in visible positions, signaling their commitment to diversity in the workplace. A handful of us passed through these newly opened doors.

The Return of the Mammy

In 1982 folklorist and literary critic Trudier Harris published a book on the image of black domestics in the writings of black authors. Although Harris makes occasional references to popular culture, her study focuses on black-authored literature. The title of Harris's book is *From Mammies to Militants: Domestics in Black American Literature.*[13] This title implies a progression. It suggests that authors *used to* depict domestics as mammies but that they now infuse domestic characters with doses of black militancy. Harris offers compelling literary evidence for her thesis; recent short stories and novels by black writers Barbara Woods, Ted Shine, and Ed Bullins offer uncompromisingly militant black female domestics. However, while the shift from mammy to militant is discernible in black-authored literature, it is not evident in popular culture. Woods, Shine, and Bullins are not household names. In the early 1980s, when Harris's book was published, most Americans—white and black—were seeing images of black women domestics on television and in popular magazines. These images were anything but militant. Television and the other highly visible purveyors of popular culture were registering a renewed affection for mammies.

In the fall of 1981 the CBS network included in its lineup a situation comedy starring stage actress and singer Nell Carter. Both physically and temperamentally, the producers and writers of *Gimme a Break* developed a character with most of the attributes of a classic, albeit updated, mammy. She is dark-skinned and overweight. But a dark complexion and a plus-size wardrobe alone do not a mammy make. Carter's character, also named Nell, worked as a housekeeper for a widowed police chief and his three daughters. The writers very carefully emphasize that Nell was not a career domestic. Formerly a cabaret singer, Nell had promised her white terminally ill best friend that she would take care of her husband and their daughters. In episode after episode, Nell's energies are devoted to fulfilling her promise to her late friend. Throughout the series, Nell was primarily a white-identified character. Although her new closest girlfriend was a black professional woman, and occasional episodes allowed her an African-American boyfriend, her life revolved around the white family whose house she called home. Similar to Aunt Delilah in *Imitation of Life*, Nell is quite content living in her white employer's home. The most telling evidence of the producers' desire to project her as white-identified came in the final season. After several years with Nell as their surrogate mother, the chief's three daughters have established their own lives and no longer need Nell's full-time care. Since the show had not yet been canceled, the writers needed to create a storyline that would give Nell something meaningful to do that would

appeal to the program's wide audience. In standard television situation comedy fashion, Nell stumbles upon a young boy in need of a
home. In this world where hundreds if not thousands of black children need good homes, Nell manages to find herself another needy
white child. With clear enthusiasm, she and the chief adopt the child,
and her position as a black woman eager to devote herself to the
needs of whites is once again assured. Thus the subliminal mammy
image cultivated in the previous five seasons is safe.

More evidence of the renewed appeal of mammy images were
evident between the pages of decorating magazines. The October
1986 issue of *Country Living* magazine displays an ostensibly real
kitchen that resembles the fictional one described at the beginning of
this chapter. In the corner of one featured kitchen, at least seventeen
ceramic, fabric, wooden, and plastic mammy icons are visible. In
addition, six pickaninnies and five pappies inhabit the shelves, cup-
boards, and walls of this Michigan kitchen. Several pages later a
kitchen containing thirteen visible mammies is featured. The owners
of the seventeen-mammy kitchen are described as collectors of folk
art, whereas the kitchen belonging to the thirteen-mammy kitchen is
featured because it shows off its owners' collection of blue granite-
ware. Mammies and other contemptible collectibles also are featured
elsewhere in the magazine. How can this renewed fondness for auntie
armies be explained? This 1986 issue of *Country Living* clearly signals and celebrates mammy's return.

Why, in the 1980s and 1990s, would anyone want to reach into a
mammy cookie jar and pull out an Oreo? The answer, it seems to me,
rests more in the liberation of white women than in the liberation of
African-American women. After all, it wasn't just black women who
received a license to leave the kitchens of white women in the mid-
1960s. The feminist movement ushered white women away from the
home and into outside workplaces. Consequently, neither white nor
black women were left minding the kitchen. The pre–civil rights
movement days described by Jo Ann Gibson Robinson in which mod-
erate-income white families could easily afford full-time domestic
help were long gone. By the 1980s and 1990s only the most affluent
could afford the wages commanded by domestic workers who exert
more control over the market for their services than their predecessors
could have ever imagined. Newspapers, magazines, and talk shows
chronicled the problems of working mothers who were forced to leave

their children in substandard day care facilities and to serve their families nutritionally deficient convenience foods.

At the same time that white women had to cope with black women's absence from white kitchens, they also had to cope with perceived competition from black women in the workplace. Virtually all of my black female friends and relatives have been subjected to the complaints of white women who seem convinced that black women are getting all of the best jobs and are singled out for promotions. Now, I don't think that white women are consciously promoting this ambivalence about black women. Instead, it emerges in subtle ways.

The spate of women's magazines that have evolved to accommodate the developing domestic/professional split constitutes a fertile ground on which to explore the impact of this phenomena. For virtually every special interest that exists, periodicals are published. There are magazines for orchid growers, fans of Walt Disney, plumbers, and trivia aficionados. Each year hundreds of new magazines are created, depleting forests and filling landfills in the name of hobbies and obsessions. But not all new magazines find a niche. The successful marketing of the glossier publications requires a keen awareness of consumer whims and trends. In recent years a glut of so-called women's magazines have begun to crowd the newsstands. Some of them are clearly designed to cater to the "outside" dimension of the new woman's life. With such names as *Working Woman* and *Entrepreneurial Woman*, they woo subscribers with promises of articles devoted to illuminating the trek from the family dining room to the corporate boardroom. Adjacent to these are old and new magazines that focus attention on the inside sphere, on the home. Titles such as *Country Living, Victoria, Country Home, Country Craft*, and *Traditional Home* evoke a discernible impulse to combine the alleged elegance and beauty of bygone days with the high-tech comforts of today. Hand-stenciled knotty-pine armoires disguise VCRs and big-screen television sets. Oak sideboards conceal microwave ovens. Pottery crocks hold blow-dryers and electric curling irons. And a handful of magazines take the position that inside and outside options are available to women who want simultaneously to have the perfect household as well as the perfect career. These magazines seem to guarantee the best of both worlds. Today's woman can have it all. Today's white woman.

Real flesh-and-blood black women, as opposed to plastic and

cast-iron miniatures of black women, rarely appear in these decorating magazines. I haven't conducted an official poll on this, but I feel secure in stating that, for the most part, black women do not share their white counterpart's affection for the good old days. Let's consider one of the most popular of the new magazines, *Victoria*. It is devoted to encouraging its readers to resurrect the charm and style of the Victorian era in their households, foodstuffs, and clothing. The pages of *Victoria* are replete with pictures of white flowers, white clothing, and white women. An article in the entertaining section might focus on how to have a proper English tea. A recent clothing article gave readers directions on how to achieve the fashion look of the film *African Queen* with 1990s clothes. *Victoria*'s decorating pages do not feature mammy memo pads—water-stained paper and crystal pen-and-ink desk sets are much more in keeping with the style the editors want to evoke. Black women are never featured in *Victoria*'s fashion pages, nor are our homes ever scrutinized and photographed as exemplars of the nostalgically correct. During the era that *Victoria* is celebrating, black women were the labor force that laundered and ironed the omnipresent white linen and lace. Black women were the ones who polished the *de rigueur* silver services.

Victoria and the other magazines do not reflect the lives lived by real white women any more than *Gone With the Wind* or *Beulah* depicts the genuine experiences of black women. Instead, they shape and sell a fantasy world in which the real complexities of women's lives at the end of the twentieth century are glossed over with platitudes and pretty pictures.

Harriet Beecher Stowe and the other mid- to late-nineteenth-century writers who "birthed" the first mammies and aunties inadvertently presented the world with a ferociously durable symbol of black feminine benevolence and self-sacrifice. The early twentieth-century moviemakers, advertisers, and other American dream merchants recognized and profited from the public's continuing love affair with the smiling faces and stocky shapes of the mythical mammies. Mammy was forced underground for an all-too-brief period of time in the 1960s and early 1970s when sensitivity to the impact of stereotypical depictions of African Americans peaked. But before long, a new, made-over mammy was resurrected. In his explanation of the appeal of the *Beulah* character, television producer Hal Kanter explained, "People thought, wouldn't it be nice to have a Beulah, to take care of us. . . ."[14] This explanation for one particular mammy's popularity succinctly describes the appeal of all of them. Mammies allow the public to indulge in wishful thinking. The idea that a selfless, sexless, black woman might want to come into your kitchen and organize your household has retained a persistent hold on the American imagination. But it is not now, and never was, true.

Mammy planter circa 1940s

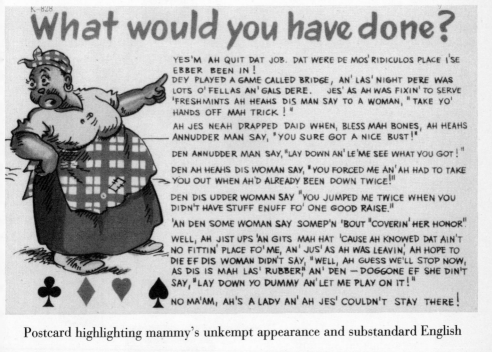

Postcard highlighting mammy's unkempt appearance and substandard English

Postcard with implicit sexual innuendoes

Mass-produced plastic
reproduction mammy
memo pad circa 1980s

Benevolent uncle
cookie jar lid
circa 1940s

Replica of a once-common
black boy hitching post

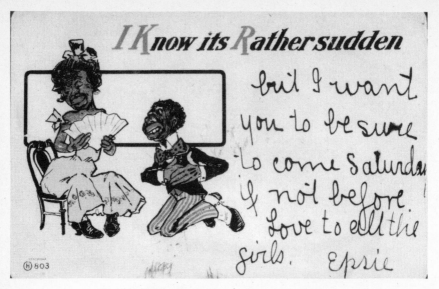

Outlandishly dressed couple on a postcard

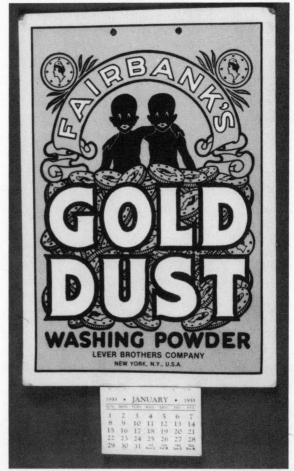

1933 calendar
featuring nude
Gold Dust twins

Happy black men in well-fitting uniforms

Sambo figure etched on
a spinning noisemaker

Alligator letter opener and
a nude black child pencil

Alligators chase a barefoot
black child up a tree

"HONEY COME DOWN" WE ALL ARE WAITING FOR YOU IN FLORIDA 557

Postcard featuring a fearless white man feeding alligators

Disproportionately large alligator with a naked black infant

Reproduction coffee label featuring an alligator and black children

Black children, out-of-doors as usual, being watched by a pair of alligators

WEIGHT
8.–3 OZS.

GHT 1912 BY
NS COFFEE CO.,LTD.

PACKED BY
NEW ORLEANS COFFEE CO.,LTD.
NEW ORLEANS, LA.

Reproduction pin (button)
featuring a semiclad black child
juxtaposed with a small animal

Darkie toothpaste, renamed Darlie
toothpaste in the 1990s

Sheet music used as part of a campaign to urge
African Americans to enlist for service in World War I

Reproduction pin (button) featuring
a creature with the head of a black
female and the body of a bird

Late 1980s wooden
"folk art" pickaninny

Reproduction sign for the
United States Fur Co.

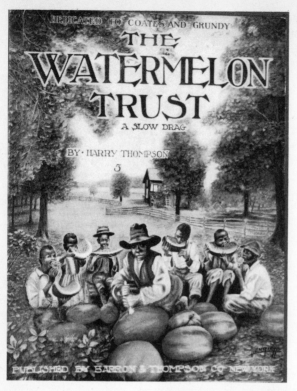

Sheet music exemplifying supposed African-American preoccupation with watermelon

Topsy/Eva or Topsy/Turvy doll

"Collectible" pickaninny
decorative plate circa 1980s

Sheet music featuring
the Duncan Sisters,
famous for playing
Topsy and Eva

Tom show poster featuring an extraordinarily well-dressed, elderly Uncle Tom and an angelic Little Eva

Poster for one of several screen versions of *Uncle Tom's Cabin*

Advertisement for a traveling Tom show

Poster for the San Francisco Mime Troupe's *I Ain't Yo' Uncle*

Lobby card for a movie serial devoted to the adventures of whites in Africa

Lunch box and thermos featuring Steve Urkel, quintessential
nerdy black adolescent

2

Blemished
Depictions

The patterns of stereotyping identified in contemptible collectibles are not limited to material culture. The ill-kept, tattered-clothed children featured on the postcards are related to celluloid pickaninnies of *Our Gang* film shorts (known as *The Little Rascals* on TV). Alligators and crocodiles have not limited their pursuit of African Americans to sterling silver spoons; they have chased their human prey in Tarzan movies. The overweight mammy permanently rendered as a cast-iron bank is clearly kin to chunky black domestics from movies such as *Judge Priest* and *Imitation of Life* and television shows such as *Beulah* and *Gimme a Break*.

No doubt the racial self-deprecation expressed by the black youngster from Pick Temple's ranch and his mother were influenced by these insidious icons as well as their counterparts in other forms of popular culture. Similarly, the other young guests—the white children —had begun to absorb messages that reinforced their own sense of racial superiority. Isolating the precise popular culture sources of such messages is problematic. In one of the early 1940s Superman cartoons shown in movie theaters, African "cannibals," complete with animal-skin loincloths and bones in their noses, dance around Lois Lane as flames snap at her heels. Superman rescues her just in the nick of time. Few would argue that such scenarios communicate the message that whites are superior and civilized while blacks are inferior and savage. The *Adventures of Superman* television series of the 1950s rarely featured blacks. In episode after episode, the caped crusader fought for truth, justice, and the American way. The "Americans" he endeavored to save were almost exclusively white. Is the cartoon episode with the obviously depreciating image of Africans *worse* than all of the episodes where blacks are nonexistent?

Certainly it is easier to find the conspicuous black sheep in the family of American popular culture. The cartoons inhabited by savages, the advertisements crowded with scraping, uniformed black servants, the movies populated by black pimps and prostitutes are fairly easy to scrutinize. Identifying the subtle ways in which popular culture contributes to racial misunderstandings is more of a challenge.

Today's merchants of popular culture descend from a long line of entreprenuers. The first in the chain were the explorers and traders who first ventured to the west coast of Africa in the 1550s. In his study of white attitudes toward blacks, historian Winthrop Jordan describes this era: "The impact of the Negro's color was the more powerful upon Englishmen, moreover, because England's principal contact with Africans came in West Africa and the Congo where men were not merely dark but almost literally black: one of the fairest skinned nations suddenly came face to face with one of the darkest peoples on earth."[1] To illustrate his point about color, Jordan cites definitions of black from a pre–sixteenth-century *Oxford English Dictionary*. The definition includes "Deeply stained with dirt, soiled, dirty, foul. . . . Having dark or deadly purposes, malignant; pertaining to or involving death, deadly; baneful, disastrous, sinister, . . . Foul, iniquitous, atrocious, horrible, wicked. . . . Indicating disgrace, censure, liability to punishment etcetera."[2] Using Elizabethan travelers' reports, diaries, letters, ship logs, and similar primary sources, Jordan builds a compelling case that within the first few decades following English involvement in the slave trade, pernicious antiblack stereotypes were commonplace.

Eurocentrism had been born. A mode of white elitism and supremacy was established and perpetuated. The chapters in Part II examine a broad spectrum of popular and folk culture texts that reverberate with Eurocentric sensibilities. Some writers, artists, politicians, and thinkers have challenged some of the consequences of white supremacy. Chapter 4 takes up the case of Harriet Beecher Stowe's *Uncle Tom's Cabin.* As Chapters 1 and 3 have already demonstrated, this one novel is virtually impossible to ignore in a study of race and American popular culture. Stowe set out to write a corrective, a story that might mitigate some of the damage being inflicted by her Southern contemporaries. Because of her own upbringing and experiences, she too was a culprit in the perpetuation of a Eurocentric worldview. She grew up in a society that privileged white over black in subtle and unsubtle ways. At the same time that she was struggling to undo some of the grosser forms of racism, her sense of white superiority infused her words.

Throughout the years Uncle Tom, a fictional black hero, assumed a larger-than-life status. Only in recent decades have real African-American heroes replaced this fictional character and infiltrated the higher ranks of American society. Chapter 5, "Jacksonalia," looks at the ways in which the masses have interpreted the achievements of three such individuals.

The remaining chapters evaluate the negative stereotypes perpetuated by television and film texts. As the youngster from Pick Temple's ranch so eloquently testified, the message that being white is better gets conveyed at a very early age. Chapter 6 looks at the largest producer of children's popular culture—the Disney studios and its affiliated companies—to determine the range of ways in which children are urged to see the world from a white perspective. Chapter 7 uses television series to contemplate the Eurocentric standards set for depictions of black intelligence. Chapters 8 and 9 critique a cluster of films from the past three decades. Very few black actors and actresses are included in them, and, at first glance, their storylines lack racial overtones. Nonetheless, they subtly reinforce a white-dominated vision of America's past and present. Chapter 10 examines a cluster of films purportedly based on real-life African Americans. In bringing such stories to the big screen, filmmakers have consistently diluted the true power of the individuals chronicled in these movies. Chapter 11 takes up films that, while physically set on the continent of Africa, offer much more insight into the workings of the European or American mind than they do about any aspect of the African experience. Chapter 12 looks at two of the best-loved films starring African-

American men. The black male stars of both movies were nominated for Academy Awards, and Sidney Poitier, the star of the first, remains the only African-American actor to win the prestigious award. The striking similarities between the films suggest that Hollywood pigeonholes African-American men in a very narrow space.

4

The Troping of Uncle Tom

We thought Uncle Tom was dead and long buried.

— TOPSY in *I Ain't Yo' Uncle*

Referring to then Supreme Court nominee Clarence Thomas, an African-American student summed up several minutes of class discussion by claiming "He's just an old Uncle Tom." "That's just what I was going to say," mumbled another student as she lowered her outstretched hand. At that point the lively discussion disintegrated because the students seemed to conclude that no more was left to be said about the Bush administration's controversial African-American nominee.[1] I asked the class to define what they meant by "Uncle Tom." While this particular group of students would have argued over the color of the blackboard, they reached complete consensus over their profile of an Uncle Tom. Describing his personality, they emphasized his supposed identification with his masters/employers and his contempt for his own (black) kind. They accused him of racial self-hate. They maintained that he was always willing to "sell out" blacks in order to placate whites and improve his personal well-being. A few students called attention to his unswerving faith in

69

Christianity. All agreed that from a political perspective, Uncle Toms were black conservatives.

I asked the class to compose a picture of a classic Uncle Tom. In describing his physical appearance, the students emphasized his advanced years, his white hair, and his stooped posture. Their Uncle Tom's visage always boasted a smile, albeit one without a full set of teeth. There was some moderate disagreement about his clothes. According to some, an image of an African-American man wearing a neat suit of servant's clothing emerged. For others, the elderly black man was attired in worn, tattered, mismatched clothing. In short, they dressed their Uncle Toms in the raiments of the adult male contemptible collectibles documented in Chapter 1. And when he removes the sloppy overalls or neat uniform, he goes to sleep; all agree that Uncle Toms are past their sexual primes.

Only a couple of hands shot up when I asked how many of the students had actually read the original *Uncle Tom's Cabin* written by Harriet Beecher Stowe. Those few students confessed that many years had lapsed since they tackled the book. But I wasn't surprised by the confidence with which the class members described a character embedded in a story so few had actually read. I know, however, that I surprised them when I claimed that it was almost an insult to Harriet Beecher Stowe's fictional Uncle Tom to associate him with all the negative qualities they enunciated in connection with Clarence Thomas. I further aggravated them by claiming that Stowe's politics had motivated her to construct a Tom who resembled the recently retired Thurgood Marshall much more than his supposed replacement Clarence Thomas.

The Original Tom

Since the first installments of *Uncle Tom's Cabin* began to appear in the abolitionist journal *The National Era* in 1851, merchants of popular culture have shaped and reshaped Harriet Beecher Stowe's fictional characters to suit their rhetorical purposes and to match the pervasive attitudes about blacks during a particular era. No single work has been reinvented with the same passion as *Uncle Tom's Cabin*. Unwittingly, Stowe gave birth to much more than a fictional hero. Aspects of her Tom fed the imaginations of generations of Americans. In literary, stage, film, and television adaptations, writers have taken enormous liberties in their characterizations of Uncle Tom. The label *Uncle Tom* is firmly entrenched, although not fully understood, in the vocabulary of most contemporary Americans: My students' definition only marginally resembled the character chronicled in the novel. "It is ironic," observes historian Wilson J. Moses, "that the humble heroism of old Uncle Tom has been transmuted into racial treason by the subtle alchemy of social amnesia."[2] This chapter examines the series of transmutations and reinventions of this basic character that merchants of popular culture have molded and remolded for more than 140 years. Each new depiction of Uncle Tom reveals much about the racial politics of a given era or group within American history. "*Uncle Tom's Cabin* was at the epicenter of a massive cultural phenomenon," notes African-American literary critic Richard Yarborough, "the tremors of which still affect the relationship between blacks and whites in the United States."[3]

If the pro-slavery congressmen who pushed for a tougher Fugitive Slave Law as a plank of the Compromise of 1850 had known that this legislation was going to inspire the writing of *Uncle Tom's Cabin*, they might have contented themselves with the old law. The new law made all blacks in the North vulnerable to capture by federal commissioners empowered to return runaways to their Southern owners. Whites were obligated to surrender any known fugitives. Harriet Beecher Stowe's sister-in-law was one of many abolitionists incensed by the impact the law was having on both free blacks and those fortunate few ex-slaves who had made their way to the free states.[4] In a letter to Stowe she wrote, "if I could use a pen as you can, I would write something that would make this whole nation feel what an accursed thing slavery is."[5] Stowe's goal was a profoundly political one; her muses were the pro-slavery congressmen who pushed through that legislation. After deciding to follow her sister-in-law's suggestion, Stowe set out to convince nonabolitionist Northerners that slaves were humans, capable of the full range of human emotions and drives so many of that era believed to be restricted to whites. Further, she intended to expose the irreconcilability of slavery and Christian piety. According to Stowe, good Christians should neither hold slaves themselves nor tolerate the presence of slavery in their nation.

This does not mean that Stowe necessarily supported racial

equality, particularly as we would define it today. In *Uncle Tom's Cabin*, the African-American characters of mixed parentage are those given the most credit for intelligence. To Stowe's way of thinking, white ancestry was clearly a prerequisite for genuine intellect. She, like Abraham Lincoln and many antebellum luminaries, posits voluntary colonization—the return of Americans of African descent to Africa—as a viable solution to the "problem" of black emancipation.

Nonetheless, in the early 1850s her beliefs about the incompatibility of slavery and Christianity definitely represented a minority opinion. The population at large did not accept blacks as residents on the same sphere of human development as whites, and good Christians did not perceive themselves to be hypocrites for owning slaves or sanctioning the perpetuation of the "peculiar institution"—the euphemism used by both Northerners and Southerners to describe slavery—in the South.[6] Stowe set out to change that. Using the slave narratives published by blacks who had firsthand experience of the peculiar institution in conjunction with abolitionist newspapers and tracts, Stowe crafted a story designed to show a Northern reading public the day-to-day existence of some Southern slaves. The public's reaction was swift and decisive. In order to meet the demand, the publisher kept three power presses running around the clock. More than 300,000 copies were sold in the first year.[7]

Tom Was No Uncle Tom

Tom as shaped by Harriet Beecher Stowe bears little resemblance to the specter of Uncle Tom who has haunted American culture. The first apparent inconsistencies emerge from Tom's age and physique. Unfamiliar with the actual novel, most people describe Tom as a wobbly, gray-haired, gap-toothed, elderly man. But without ever actually revealing her hero's age, Stowe paints a picture of a healthy, robust family man. When readers first cross the threshold of Tom's cabin in Chapter 4, they meet a family consisting of Tom, his wife, Chloe, and their three young children. Stowe describes her hero as "A large, broad-chested, powerfully made man, of a full glossy black, and a face whose truly African features were characterized by an expression of grave and steady good sense, united with much kindliness and benevolence."[8] Clearly, the children are all quite young, probably under five years of age. Chloe is still breastfeeding at least one of them. Throughout the novel, Stowe continues to emphasize Tom's physical strength and stamina. En route to New Orleans by riverboat, he rescues his future mistress, Little Eva, who has fallen into the water. "A broad-chested, strong armed fellow, it was nothing for him to keep afloat in the water, till, in a moment or two, the child rose to the surface, and he caught her in his arms, and swimming with her to the boatside, handed her up, all dripping, to the grasp of hundreds of hands, which, as if they all belonged to one man, were stretched eagerly out to receive her."[9] To be sure, some of Stowe's descriptions do contribute to the confusion over Tom's age. Chloe affectionately refers to him as "old man." And in defending him to a slave trader, his master speaks readily about his strength of character and trustworthiness. Stowe's vagueness no doubt stemmed from her desire to maximize her hero's capacity to evoke a reader's sympathy. By showing Tom's last supper with his family before being removed by a slave trader, she demonstrates how easily slave families could be broken up. By painting him as wise, venerable, and kind, she shows her reader a worthy hero. By depicting his ability to save a child's life and work long days in the field, she delivers a brave, physically capable hero whose abilities contradict the lazy slave stereotype then being actively promoted by pro-slavery Southerners. The elderly, stooped-over, slow-moving Uncle Tom of contemporary popular culture could never have fulfilled the political ends sought by Stowe.

Further marked inconsistencies are discernible between the values and principles of the reconstructed Uncle Tom and Stowe's original hero. Both are devout, stalwart Christians. Both are unflinching in their loyalty. But the reconstructed Uncle Toms are passive, docile, unthinking Christians. Loyal and faithful to white employers, they are duplicitous in their dealings with fellow blacks. Stowe's Tom is a proactive Christian warrior. He does more than accept God's will, he endeavors to fulfill it in all of his words and deeds. He is loyal to each of his white masters, even the cruel Simon Legree.

Yet his allegiance to his fellow slaves is equally strong. Stowe reveals the depth of his Christian principles to readers by showing how he responds to a series of challenges that might confront any slave. The first major obstacles derive from the information that his "good" master has been forced to sell him in order to offset debts.

Stowe's plot gives Tom the opportunity to run away the night before Haley, the slave trader, is scheduled to add the faithful servant to his human inventory. But rather than accompany Eliza, a mulatto compatriot who has opted to rescue her son from Haley's chains by running with the youngster toward Canada, Tom decides to acquiesce to their master's design. Explaining his decision to Chloe, he reasons, "If I must be sold, or all the people on the place, and everything go to rack, why, let me be sold. I s'pose I can b'ar it as well as any on 'em, . . . It's better for me alone to go, than to break up the place and sell all. Mas'r an't to blame, Chloe, and he'll take care of you and the poor. . . ." Stowe stresses that Tom decides to let himself be sold in order to keep the rest of his family intact. Acquiescing to his master's plan gives Tom the best guarantee that Chloe and their children will be able to maintain a family unit.

Throughout the remainder of the novel, Tom faces many more physical and mental obstacles. At each juncture, he bases his action on his interpretation of God's will. In his last challenge, Tom's faith is put to the ultimate test. In the final chapters of the novel, Stowe places Tom under the control of a truly reprehensible owner. Indeed the very name Simon Legree still conjures up images of an intractable, uncompromising oppressor. Legree subjects Tom to virtually every kind of corporal and emotional abuse a male slave could suffer. For Tom, the worst punishment of all is being forced to witness Legree's sexual mistreatment of the female slaves Cassy and Emmeline. After the women escape his lair, a near-mad Legree insists that Tom lead him to their hiding place. Knowing all too well the extent of Legree's malice, Tom stands his ground and says, "I know, Mas'r [where they are]; but I can't tell anything. *I can die.*"[10] As a result of the beating that Legree commands, Tom dies. A good Christian, Tom refuses to lie about Cassy and Emmeline's whereabouts. A good Christian, he accepts a painful death rather than reveal their hiding place. Convincing her antebellum readers to abhor slavery required Stowe to deliver a likable, equitable, sympathetic hero. Willing to sacrifice his life for fellow slaves, Tom emerges as the consummate Christian.

The Troping of Uncle Tom

For every enlightened abolitionist like Harriet Beecher Stowe, antebellum America boasted a good many more reactionary individuals appalled by any suggestion of emancipating the slaves. Even before the novel itself was published, a Baltimore-based "scholar" decided to undo some of the antislavery political sentiment being triggered by the serialized chapters of *Uncle Tom's Cabin* still appearing in the *National Era*. He presented a theater manager with a script in which "Uncle Tom is not portrayed as a martyr, nor shown in less piety, but with absolute devotion to his master."[11] Both the amateur playwright and the theater manager knew that Baltimore's largely pro-slavery population would be more likely to embrace an Uncle Tom who proclaimed, "Sha! I was born a slave, I have lived a slave, and, bress de Lord, I hope to die a slave!" than the less servile stance assumed by Stowe's Tom. They gave Baltimore a Tom who matched its pervasive political philosophy.

The troping of Uncle Tom had begun. I use the word trope in this chapter to convey the message that few, if any, popular and folk culture depictions of Uncle Tom are true to the Stowe original. Instead, the term Uncle Tom has become a trope, a figure of speech intended to trigger a set of assumptions, assumptions not always based on the actual novel. Since the 1850s Americans have never been Tom-less. Each new generation of artists continues to find the Uncle Tom trope serviceable. The appeal is extensive. My Native American students inform me that a sellout in their culture is often labeled an "Uncle Tomahawk." Similarly, Chicano and Latino students refer to "Uncle Tomas," and Asians know what is meant by an "Uncle Tong." Show me the way a given populace has depicted its Uncle Tom and I'll tell you about the racial politics of the time.

This particular production of a theatrical rebuttal to Stowe flopped. However, its failure did not prevent other playwrights from appropriating the story. Just as made-for-television movie producers and feature filmmakers vie for the broadcast rights to today's best-selling novels, their nineteenth-century counterparts in the theater world were eager to cash in on the success of a novel as popular as

Uncle Tom's Cabin. The most influential of the antebellum theatrical versions was scripted by writer George Aiken and staged by producer George Howard. Aiken's rewrite was not intended to present a pro-slavery message. Nonetheless, he made profound changes in Stowe's original story. At Howard's urging, he shifted the attention away from Tom and his experiences to the novel's white and near-white characters. Aiken focused on the relationship between Uncle Tom and the young white child whose life he saved. Little Eva, not Tom, was clearly the star of his play. The child's angst-producing death was promoted and emphasized much more than Simon Legree's fatal beating of Uncle Tom.

Aiken may have been motivated by the realities of the theatrical world of the 1850s. A precocious child actress, Cordelia Howard, was the undisputed star of her father's theatrical company. Any play mounted by the company needed to capitalize on her appeal. Casting a respectable actor to play Tom presented another set of problems. On the one hand, no producer North or South was going to cast a black man in a prominent stage role. On the other hand, most legitimate white actors were loath to "blacken up" in order to play a slave. Such portrayals had heretofore been the province of more pedestrian, lower-status minstrel shows. Actors who had enjoyed any success in the "legitimate" theater considered blacking up beneath them. According to one source, G. C. Thurmon, the actor first offered the part, refused on the grounds by saying "I'm not going to play a Jim Crow darkey. It will jeopardize my reputation."[12] Howard and Aiken were able to convince Thurmon to take the part. Top billing, however, went to Cordelia Howard, who played Little Eva from her childhood years until she married. During most of her reign as star of the show, the play was subtitled "The Death of Eva."

Audiences enthusiastically responded to the Aiken version of *Uncle Tom's Cabin* and the many spinoffs it generated. Little Eva became America's darling. Aiken came up with an ingenious plot device to keep her in the play even after her climactic deathbed scene at the end of the third act. When Tom dies in a much less elaborate sequence at the end of the play, the stage directions dictate: "Eva, robed in white, is discovered on the back of milk-white dove, with expanded wings, as if just soaring upward. Her hands are extended in benediction over St. Clare and Uncle Tom who are kneeling and gazing up to her. Expressive Music. Slow Curtain."[13] In the novel, Tom's final words testify to his concern for Chloe and his anxiety about her well-being. In the Aiken and many subsequent adaptations, a "happier" death scene is proffered—one in which Tom eagerly ascends into Eva's angelic arms. Aiken's distortion conveys the attractive (to antebellum whites) notion that the slaves' love for their masters exceeded their love for their own families.

Oddly enough, Stowe's position that no truly good Christian person could sanction slavery became even less tenable in the aftermath of the Civil War. The political climate had shifted. In the 1850s antislavery activists were compelled to convince the masses that slavery was an evil institution, slaveholders were selfish people, and slaves were human beings who deserved freedom. After the war, the need to restore the Union was paramount. Only a radical minority of former abolitionists advocated punishing individual members of the Confederacy. Cued by Abraham Lincoln's second inaugural speech in which he envisioned overseeing a reconstruction "with malice towards none," Northerners softened their stance on former slaveholders. Forgiveness was the order of the day as Lincoln presided over pardon after pardon for Confederate soldiers. As soon as Andrew Johnson assumed office upon Lincoln's death, he set the wheels in motion that would allow Southerners to reclaim their land and their personal property (except slaves). Contrite Confederates were not tried for war crimes. Lincoln and then Johnson perpetuated the notion that the war had been caused by a handful of charismatic insurgents who seduced their well-meaning, God-fearing Southern brethren into an unwanted conflict. For the purpose of political expediency, the dominant message being articulated about the peculiar institution in the late 1860s was contrary to Stowe's message in the 1850s. The vast majority of slaveholders were suddenly well-meaning victims of the Simon Legrees of their world. Because a minority of slaveholders had acted in such a ignominious manner, the whole institution of slavery had to be abolished.

The Civil War and Reconstruction did not diminish the popularity of either the play or the novel. Postwar theatrical adaptations veered even farther away from the Stowe novel and reinforced the prevailing attitude about *former* slaveholders. Stowe had taken great pains to censure the whole institution of slavery. Tom was never safe, not even when he was in the hands of the so-called good masters Shelby and St. Clare. In most of the popular postwar versions, Tom is depicted as reasonably content with slavery until he is placed under the whip of Simon Legree. Instead of indicting the institution of slavery as a whole, these versions merely find fault with some particularly cruel masters.

Theatrical versions of *Uncle Tom's Cabin* were so popular they spawned their own vocabulary. They were called Tom shows, and the actors and actresses who performed in them were called Tommers. With ramshackle props, crude costumes, and flimsy scenery, Tommers crisscrossed rural and urban America, mounting the play anywhere they might be able to entice an audience. Theaters and stages were optional; inveterate Tommers would perform in barns or railroad stations. By 1879 there were at least forty-nine traveling companies performing *Uncle Tom's Cabin* in the United States. Because the companies were small and the number of roles in the play large, most of the performers played several different parts. The same actor might play George Shelby, Augustine St. Clare, and Simon Legree. The same actress might play both Topsy and Eva. Until the mid-1870s virtually all of the Toms were white actors in blackface. Looking for a new twist on the now nearly twenty-year-old play, producer Gustave Frohman came up with the inspiration, "Why not have a real Negro play Uncle Tom?"[14] Sam Lucas, one of the best-known African-American entertainers of the era, accepted the role. Still, such mixed-race productions were the exception rather than the rule well into the twentieth century. As Jim Crow–style segregation—the establishment of separate facilities for blacks and whites—became increasingly codified, most productions of *Uncle Tom's Cabin* remained whites only.

Once again, the politics of *Uncle Tom's Cabin* productions are indicative of the racial climate of a given era. Casting Sam Lucas or any other African-American actor to play Tom or one of the supporting roles was as much a promotional gimmick as incorporating real bloodhounds into the play. From the 1870s until the turn of the century, African Americans were nearly as mute as they had been before the Civil War. The radical Republican push to secure blacks in state legislatures and the U.S. Congress was over, and these governing bodies returned to their all-white composition. Grandfather clauses and poll taxes had been established to prevent blacks from voting. For many African Americans, chattel slavery had been replaced by peonage and sharecropping relationships that shackled the sons and daughters of former slaves to the sons and daughters of former slave owners. Segregation was accepted practice, and African-American performers faced compelling restrictions when trying to practice their craft. Forced to compete with white actors in blackface and ostracized from mainstream venues, they could rarely get any kind of meaningful role—not even in *Uncle Tom's Cabin.*

As the decades passed, the horrors of slavery chronicled by Stowe were further diluted. Audiences came to favor musical versions of the play. Minstrel-style songs were incorporated into the plot so that audiences could hear Uncle Tom sing a spiritual or Topsy bellow a slapstick ditty. Productions by the more successful troupes also included animals. Playbills promising to show Eliza being chased across the icy river by live bloodhounds, Eva ascending to heaven on white ponies, and Lawyer Marks parading about on a trick donkey fueled ticket sales. The fates of Tom, Chloe, Topsy, Eliza, and George had become fodder for musical entertainment.

Uncle Tom at the Turn of the Century

In 1903 Edwin S. Porter produced the first of several film versions of *Uncle Tom's Cabin* for the Edison Company. In this twelve-minute silent, black-and-white version, Tom was once again played by a white actor in blackface. The influence of fifty-one years of stage plays is apparent. The film highlights Eliza's treacherous escape across the ice and Little Eva's death. "Silence" takes on a dual meaning in this film. In addition to the fact that the film doesn't have sound, it also refers to the ways in which Tom's character is robbed of the agency and power given him by Stowe. In his dealings with his masters, Tom always seems to be bowing and scraping. His loyalty to Little Eva is depicted as his noblest attribute.

Between 1903 and 1927 several more photoplays and films based on all or part of the Stowe novel were produced. It wasn't until 1914 that an African-American actor, the seventy-two-year-old Sam Lucas, was cast to portray Uncle Tom. Given the actor's advanced years, it is easy to see why this version does not present Tom as the father of young children. Black children are shown, but the smiling and happy youngsters are not presented as Tom and Chloe's offspring. In the role of Aunt Chloe is an actress so stout that it seems likely that some padding was used to make her appear enormous. The audience isn't given any kind of clue as to why Tom chooses to be sold rather than to run away. Simon Legree is the only flawed white character in this version. The final beating that he gives Uncle Tom seems much too mild to have resulted in death. Film historian Daniel J. Leab points out that the presence of black actors in this and other films astounded reviewers, who made comments such as "well-acted, considering that the cast is made up of genuine colored people. . . ."[15]

By the standards of the early twentieth century, the 1914 version was an elaborate, expensive production. From then on any black screen image that even approximated this docile depiction was labeled a Tom. African-American film historian Donald Bogle titled his seminal book on the black images in motion pictures *Toms, Coons, Mulattos, Mammies & Bucks.* Summing up the attributes that made a good cinematic Tom, Bogle maintains, "Always as Toms are chased, harassed, hounded, flogged, enslaved, and insulted, they keep the faith, n'er turn against their massas, and remain hearty, submissive, stoic, generous, selfless, and oh-so-very kind."[16]

Offstage, the public was refusing to hear accounts of slavery that diverged from the now-pastoral panoramas promoted by the silent Tom movies and the traveling Tom shows. It is probably not a coincidence that by the turn of the century the most popular African-American leader was an ex-slave who, like the reconstructed hero of the Tom show circuit, acquiesced humbly to many forms of second-class citizenship. Booker T. Washington appealed to white America because he did not threaten the racial status quo. He persuaded wealthy individuals to contribute to black colleges such as his own Tuskegee Institute by reasoning that well-trained blacks could better serve their white employers. Speaking before an Atlanta audience at the 1895 World's Fair, he maintained that "In all things that are purely social we can be as separate as the fingers, yet one as the hand in all things essential for mutual progress."[17] Historian Wilson J. Moses argues that Washington, "cunning and slippery, played upon the Uncle Tom stereotype" in order to guarantee his position as white America's favorite black son.[18]

In 1903, the same year the first film version of *Uncle Tom's Cabin* was produced, W. E. B. DuBois, one of Booker T. Washington's more outspoken African-American critics, prefaced his manifesto *The Souls of Black Folk* by prophesying "The problem of the Twentieth Century is the problem of the color line."[19] When DuBois and other African-American leaders such as Ida B. Wells-Barnett and William Monroe Trotter threatened Washington's autonomy, he used unscrupulous means to undermine their efforts. Stowe's original Tom refuses to betray other slaves. He declined to whip them, preferring to submit himself to the lash rather than inflict it upon others. He respected Eliza's decision to steal herself and her son from their master. He did not betray her. These sequences were usually absent from stage productions by the turn of the century. In those Tom shows, the hero's amicable relationship with his masters is highlighted at the expense of references to the nuances of his relationships with and defense of other slaves. On stage and off, America was willing to embrace only those blacks who put the needs of whites ahead of their own.

In the first decades of the twentieth century, African Americans who were willing to risk the wrath of white America were, at best, ignored and, at worst, punished for speaking out. Ida B. Wells-Barnett recalled the attempts she and several African-American leaders made to get President Woodrow Wilson to rescind orders enforcing segregation in the federal workplace. After the president had promised to look into the matter, the delegation heard nothing from him and the rules that prohibited integration remained in place. A second meeting was called. Wells-Barnett recalls, "the president became annoyed over Mr. Trotter's persistent assertion that these discriminations were still practiced and that it was his duty as president of the United States to abolish them. President Wilson became very angry and he told the committee that if they wanted to call on him in the future they would have to leave Mr. Trotter out."[20] Other prominent African Americans were silenced for any hint of defiance. After African-American prizefighter Jack Johnson defeated white opponent Jim Jeffries in 1910, Congress enacted legislation that prohibited the filming of live fights.[21] Marcus Garvey, one of the twentieth century's first outspoken black nationalists, was prosecuted for embezzling funds from followers of his back-to-Africa movement. World War I black veterans who returned to the South were sometimes met at the train station by white supremacists who forcibly stripped them of their military uniforms.

Celluloid and theatrical Toms reinforced the apologist stance toward the old South that was gaining credence within the academic community. Ulrich B. Phillips's noteworthy *American Negro Slavery* was published in 1914. This book became the standard sourcebook on slavery for generations of professional historians. Phillips's vision of life on the magnolia-lined plantations bore a remarkable resemblance to the portable stage sets of Tom shows. The masters were benevolent, the mistresses were kind, the children were scamps, and the male slaves were venerable old darkies. Sure, there were some heavy-handed masters, but they were outnumbered by their more even-tempered counterparts. As serious students of history contemplated the benevolences of the peculiar institution, moviegoers were treated to a cinematic study of the same themes.

Filmmaker D. W. Griffith's 1915 saga of life in the old South, *The Birth of a Nation*, is another example. Had *Uncle Tom's Cabin* never been written, *The Birth of a Nation* would most probably never have been made. That's because Thomas Dixon, author of the novel on which the film was based, maintained that a Tom show had inspired him to become a writer. Dixon, an unapologetic white supremacist, was "angered by what he considered the play's unjust treatment of the South, [and] he left the theatre vowing to tell the South's true story."[22] Actually, he told his version of the history of the South in three very successful novels. All three function as rejoinders to Stowe. *The Birth of a Nation* is based on *The Clansmen*, the second book in the trilogy. The film's "house slaves" are portrayed as loyal servants, anxious to remain with their masters even after the Emancipation. Much more of the film is devoted to the threats presented by the ungrateful former slaves and Northern-born blacks who uncritically follow the directions of no-good Union-bred carpetbaggers. After a particularly bold Northern African-American soldier tries to force himself on an innocent young Southern white woman, the brave sons of the Confederacy organize their forces, garb themselves in white robes, and drive away the marauding black soldiers and their sympathizers. Griffith's own prejudices prevented him from even casting blacks in prominent roles in the film.

Woodrow Wilson's impatience with William Monroe Trotter and the delegation that called upon him to integrate federal workplaces is better understood when we consider that the president, himself an academic, heartily endorsed Griffith's film. The same man who gave a stamp of approval to a film that depicted the Ku Klux Klansmen as the South's unsung heroes was unlikely to tolerate the aggressive demeanor of an African-American leader who dared to suggest that black employees were entitled to the same opportunities to work for the government as whites. Wilson's endorsement functioned as a part of an elaborate shield that protected *The Birth of a Nation* from the boycotts led by African-American activists in most major cities. As a result of the film's popularity, the Ku Klux Klan enjoyed a resurgence of interest. Antiblack violence increased mightily as those blacks who did not conform to the stereotyped Uncle Tom image promoted in the Tom shows and films were subjected to random attacks.[23]

One Hundred Years of Uncle Tom

As the twentieth century trudged toward the halfway mark and the Stowe novel approached its hundredth anniversary of publication, DuBois's prediction that the color line would confound Americans was being borne out. The status of Uncle Toms of this era and the preceding decades suggests that blacks and whites were approaching the color line from two very different directions. For white producers, *Uncle Tom's Cabin* remained a Bible from which "truths" about slavery could be extracted. For African-American writers, *Uncle Tom's Cabin* was more a profane than a sacred text.

Both white filmmakers and theatrical troupes continued to script all or parts of the story. There can be little doubt that the popular depression-era films starring Shirley Temple and Bill "Bojangles" Washington owed their success to the public's love affair with the Little Eva/Uncle Tom team. Describing Robinson as a "cool-eyed Tom," film critic Bogle declares the relationship between America's sweetheart and the tapdancer "the perfect interracial love match."[24] With laws against miscegenation on the books in many states, the match between Shirley Temple and Bill Robinson was the only one that would be tolerated.

Uncle Tom's Cabin was elevated to a new plateau in American musical theater history when Rogers and Hammerstein incorporated an elaborate Siamese version of the story within *The King and I*. Once again racial politics are sacrificed in favor of a message about sexual politics. One of the king's concubines has recognized the similarities between the separation inflicted upon her and her lover and the separation forced upon Eliza and George in Stowe's novel. Anxious to plead her case to the king as well as to facilitate her own elaborate escape plans, the concubine entertains the king and his British guests with a production that highlights the predicament of Eliza and George.

These and other early to mid twentieth-century versions of *Uncle Tom's Cabin* shed light on a white America chained to a romantic, sentimentalized vision of the institution of slavery. As African-American activists were making moderate headway in the early civil rights struggles, whites bought their tickets to see dancing Uncle Toms and coy little Evas.

The 1920s marked the beginning of an era of unprecedented political and literary empowerment for African Americans. In increasing numbers, black writers and artists asserted their right to tell their own stories. Most white Americans weren't quite ready to hear the black stories just yet. In 1927 Hollywood opted to make yet another large-scale production version of *Uncle Tom's Cabin* with an African-American male lead. Noted for his work on stage in Eugene O'Neill's *Emperor Jones*, actor Charles Gilpin was cast to play the much-beloved slave. Gilpin, however, could not convince the film's white director to alter some of the more offensive aspects of a stock Uncle Tom character. As a result, Gilpin quit the cast. Another actor, James Lowe, took over the part, and Gilpin returned to the job as an elevator operator that he relied on to tide him over between stage parts.[25] Gilpin's rejection of the opportunity to play a facile Uncle Tom signaled a growing defiance on the part of African Americans determined to devise their own revisions of *Uncle Tom's Cabin*.

In spite of their best efforts to construct their own aesthetic architecture of the African-American experience, many black writers opted to lease some creative space to *Uncle Tom's Cabin* and its offshoots. Discussing the influences that shaped his celebrated novel, *Invisible Man*, Ralph Ellison recalls:

> I had seen, in a nearby Vermont village, a poster announcing
> the performance of a "Tom show," that forgotten term for
> blackface minstrel versions of Mrs. Stowe's *Uncle Tom's Cabin*.
> I had thought such entertainment a thing of the past, but there
> in a quiet northern village it was alive and kicking, with Eliza,
> frantically slipping and sliding on the ice—and that during
> World War II—to escape the slavering hounds.[26]

Ellison's contemporary Richard Wright used the title *Uncle Tom's Children* for his anthology on several black stances common in the depression-era South. Several decades later Ishmael Reed named his protagonist in *Mumbo Jumbo* Jes Grew in recollection of Topsy's lament that she hadn't been born, she "just grew."

Blacks were seeing a very different America in the early to mid-twentieth century. The image of the dancing Uncle Toms that whites clung to had become a cumbersome and odious albatross for African Americans. Ellison's protagonist in *Invisible Man* finds himself unable to discard the jolly nigger piggybank he has inadvertently become guardian over. The more African Americans tried to leave Uncle Toms behind them, the more the tenacious Tom image followed them.

Uncle Tom—140 Years and Counting

In the late 1980s and early 1990s, 140 years after the publication of *Uncle Tom's Cabin*, the story and its spinoffs continue to stimulate creative activity. Two efforts—one largely a white production and the other a black one—can be used to measure the persistence of discordant views on who the slaves were and who their heirs have become.

Produced in 1987 for the cable channel, Showtime, *Uncle Tom's Cabin* was then issued on the home video market and is available at many variety stores for under ten dollars. Without question, this version eliminates most of the caricatured distortions discernible in post-Aiken productions. This strong, virile, middle-aged Tom never scrapes or bows. His English is clear and undistorted. His demeanor is serious. The label Uncle Tom is studiously avoided throughout. The audience is made fully aware that his decision not to run away with Eliza is driven by the knowledge that if he is sold, his family will probably remain intact whereas if he runs away, they are likely to be separated. Although he does bond with Little Eva, he never replaces her love for the love of the family he has been forced to forsake. He does sing the occasional sacred song, but, at least, the songs are plaintive celebrations of spirituality, as opposed to raucous coon songs of earlier Tom shows. Even Topsy's rambunctiousness is understated.

In short, this is a politically correct Uncle Tom. Able to hold his own with blacks and whites, this Tom is a flawless specimen of Christian nobility and all-American common sense. Stowe was interested in depicting a black man who could invoke concern in white readers. The Showtime Tom is just such an individual. He is also just the kind of Tom that most whites would embrace. But the very qualities that may make him appealing to whites contribute to the kind of ambivalence he generates in some African Americans.

If the Showtime version is politically correct, the 1991 production of *I Ain't Yo' Uncle: The New Jack Revisionist "Uncle Tom's Cabin"* by African-American playwright Robert Alexander is politically inflammatory. Well aware of the distortions and manipulations Stowe's original text underwent, Alexander decided to funnel the core story through the point of view of the black characters. He gives Stowe a voice, and in the play's prologue, Topsy, Eliza, George, and Tom propose to put her on trial for "creatin' stereotypes." Tom then sentences her to listen to their version of the story:

> I said we're doing this play! Wid new dialogue . . . and scenes YOU left out! Scenes that show me in a new light. A true light. I want to git paid my proper respect, especially from the brothuhs and sistuhs who turn their backs. None of y'all would be here if it wasn't for me. I stayed behind so y'all could git ahead, So tonight—let me lift my voice and sing, 'til the earth and heavens ring . . . ring with the harmony of my New Jack Swing.[27]

Although Alexander endows his Tom with defiance, wit, and determination lacking in the earlier Toms, an upstart Topsy proves to be the most profound character in the play. Toting a boom box and garbed in conspicuously ethnic clothing, she taunts the audience during the final act:

> TOPSY: Dat's right. Topsy Turvy in effect. This ain't no
>   motherfucking play. I'm the governor of this bullshit
>   story. Harriet didn't make me up. Well, well, well
>   . . . look at all these crackers and peanut butter.
>   We'se ready for a picnic (THESE TWO LINES VARY
>   ACCORDING TO THE RACIAL MIX OF THE
>   AUDIENCE) What you lookin' at?! I oughta fuck you
>   up! I see the way you look at me when I get on the

bus . . . you sit there, scared . . . tensed . . .
clutchin' yo' purse . . . hoping I don't sit next to you.
Well, fuck you! I shot a bitch cause she looked at me
wrong. I burned down Uncle Tom's condo with the
nigger still in it. I love to hear glass break. I love to
watch shit burn. I love to hear motherfuckers scream.
Word!! (TOPSY FREEZES)

TOM: Any volunteers to take Topsy? Ya'll think she come from
nowhere? Do ya 'spcts she just growed?[28]

I Ain't Yo' Uncle has enjoyed a great deal of the kind of critical
success that the work of an up-and-coming playwright can garner. It
has been staged in several cities on the East and West coasts. Nonetheless, its audience is pretty much limited to that small segment of
the population inclined to buy tickets and spend an evening at the
theater. In other words, it is unlikely to reach even a fraction of the
public reached by the standard Showtime version. In my lifetime, I
doubt I'll be able to walk into a store and find a video version of *I
Ain't Yo' Uncle* for under ten dollars.

Once again the status and commodification of *Uncle Tom's Cabin*
productions is emblematic of race relations as a whole in the United
States. A safe, even-handed version is produced and aired on cable
television where it is sure to reach a sizable audience. The Showtime
producers rework the Uncle Tom trope to tell a story about a past
remote to most of the audience. An idealized, almost too perfect, an-
ger-free African-American man is offered to the masses. Few real
African-American people could live up to the noble standard set by
this Tom. Few would want to.

Following in the tradition of Richard Wright, Ishmael Reed, and
other African-American artists, Robert Alexander has seized the characters and basic scenario to tell a different story. He uses the Uncle
Tom trope to tell a story about a continuum between slavery and the
present. The strong language and confrontational attitudes discernible in Alexander's story express 1990s black anger. Connections between slavery and contemporary social problems are at the center of
the production. This Tom draws a direct link between the economic,
social, and cultural frustrations that plague so many contemporary
African Americans and the institution of slavery.

Two Uncle Toms. One version shows audiences how horrendous an institution slavery used to be. After turning off the Showtime version, audiences can commiserate over the fates of these characters who lived and died well over one hundred years ago. The film implies that slavery is a thing of the past, unconnected to the day-to-day lives of African Americans. Since slavery is dead, contemporary blacks should take this hardworking, pious Uncle Tom as a role model and apply themselves to the tasks at hand. Without anger, they should move forward into the twenty-first century. The Alexander version holds the institution of slavery and the descendants of slave owners accountable for today's racial dilemmas. Audiences are asked to think of Topsy every time they see a sullen African-American adolescent with a boom box. Apparently, the Uncle Tom trope has yet to live out its usefulness.

5

Jacksonalia

Would we take Jesse Jackson? Hell, we'd take Michael Jackson!

—"RE-RON," Gil Scott-Heron

In Spike Lee's film *Do the Right Thing*, the protagonist Mookie (played by Lee himself) confronts the white son of his employer who wears his smug racism proudly, as if it were an essential component of the smoldering urban Mediterranean machismo he cultivates. Mookie wants to know how he reconciles his obvious contempt for the young black customers who patronize his father's Brooklyn pizzeria with his unflagging admiration for black musicians and athletes—seeing no incongruity. Pino (John Turturro) claims that the singers and basketball stars in question aren't really black. He tries to make a case that their talent is so profound that it has eclipsed the color of their skin. When he sees the black men whose photos Buggin' Out (Giancarlo Esposito) wants to put on the walls of the restaurant, he does see black and no talent that serves his needs. The accomplishments of Malcolm X and Martin Luther King, Jr., remind him of their blackness and the blackness of the patrons of his father's restaurant. Implicit in his comments is the notion that blackness is all he sees when he sees black political figures. Athletes and singers who entertain him are acceptable men and women for him to admire, but black public figures and politicians who serve black constituencies are anathema.

Do the Right Thing was produced in 1989. But the attitudes Lee illuminates through Pino's character predate the 1980s—for that matter, the 1890s. At least since the Civil War, African-American entertainers have been able to reap the rewards of the American dream better than any of their kin.[1] In particular, blacks with muscles or melody have been feted by the dominant culture. Blacks who have chosen professional paths or public service routes have faced more roadblocks and detours in their careers.

But even as African Americans have achieved success within the fields of entertainment, their accomplishments are still frequently filtered through the lens of race. The statistics on Jack Johnson, Jesse Owens, Joe Louis, Jackie Robinson, and Wilma Rudolph frame their records in racial terms. Johnson was the first black heavyweight champion; Owens's Olympic gold medal and Louis's defeat of Max Schmelling were triumphs for the race as much for the men and their country; Robinson integrated America's favorite pastime; Rudolph was the fastest black woman on the track. Similarly, the talents of Paul Robeson, Lena Horne, Pearl Bailey, and Sidney Poitier are prefaced with references to their race. But at least these figures have a place in the history records. African-American public figures from outside of the entertainment orbit frequently fade into the outer fringes of public awareness. I find that students in my introductory African-American Studies and American Studies classes can at least say *something* about the entertainers just mentioned. But more often than not, the names and deeds of Frederick Douglass, William Monroe Trotter, Ida B. Wells-Barnett, and Asa Philip Randolph are unknown to them. In fact, in 1986 a bright eighteen-year-old college freshman asked me who Martin Luther King was. It would be nice to think that the past tense could be used here to suggest that black entertainers *used* to be measured in terms of their melanin and that the achievements of other notable blacks *used* to be undocumented. But the stereotypes associated with blacks still get tangled up with their reputations. This pattern can be seen in the careers of many accomplished black men and women. And for those whose surname is Jackson, a double burden is often applied.

Michael Jackson, the pop entertainer, Reggie Jackson, the hitter and outfielder extraordinaire, and the Reverend Jesse Jackson, the religious leader, social reformer, and former contender for the Democratic nomination for president, share many attributes. They are all black. They are all male. For outstanding achievement in their respective fields during the 1970s and 1980s, they all commanded the attention of the American public. I think it is safe to state that no African-American baseball player captured the imagination of the sports fans and, perhaps more important, the sportswriters than record-breaking Reggie Jackson, aka Mr. October. No black performer's high sopranic crooning, flashy wardrobe, and fast moves attracted more air time and media speculation than Michael Jackson, and no black politician's oratorical flourish and commanding presence seized the voter's attention and the often bewildered speculation of the press corps more than the Reverend Jesse Jackson. As their prominence increased, so too did a body of folklore chronicling their successes and failures.

Michael Jackson

Michael Jackson's star began to rise when he was six years old and Motown diva Diana Ross arranged for the Jackson Five to audition for the legendary Detroit record company. The audition tape that snared the group a recording contract still finds its way onto documentaries and rock-and-roll retrospectives. Singing his heart out, strutting through the studio, and pivoting like a smurf-size James Brown, young Michael outshines his talented brothers. Shaped and packaged by the Motown machine, the Jackson Five were an unqualified success, especially with younger listeners. But Michael's status as a folk hero was really solidified after he embarked on a solo career. In 1983 his second solo album, *Thriller*, began climbing the charts, where it remained at the top for an unprecedented length of time. In May of that year Michael appeared on the *Motown 25* special and gave the public its first real opportunity to see his new hairstyle, new nose, heavy makeup, new moves (the Moonwalk), and one beaded glove. While his dancing talents had always been applauded, the tight, precise, innovative moves with which he performed his hit single "Billie Jean" astounded the television audience. According to Michael, one of the many calls he received the day after the special aired came from dancer Fred Astaire, who praised the choreography. Ironically, Michael and his record company had to fight to get the then fledgling Music Television Network (MTV) to air the videos produced in conjunction with *Thriller*. Using one of the most bizarre lines of reasoning ever articulated about music history, MTV officials claimed that they were reluctant to air Michael Jackson and other black artists' videos because African Americans had so little to do with rock and roll.[2] This is akin to saying that the founding fathers didn't have anything to do with the American Revolution.

Following the release of the *Thriller* album and his *Motown 25* appearance, the American public was inundated with press coverage of Michael's every move. No doubt his record company's publicity machine and his own knack for scene-stealing fueled the hype. Responding to the hype, the entertainment reporters had Michael's fans (and nonfans as well) contemplating such earth-shattering questions such as: Did he have plastic surgery? Was he gay? Why did he wear one beaded glove? What was happening to his complexion? Many celebrities can orchestrate their foray onto the entertainment pages. But Michael's idiosyncrasies propelled him into the vernacular discourse of the folk as well.

Michael's habit of wearing one sequined glove while performing provoked curiosity:

Q: What do the San Francisco Giants and Michael Jackson
     have in common?
A: They both wear one glove for no apparent reason.

The Giants were not the only team targeted by this riddle; any team not performing to fans' satisfaction during the mid-1980s was apt to be mentioned. The riddle lampoons the team in question much more than it does Michael. The skill with which a baseball player uses his glove has a measurable impact on his success, whereas Michael's glove was a costuming choice. Before long, questions about the glove were wedded to questions about Michael's sex life. Following his appearance on the Motown special, Michael appeared at an awards ceremony accompanied by then Princeton undergraduate Brooke Shields. Now this, of course, was prior to her public confession of chastity. Her relationship with Michael garnered much press attention and the following riddle:

Person A: Did you hear that Brooke Shields had to have an operation?

Person B: No, what was the matter with her?

Person A: They still don't know, but they found the other glove!

Another version of this riddle highlights the ambiguity surrounding Michael's sexual orientation:

Person A: Did you hear where they found Michael Jackson's other glove?

Person B: In Boy George's pants.

Like Michael, British rock star Boy George favored heavy makeup and an overall sexually androgynous look.

In 1983 Michael signed a very lucrative contract with Pepsi-Cola to do a series of highly produced commercials for the soft drink company. While filming the special effects for one of the first commercials, Michael suffered mild burns. The jokes were circulating before the flames were extinguished:

Person A: Did you hear that Brooke Shields broke up with Michael Jackson?

Person B: No, why?

Person A: She won't go out with a guy that smokes!

Of course, Michael was not the first black celebrity to be injured in a very public fire. The folk soon began to compare Michael's predicament with that of comedian Richard Pryor, whose accident occurred while he was free-basing cocaine:

Person A: Did you hear that Michael Jackson and Richard Pryor started a new foundation?

Person B: No, what is it?

Person A: They are going to call it the Ignited Negro College Fund.

Person A: Did you hear what Michael Jackson said to Richard Pryor?

Person B: No, what?
Person A: I swear to God it was Pepsi!

Q: What's the difference between Michael Jackson and
     Richard Pryor?
A: Richard Pryor got burned by coke; Michael Jackson got
     burned by Pepsi.

As the following jumprope rhyme suggests, both Michael's sexual
orientation and accidental singeing were pondered on the playground:

> I pledge allegiance to the flag
> Michael Jackson is a fag
> Pepsi-Cola burned him up
> Now he's drinking 7-Up
> Don't feel shy
> Don't feel blue
> Cause Richard Pryor got burned too

Motown 25 included footage from the Jackson Five's original audition tape. Anyone who looked closely at the finger-snapping young
Michael and the moonwalking, one-gloved singer who stole the show
that night would notice that the young man had matured in many
ways, some logical and some illogical. In addition to being older and
taller, as one would expect, Michael's complexion was inexplicably
lighter. It would be almost a decade before Michael acknowledged
that because of a skin disease, he applies very heavy makeup in order
to even out his skin tone. Before Michael went public with this revelation, many of his fans maintained that his insistence on light skin, a
thinner nose, and straightened hair indicated a lack of pride in being
black. In the mid-1980s Jackson recorded a song titled "Ebony and
Ivory" with former Beatle Paul McCartney. A riddle that reflects the
folk's perception of the complexion change follows:

Person A: Did you hear that Paul McCartney and Michael
            Jackson are going to do another song together?
Person B: No.
Person A: It's called "Ivory and Ivory."

In recent years, Michael's celebrity stature has fluctuated. When a new album or video is released, he garners enormous attention. Most of the folklore about Michael is still triggered by his extraordinary physical appearance and his unconventional lifestyle. With each new public appearance, he looks more and more androgynous. The makeup he wears gives him a pasty-white surreal complexion. He often wears his hair in shiny corkscrew curls that fall over his eyes. His relationships with his siblings and parents are apparently quite charged. Aside from an occasional appearance with Brooke Shields or Elizabeth Taylor, he is rarely seen in public with adult women. He speaks in a high-pitched childlike voice, and he lobbies eloquently on behalf of the underprivileged children. His estate contains both a small zoo and an amusement park. Given the fact that even more mundane heroes generate media attention, it is not surprising that Michael has encountered such a persistent cycle of rumors.*

Reggie Jackson

While Michael Jackson was flaunting his sequined glove as he danced across the stage, baseball player Reggie Jackson was using his leather one to catch speeding baseballs. As "Mr. October" made his way from Charlie Finley's Oakland A's in 1967, to the Baltimore Orioles, to the New York Yankees, and finally to the Anaheim Angels and back to the A's, his stature and reputation increased. From opening day through the summer and into the early fall, Reggie Jackson was as good as the best of baseball's sluggers. His nickname came from the extraordinary success he had as the leaves started changing colors, when his performances were generally several notches above his regular season standards.

His alleged prowess away from the baseball diamond commanded as much attention as his on-field heroics. Reggie himself invited much of the attention. While he was still with the Orioles, Reggie found himself surrounded by several members of the New York press corps. With Reggie's help, the Orioles had just defeated the New York Yan-

---

* Just as I was finishing writing this book in the fall of 1993, allegations of sexual misconduct were leveled at Michael Jackson. In the aftermath of these charges, Jackson canceled his concert tour and checked himself into a substance abuse program. Needless to say these developments have contributed to new joke cycles. The publishing deadline for this manuscript does not allow for the consideration of these cycles here.

kees. Asked about the possibility of ever playing in New York, Jackson responded, "If I played in New York, they'd name a candy bar after me."[3] Although the popularity of Reggie Bars never matched that of their namesake, the following item of Xerox lore suggests that they did contribute to his lady-killer image:

> One *Pay Day*, *Reggie*,
> Wanted a *Bit of Honey*,
> So he took *Mr. Goodbar*'s secretary,
> Ms. *Hershey*, out behind the
> *Power House* in *Fifth Avenue*
> Where he began unsnapping her
> *Milk Duds* from her *Reese Cups*.
> He began to feel her *Mounds* with
> His *Butter Fingers*, then the
> *Three Musketeers* showed up and it
> Turned into a real *Almond Joy*.
> As she *snickered*, *Reggie* slipped his
> *Whopper* into her *Milky Way*. Then she
> Screamed; it feels like a *$100,000 Bar*.
> She squeezed his *Whatchamacallit* and
> *U-No* that's how they got *Oh Henry*
> and *Baby Ruth*.

Reggie's reputation as a ladies' man takes a curious twist in a well-known cycle of contemporary legends. Since these stories began to circulate in the early 1980s, they have been attached to several other prominent black male entertainers. Most of the stories go something like this:

> Several older white women [in many versions the women are Mennonites, Mormons, or members of similarly sheltered religious subcultures] took a bus tour to New York City. Their husbands and friends had cautioned them about the dangers of the big city. The first night they decide to play it safe and have dinner in their hotel's restaurant. On their way they find themselves alone in the elevator with a "large" black man with a big dog. The huge black man commands "Sit, Lady." The

ladies gasp obediently and sink to the floor. The black man
explains that his dog's name is Lady and the chagrined women
get up. When they ask for their check after dinner in the hotel
dining room, the waiter explains that their check has already
been paid. When they ask who has paid it, the waiter says
something like Reggie Jackson over there paid your check, he
said you ladies gave him the best laugh he's had in a long time.
As he points to Jackson from across the room, the ladies realize
that Jackson was the man in the elevator.

Reggie has repeatedly denied this story. However, Matt Merola,
his press representative, frequently affirms its truth because it makes
his client look like such a nice guy.[4] Popular for well over a decade
now, the legend refuses to die. Various African-American celebrities—
"Magic" Johnson, Mean Joe Green, Wilt Chamberlin, and Lionel
Richie—have been identified as the dog-lover; I have never heard a
version in which a white celebrity is named.

Since the man in the elevator is always African American, it
seems reasonable to conclude that the ladies have been led to believe
that black men are a particular source of danger. Perhaps the key to
the legend's tenacity can be found in one fairly common motif discernible in most versions. The women usually have been warned by a
husband or son about the dangers a black man may pose.[5] The narrative rarely ends with the chagrined women merely exiting the elevator. In many versions Reggie has a bottle of champagne sent over to
their table, and in others they find that Reggie has paid their entire
hotel bill when they check out. Ever since the races first came into
contact, whites have articulated concerns about the black man's purported sexual superiority. For the white male, the belief that black
men are eager to defile every white woman with whom they come into
contact is probably only somewhat less frightening than the possibility that the white woman might actually enjoy or prefer the black
man's sexual prowess.

The "elevator incident" takes on new meaning when viewed from
this perspective. White husbands and sons have so terrified their
wives and daughters that the women anticipate the "worst" when
face to face with an African-American man. The black man in question, however, spoils the scenario by asking nothing of the women.

Yet the conclusion of the story frequently finds the women enjoying a meal, a bottle of champagne, or a room provided by a black man. Any one of these three items could easily symbolize a form of sexual satisfaction. Food and drink are common substitutes for sex, and a hotel room is not an uncommon setting for sex. Thus, in spite of the white male's efforts, the white women featured in this legend find immense satisfaction from gifts presented by an African-American male.

Jesse Jackson

What Michael Jackson was to the entertainment pages, and Reggie Jackson was to the sports pages, the Reverend Jesse Jackson was to the political pages of the mid-1980s. In 1984 and 1988 a third African-American named Jackson received nationwide attention, this time as a candidate for the Democratic Party's nomination for the presidency. Although he had never been elected to political office, the Reverend Jackson had been a well-known African-American leader for two decades. He first became prominent at the side of the Reverend Martin Luther King, Jr. Following King's assassination, Jackson survived a tough period—other King associates and the press questioned his behavior immediately following King's Memphis shooting.[6] On Christmas day, 1971, Jackson developed and led a grassroots organization called Operation PUSH (People United Serving Humanity). On behalf of PUSH, Jackson urged white-owned corporations and small businesses to hire African-American employees. Another of PUSH's primary goals was to encourage young African Americans to stay in school. On behalf of the organization, Jackson made numerous public appearances throughout the United States. By the early 1980s crowds were chanting "Run, Jesse, Run" following his always-inspiring speeches.

Jokes about politicians and similarly respected figures frequently hinge on the public's fascination with any flaw that surfaces about a particular leader. In order to run for high political office, many men and women feel compelled to present themselves as near-perfect individuals. When chinks in the armor are exposed, when Achilles' heels are found, the media and the public enjoy them. The kinds of flaws that capture our imagination are often ones related to deeds or misdeeds of politicians.

Senator Kennedy and Mary Jo Kopechne were driving along a road. She tries in vain to get his attention: "Ted, there is something we simply must discuss." "Later, later," he replies. "No, Ted, there is something important that we must discuss." "Later, later," he snaps. "Ted, supposing that I'm pregnant." "We'll cross that bridge when we get to it."

The incongruity of certain characteristics and the office an individual aspires to is often at the root of jokes about him or her. As an African American, Jackson's race was a major Achilles' heel in the mind of the public. Jokes about the unsuitability of blacks for the white-collar world are commonplace.

Q: What do you call a black guy who's a millionaire, has a Ph.D., and is just incredibly successful?
A: A nigger.

Q: What do you call a black man in a suit?
A: A defendant.

Q: What's the first thing you say to a black man in a suit?
A: Would the defendant please rise?

Jackson's political coup in 1983 came on the heels of his official entry into presidential politics. The Reverend Jackson went to Syria and secured the release of Robert O. Goodman Jr., a navy bombardier who had been taken prisoner after his plane had been shot down. Probably the most frequently cited joke about the Reverend Jackson is one that he himself offered when he did a guest stint as host of TV's *Saturday Night Live.* Like many successful jokes first told on television, this one developed a life of its own.

After obtaining Lieutenant Robert Goodman's release from the Syrians, the Reverend Jackson decided to have a meeting with the Pope. In order to secure complete privacy, they held their meeting on a boat in a river. Of course, the press found out about the meeting and they rented a boat of their own from which they followed Jackson and the Pope. During the meeting the Pope's cap blew off. The Reverend Jackson walked across the water, retrieved the Pope's cap, and returned it to him. The next day the headlines in all of the newspapers read "Jesse Can't Swim!"

By running for the Democratic nomination for president, the Reverend Jackson broke a multitude of political "rules." After all, few individuals who have never been elected to any political office start out seeking the presidency. No African American had ever been considered a serious contender for the nation's highest office. For that matter, no clergyman had been considered a serious contender for the Oval Office. Although he was running for the Democratic Party's nomination, he had long criticized the party. In spite of these and other ostensible drawbacks, Jackson developed a serious following. He handled himself well in the debates and showed an impressive command of domestic and international affairs. The preceding joke reinforces Jackson's image as a politician who was truly "damned if he did and damned if he didn't." A large part of Jackson's credibility problem ostensibly stemmed from his lack of experience in world affairs.

After he declared his candidacy, the reporters asked Jesse Jackson what he thought about Beirut. He said, "Babe Ruth? Well, he was a good ballplayer, but I must confess I personally prefer Hank Aaron."

Although this joke contains no overt reference to race, Jackson's identity as an African American undergirds it. The public anticipates an African American to have a greater command of sports history than Middle Eastern affairs. Further, since Babe Ruth was a legendary white baseball player and Hank Aaron a black one, audiences expect Jackson would prefer the latter athlete. The following variation on a well-known joke formula also targets Jackson's intelligence.

There was a plane, and there was a pilot, a copilot, a priest, a Boy Scout, and Jesse Jackson aboard. Suddenly the pilot and copilot burst out of the cockpit and said, "Man, we are all going to die. The engines just went out." There's only four parachutes. The pilot and copilot each took one parachute and jumped out. Jesse Jackson stood up and said, "Man, I can't die.

People look up to me. I'm going to be a great leader some day. I might even be president one of these days." So he took one and jumped out. Then the priest said to the Boy Scout, "Son, you're young. You have a great life ahead of you. You take the parachute. I'll stay with the plane." Then the Boy Scout goes, "Naw, man, we're both saved. That stupid nigger just grabbed my knapsack."[7]

Jackson did not earn the party's nomination in 1984, but he entered the arena again in 1988. By the mid-1980s the media and the public had begun to express interest in the intimate details of the personal lives of politicians and other public figures. When a politician's "zipper problems" were exposed, numerous jokes circulated. For the sake of brevity, I'll cite only those in which the misadventures of two or more politicians are exploited.

Q: What was Gary Hart's greatest regret?
A: He didn't ask Ted Kennedy to drive Donna Rice to the airport.

Q: Did you hear about the new law firm: Richard Nixon, Gary Hart, and Ted Kennedy?
A: It's called Trick 'em, Dick 'em, and Dunk 'em.

Magazines such as *Playboy* and *Penthouse* made very open offers of huge sums of money to the young women whose names were linked with public figures. Jessica Hahn cashed in on the notoriety her affair with televangelist Jim Bakker earned her by posing nude. Jesse Jackson's name was never definitively linked with any woman other than his wife, so the better-known jokes about his sexuality stemmed from speculations about his relationship with her.

Q: Did you hear that Jesse Jackson had to withdraw from the presidential election?
A: His wife was found posing nude for *National Geographic*.

Once again Jackson's race is his Achilles' heel. For many years *National Geographic* was the only "reputable" periodical to feature bare-breasted women. The women, however, were "tribal" ones, usu-

ally living in Africa. In other versions of the same joke Jackson's
parents are foregrounded.

Q: Did you hear that Jesse Jackson had to pull out of the race?
A: His parents posed naked for *National Geographic.*

Person A: You know why Jesse Jackson dropped out of the
presidential race?
Person B: No, why?
Person A: He found out his mother was a centerfold in
National Geographic.

Jacksonalia

Michael Jackson lore focuses on his questionable sexual orientation, his relationship with Brooke Shields, his "fire" escapade, and his
relationship with the Pepsi-Cola corporation. The legends and jokes
about Reggie Jackson trade on his sexual exploits, his arrogance, and
his status as an African-American folk sports hero. Some of the material about the Reverend Jesse Jackson hinges on flaws comparable to
the type that trigger jokes about any politician. Other jokes reflect a
public that still perceives race as an impediment to political success.
This pattern is also discernible in a cycle of material that purposely
confuses Michael, Reggie, and Jesse Jackson. Far and away the largest
body of this material bestows the traits of Reggie Jackson, the sports
hero, or Michael Jackson, the pop entertainer, on the Reverend Jackson. For example:

Person A: Did you hear that President Reagan called Jesse
Jackson?
Person B: No, what did he say to him?
Person A: He said he was sorry to hear about his hair.

This joke is of course dependent on the audience's knowledge that it
was *Michael* Jackson who accidentally burned his hair. In another
example, a student recalled part of a joke she heard within a few days
of Jackson's noteworthy address to the Democratic National Conven-

tion in 1984. Someone (white) said to her, "That Jesse Jackson sure is something, isn't he?" After her response of yeah, the other party said, "Yeah, not only can he hit home runs, sing and dance, but he can speak too!"

The media also indulged in this impulse to confuse Jesse Jackson with Michael or Reggie Jackson. Following Jesse Jackson's address to the Democratic National Convention, ABC's *Nightline* featured him in an interview with its host, Ted Koppel. Koppel scored a coup by having Jackson, who had surprised his critics by delivering a quite powerful address, as his guest that night. Jackson's comments were interspersed with those by columnist George Will, a guest commentator. At the end of the program, Koppel allowed Will to have the final word. He began by conceding that, in fact, Jackson had delivered a good speech but that he could learn a few lessons from Michael Jackson. The print media also intentionally linked Michael and Jesse Jackson. A newspaper article on Jackson's ostensibly disorganized campaign tour was titled "Allegations and Alligators—Jackson Campaign: A Thriller." The headline of an article in *The New Republic* about Jackson's trip to Cuba and Central America read: "The Jackson Tour."[8]

At first glance, this tendency to juxtapose Jesse with Michael or Reggie Jackson might seem to be merely a play on the coincidence embodied in having three black celebrities, indeed heroes, with the same surname. One might even go a step further and claim that this juxtaposition reinforces the notion that whites have trouble differentiating between one black (or one Jackson) and another. However, if that were the case, then we would probably find examples in which the traits of Jesse Jackson were transposed upon Michael or Reggie Jackson. But we don't. Or, at least, I didn't. What I found were examples in which Michael's or Reggie's traits were imposed upon Jesse—in other words, examples in which the traits of a black performer or sports figure were transposed upon a political figure. Thus jokes such as "What did Jesse Jackson drink after the Democratic Convention?" Answer: "It sure wasn't Pepsi!" reflect an impulse to place a African-American hero within the acceptable role of a sports figure or entertainment figure. The perpetuators of these jokes, the writers of the cited newspaper and magazine articles, and George Will are all refusing to accept a black man as a viable political figure. When they derive humor and interest in his campaign by intentionally confusing him with a singer or an outfielder, they are implicitly stating that they are more comfortable with blacks who excel in the accepted arenas of entertainment and sports.

The Pino character in *Do the Right Thing* echoes a sentiment shared by many. He is fond of African-American sports figures and entertainers. He embraces those blacks who perform. He can be a recipient of their talents. But he doesn't want pictures of African-American political leaders on the walls of his father's pizzeria. The talents of Malcolm X, Martin Luther King, Jr., and contemporary African Americans are not devoted to making his life better or more enjoyable. Instead, such individuals have committed their lives to improving the standard of living for black Americans. To the Pinos of the world, bettering the day-to-day life of black Americans translates into diminishing the potential of themselves and other Americans. And such individuals are just more comfortable with black sports figures and entertainers than they are with political and social activists. Those jokes that confuse Michael and Reggie Jackson with Jesse Jackson suggest that this is a pervasive view.

6

Everything Is *Not* Satisfactual

*The kind of work I have always wanted to do requires me to
learn how to maneuver ways to free up the language from its
sometimes sinister, frequently lazy, almost always predictable
employment of racially informed and determined chains.*

—TONI MORRISON, *Playing in the Dark: Whiteness and
the Literary Imagination*[1]

The American toy chest that comprises children's popular culture is
a cavernous container with almost infinite room for growth. It contin-
ually expands to accommodate the mass-produced books, comics,
backpacks, T-shirts, toys, games, theme parks, cereal box premiums,
Happy Meal give-aways, movies, commercials, and television programs that children begin to consume shortly after their umbilical
cords are cut. It starts when they are put in diapers adorned with
cartoon characters around the waistline or are given bottles on which
such characters dance, and it lasts well into the adult years. These
commercially constructed entities contribute to the youngsters' value
system and worldview. The literature they read, the videos they
watch, the toys they play with, and even the lunchboxes they tote
influence children's sense of who and where they are in the world. No
single conglomerate claims more space in the toy chest of American

popular culture than the myriad of companies and enterprises connected with the Walt Disney Company. Since the 1930s the film studio founded by the son of a midwestern farmer has increasingly dominated the creation and distribution of the cultural artifacts of American children.

Like most Americans of my generation, Disney-related products were a significant part of my childhood. I raced home from school to watch reruns of the *Mickey Mouse Club* in the early 1960s. *The Sword in the Stone* (1963) was my first "movie theater" movie. I felt enormous pride when I memorized the lyrics to "Supercalifragolisticexpialidocious," a hit song from the movie *Mary Poppins*. I saw *That Darned Cat* at least three times. My students, most of whom were born in the 1970s, can also measure the landmarks of their early childhood with Disney milestones. My own son, born in the late 1980s, sleeps under a *101 Dalmatians* comforter and can recite most of the dialogue and lyrics to *Beauty and the Beast.* When I take him to a movie or rent a video for him, and he sees the trademark castle materialize on the screen, he says "It's a Disney one!" and sits back to absorb the story that follows. When I sent the final galley proofs of my first book back to the editor, I announced to my family, "Okay, Mommy has just finished her first book! What are we going to do next?" "We're going to Disneyland!" was the exclamation, and we headed off for two days in the Magic Kingdom.

On a Disney-idolatry scale, I would position my family somewhere smack in the middle. I have friends and colleagues who eschew any blatantly commercial children's popular culture. Their kids don't watch television (at home, anyway), they read only those books that have won children's literature awards, their vacations are taken in educationally correct settings, and their clothes are all natural fibers and are never inscribed with images of cartoon characters. On the other hand, I have friends and colleagues who enthusiastically pursue as many of the Disney products and paraphernalia as their pocketbooks will permit.

The amount of space commanded by Disney products in America's toy chest is no accident. Walt Disney, the company's founder, was without question one of the shrewdest twentieth-century merchants of popular culture. As his biographers have pointed out, he possessed an innate ability to predict and deliver stories that delight and assuage the American masses. An intrepid entrepreneur as well as a storyteller, Walt Disney delivered much more than the stories themselves. This dimension of his influence began in the 1930s, when he signed an agreement allowing a manufacturer to inscribe Mickey Mouse's image on a note pad. Today the mouse reigns over a battalion of Disney-spawned items. From waffle makers to telephones, there are few products that cannot be obtained with Mickey's smiling image on them. More and more shopping malls have Disney stores in them. Foundations exist that raise money so that terminally ill children can visit Disneyland or Disney World, the most popular family vacation destinations in the world. Most cable systems carry the premium Disney Channel, a television network dominated by Disney-produced programs. Most movie complexes always present at least one Disney-produced feature at any given time.

Written in the late 1960s and revised in the mid-1980s, film scholar Richard Schickel's biography of Walt Disney, *The Disney Version*, is an excellent study of the love affair cultivated by the man behind the mouse and the American consumer. Schickel's title choice was particularly appropriate. The stories told by Disney were one man's *version* of the heroes and heroines whom he felt confident about redoing for his American audience. Disney credited his success to his own ordinariness. He believed he could predict what stories would appeal to middle-of-the-road consumers because he was cut from the same cloth as they. Walt Disney modified traditional folktales to fit the standards of American's national literature. Consequently, the Disney "versions" were fundamentally white ones. In her critique of the function of a black presence in American "high" literature, African-American author and critic Toni Morrison has noted, "National literatures, like writers, get along the best way they can, and with what they can, yet they do seem to end up describing and inscribing what is on the national mind. For the most part, the literature of the United States has taken as its concern the architecture of a *new white man*."[2] Morrison's approach to Willa Cather, Ernest Hemingway, Mark Twain, and several other American "adult" creative artists is applicable to Walt Disney as well. Like the writers analyzed by Morrison, Disney told stories that reinforced the prevailing status quo of his times. His professional heirs have done much the same. "Good" Disney stories do not violate the truths held by the majority. "Good" Disney stories adhere to a hierarchy in which white reigns supreme over black.

"Good" Disney versions can be mined for insight into the ways in which attitudes toward race, class, and gender have evolved in the twentieth century. At first glance, the sheer productivity of the Disney Studios emerges as an obstacle. Throughout the years, the company has produced thousands of cartoons, scores of movies, and an abundance of spin-off items. Rather than proceed product by product, I have opted to approach the Disney corpus from a different perspective. First, I look at how color is used to evoke goodness and evil in several of the full-length movies. Most of this analysis rests on Disney's first major effort, *Snow White and the Seven Dwarfs* (1937). Almost ten years after *Snow White*'s debut the Disney company produced its first feature (and one of its last) in which an African-American actor played a prominent role. Therefore, *Song of the South* (1946) warrants a prolonged consideration.

Since Walt Disney's death in 1966, the company has undergone many profound changes. Whereas Disney himself insisted that every product be thoroughly saccharine and wholesome, the heirs to his creative legacy have been eager to cash in on the public's desire for slightly more sophisticated merchandise. In order to reap some of the profits to be earned, the Disney studios created a second label, Touchstone, under which it markets movies suitable for an older, somewhat more sophisticated crowd.[3] Noteworthy among these efforts is *Who Framed Roger Rabbit*, made in collaboration with Robert Zemeckis and Amblin Entertainment.

My goal here is not to indict the man or his company as "racist." If the racial subtexts of Disney's productions had contradicted or alienated American consumers, audiences would have rejected the movies, cartoons, television shows, and all of the spin-offs. But Disney versions are rarely, if ever, rejected. Their space in the toy chest of American popular culture is secure.

Disney's Palette

In either its live-action or animated features, the productions of the Disney studios are not overpopulated by depictions of real African-American people. During Walt Disney's own lifetime, very few black performers or other employees took home paychecks from the Disney studios. Of course, the payrolls of other major Hollywood studios didn't have a whole lot of African-American names on them either. Disney's animators were, however, making steady use of the darker colors on their palettes. With remarkable consistency, they portrayed their good characters in lighter tones, with paler clothes, and fairer hair, while the darker shades were used for the evil characters. The Disney animators were certainly not the first to use dark colors to evoke evil. Western culture has long linked darkness and evil. By persistently wrapping evil characters in dark cloaks, capes, cowboy hats, and hoods, and rendering the good ones in starched white aprons, gowns, and uniforms, the Disney studios ensured that several generations of American children would shudder with apprehension when darkness appeared on the screen and would utter sighs of relief at lightness.

Disney chose *Snow White and the Seven Dwarfs* as the story for his first full-length film. Folklorists recognize "Snow White" as a staple narrative in the fairy tale collection assembled in the early nineteenth century by Jacob and Wilhelm Grimm. Disney did not remain true to this or any other Grimm version he adapted for the screen.[4] Most of Disney's modifications were motivated by the desire to mitigate some of the more unsavory and sanguinary twists of the plot. This is particularly ironic when we consider that the most pervasive criticism of *Snow White and the Seven Dwarfs* originated from observers who argued that the final product of five years' work by the Disney studios was too frightening for children. Disney and company had already eliminated some episodes within the narrative likely to terrify children or offend their parents. For example, in the Grimm version, the evil stepmother, disguised as an old crone, makes three attempts on Snow White's life. For the movie, Disney scaled back to just one. The Grimm version ends at the wedding of Snow White and her Prince. The happy royal couple have devised their own punishment for the evil queen:

> But iron slippers had already been put upon the fire, and they were brought in with tongs, and set before her. Then she was forced to put on the red-hot shoes, and dance until she dropped down dead.

Disney's much tamer ending comes when the Prince rescues the sleeping Snow White. The aura of evil in the Grimm version is driven by gruesome deeds and vulgar actions. After one of the old crone's visitations, the Seven Dwarfs return home to find a collapsed Snow White. They proceed to search her body and find that she is being slowly strangled by a corset the Queen had tricked her into wearing. No doubt the puritanical Walt Disney had no intention of requiring his animators to design scenes showing the Seven Dwarfs feeling up Snow White and removing her corset. Disney substitutes subtle but nonetheless potent markers of evil. The extent of the old crone's evil is suggested by her elongated nose and flowing black cape. Rather than showing her evil through her sordid deeds, Disney relies heavily on her abhorrent appearance to repel the audience.

The Grimms did not specify black as the primary color in the evil stepmother's wardrobe. Aside from references to an ebony window frame and Snow White's black-as-ebony hair, *Snow-White* lacks references to dark colors. In the Disney version, Snow White's stepmother, the Queen, is the first human character portrayed. The audience sees her from the rear. She wears a flowing black cape, over a deep regal purple gown, and a black turban. Within seconds after she appears on screen, we hear her uttering the infamous "Magic Mirror, on the wall . . ." Learning that "Snow White is the fairest of them all" enrages her. When the audience first sees Snow White, the young princess is surrounded by white doves. Soon "her Prince" rides up on a white horse.

The light/goodness and the dark/evil pattern continues throughout the movie. Imagining that tree limbs are tentacles and felled logs alligator mouths, Snow White keels over from fear in the dark forest she has fled to after the huntsman is unable to carry out the Queen's order to kill her. In the bright light of day, the creatures the princess feared in the dark night turn out to be cuddly, furry, friendly animals. They escort her to the dwarfs' cottage, where the first order of business is cleaning the place up. Before the seven little men are fully welcomed back into their own home, they too are compelled to bathe. The huntsman's substitution of a pig's heart for Snow White's doesn't fool the magic mirror. When the Queen learns that her murder plot has failed, she descends into the dark castle basement where she consults her web-covered books on black magic in order to find the spell that will help her rid the landscape of the fair Snow White. She transforms herself into an ugly old crone shrouded in a black, hooded robe. The poisonous apple she concocts is also black until she disguises it red. A black crow observes all of her machinations in the castle, and a pair of black buzzards watch over her when she reaches the dwarfs' cottage. In her final scene, the seven little men have chased her to the top of a rain-soaked mountain. She stands in her black robe posited against a dark mountain under a gloomy and turbulent sky. Then she falls into a dark abyss. Meanwhile, on a beautiful grassy hill, the dwarfs have displayed Snow White in a glass coffin surrounded by flowers. She is bathed in sunlight as her Prince, on his white horse, comes to bestow love's first kiss on her lips.

I am using *Snow White and the Seven Dwarfs* as a case study here for several reasons. It bears scrutiny because it was the first such animated feature brought to the screen. Both a critical and commercial success, it has earned in excess of $100 million.[5] Perhaps because of its immediate success, Disney and his creative team continued to rely upon narrative strategies developed for *Snow White*. Since audiences liked stories of innocent princesses, brave princes, and cuddly animals, the Disney people have continued to give them to us.

Over the years the Disney palette has expanded. A much broader selection of colors is available now than when the original *Snow White* cels were painted during the mid-1930s. Yet, as before, more often than not colors from the darker end of the spectrum are selected to suggest evil. The voluptuous Ursula the Sea Witch in *The Little Mermaid* (1989) wears a strapless black gown. Darkness pervades whenever there is trouble in the seas inhabited by Ariel, Flounder, and King Triton. When the magic spell is broken in *Beauty and the Beast* (1991), a dark, gray film evaporates from over the castle and it seems to undergo a magical paint job, rendering it white from moat to turret. Jaffar, the wicked character in *Aladdin* (1992), is draped in black from head to foot. Whenever the characters are in the general vicinity of the evil sand castle, darkness sweeps over the screen. In *Cinderella* (1950), the magic coach and horses are white, her evil stepmother is shaded in dark hues. Her Prince shows up in white uniform to put the glass slipper on her foot and whisk her away to live happily ever after.

It is easy to imagine the Disney studios defending themselves by accusing me of underestimating the critical sensibilities of children with my assumption that just because the bad guys in some of their films are dressed in black, they become apprehensive toward black people as they grow up. Few, if any, children see these movies in a vacuum. At the same time that the first audience of children was watching *Snow White and the Seven Dwarfs*, they could have been easily reciting "Eenie, meanie, miney, moe/Catch a nigger by the toe." Their parents could easily have been reading them *Little Black Sambo, Dr. Doolittle*, or *Mary Poppins*.[6] Some of Disney's staunchest fans grew up to become filmmakers. George Lucas, for one, acknowledges his creative debt to Walt Disney. His *Star Wars* trilogy subscribes to a similar color code. Luke Skywalker and Princess Leia, the good characters, are swathed in white. Darth Vader's hooded robe closely resembles that worn by the old crone in *Snow White*. Single portrayals of good/light and evil/dark might not convey the message that white people are superior to black. But when all of the toys in the toy chest reinforces the dichotomy, it is sure to have an influence.

Song of the South

Jacob and Wilhelm Grimm and Hans Christian Andersen were not the only folklore collectors embraced by Walt Disney. He also modified the books of Joel Chandler Harris, a late nineteenth-century white journalist for the *Atlanta Constitution*. Harris set himself to the task of collecting and preserving the folktales that he had overheard slaves tell during his childhood. Disney had enjoyed Harris's stories and was eager to bring them to a new generation of American children.

Scholars who have investigated these tales now agree that Harris's collection represents the most significant compilation of genuine slave folklore available from the nineteenth century. African antecedents can be found for more than half of the tales. The chief protagonist in these tales is the trickster Brer Rabbit, who uses his wit, guile, and spunk to sabotage the efforts of ostensibly stronger animals in the forest.

In presenting these trickster stories, Harris embroidered the core tales with a frame story about a docile, aged slave who spends his evenings telling the tales to a young white boy. It is easy to understand why Harris felt the need to add this seemingly innocuous frame story. He was writing from the South in the aftermath of Reconstruction. Clearly he had to present the tales in a way that would be palatable to his white readers. Recasting the stories in the 1940s, Walt

Disney was clearly also concerned about reactions of his white audience.

The Slaves' Stories

By focusing on the frame story, however, Harris and Disney performed a grave disservice to these tales and to African Americans. During the era of slavery the trickster tales constituted the largest component of slave oral literature. They were not merely moral or entertainment stories for children but, instead, functional narratives for the adult African-American population. In slave reminiscences collected by the Federal Writer's Project in the 1930s, countless elderly slaves recalled the days in which the Brer Rabbit stories were shared among the adults when masters were far out of hearing range. While adults may have occasionally shared the tales with a white youngster, such storytelling situations were the exception and not the rule. With his quick wit, unrelenting verve, and voracious appetites Brer Rabbit was the perfect hero for a people who had to rely on verbal facility rather than physical strength in order to exercise any control over their day-to-day lives. In the world the slaves made, Brer Rabbit symbolized the most successful slave, the one who could minimize his workload, maximize his food intake, and all the while escape punishment. Brer Fox, Brer Bear, or any other enemy in the forest symbolized the masters and overseers who were so persistent in their attempts to harness the wily rabbit.

Disney's twentieth-century re-creation of Harris's frame story is much more heinous than the original. The days on the plantation located in "the United States of Georgia" begin and end with unsupervised blacks singing songs about their wonderful home as they march to and from the fields. Disney and company made no attempt to render the music in the style of the spirituals and work songs that would have been sung during this era. They provided no indication regarding the status of the blacks on this plantation. Joel Chandler Harris set his stories in the postslavery era, but Disney's version seems to take place during a surreal time when blacks lived on slave quarters on a plantation, worked diligently for no visible reward, and considered Atlanta a viable place for an old black man to set out for.

Kind old Uncle Remus caters to the needs of the young white boy whose father has inexplicably left him and his mother at the plantation. An obviously ill-kept black child of the same age named Toby is assigned to look after the white boy, Johnny. Although Toby makes one reference to his "ma," his parents are nowhere to be seen. The African-American adults in the film pay attention to him only when he neglects his responsibilities as Johnny's playmate-keeper. He is up before Johnny in the morning in order to bring his white charge water to wash with and keep him entertained.

The boys befriend a little blond white girl, Ginny, whose family clearly represents the neighborhood's white trash. Although Johnny coaxes his mother into inviting Ginny to his fancy birthday party at the big house, Toby is curiously absent from the party scenes. Toby is good enough to catch frogs with, but not good enough to have birthday cake with. When Toby and Johnny are with Uncle Remus, the gray-haired black man directs most of his attention to the white child. Thus blacks on the plantation are seen as willingly subservient to the whites to the extent that they overlook the needs of their own children. When Johnny's mother threatens to keep her son away from the old gentleman's cabin, Uncle Remus is so hurt he starts to run away. In the world that Disney made, the blacks sublimate their own lives in order to be better servants to the white family. If Disney had truly understood the message of the tales he animated so delightfully, he would have realized the extent of distortion in the frame story.

From Brer to Roger

Brer Rabbit was not the last hare to command center stage in a Disney-related production. Forty-odd years later, in 1988, *Who Framed Roger Rabbit* emerged as an unqualified commercial and critical success for Disney's Touchstone label. Both productions broke new technological ground in weaving live-action sequences with animated ones. Aside from a few scenes of Uncle Remus ambling along singing as animated birds flit to his shoulders and cartoon squirrels dart through his legs, most of the animated characters in *Song of the South* are segregated from the humans in their own stories. In *Roger Rabbit* the human characters and animated ones coexist in an imagined view of Los Angeles in the 1940s. Only one plot undergirds *Who Framed Roger Rabbit*, but within it an interesting message about segregation does emerge.

The Los Angeles imagined by the filmmakers consists of two communities—one human and one animated. It goes without saying that the humans are depicted as the superior, dominant population and the animated characters, the toons, are portrayed as the inferior, subordinate community. In assigning characteristics to depict toon inferiority to the audience, the filmmakers bestowed upon them several attributes traditionally associated with blacks.

The toons work for the humans. By day they come to the several film studios in the city to make movies. Toons specialize in broad, slapstick-style comedy. By night they return to Toontown—a very standard kind of ghetto. Toons live there, but the property is all owned by a human, Marvin Acme. Most humans avoid going into Toontown. At first an undesirable tract of property, from a human perspective anyway, Toontown's value has increased as the needs of Hollywood's film community have expanded. Thus, when it is learned that Toontown's quirky landlord intends to bequeath the land to the Toons, his business competitors set out to undermine his plan.

Toons exemplify the attributes of an idealized, fantasy minority group. With the exception of a cadre of nefarious law-enforcement weasels, most toons are content singing, dancing, and performing comedy routines. As Roger Rabbit says, "My whole purpose is to make people laugh." Toons can suffer a multitude of physical abuses. They experience no long-term pain even though they are thrust through walls, dropped from windows, strangled, and crushed. Until they see Judge Doom's fatal toon "dip," humans believe that it is impossible to kill a toon. Toons themselves are not eager for liberation; they are not fighting for the chance to own Toontown.

Roger and Jessica Rabbit are the most prominent toon characters in the film. At first glance, Roger is just a silly-looking rabbit. In some respects he resembles the happy-go-lucky coon (toon?) characters immortalized by black comedian Stepin Fetchit (Lincoln Perry) in the 1920s and 1930s. African-American film historian Donald Bogle identifies several telltale features of the coon persona as exemplified by Fetchit in the 1930s.[7] These include (1) outlandish, oversized clothing; (2) an inability to pronounce correctly multisyllabic words; (3) dimwittedness; and (4) never a threat to his often-coarse master.

Roger Rabbit's clothes are fairly outlandish, consisting of baggy red overalls and an oversized polka-dot bow tie. He too has trouble with multisyllabic words. Meaning to say "corroborate," he says "corrugate." He substitutes "prostate" for "probate." Even for a toon, he emerges as particularly dimwitted. Knowing that Judge Doom intends to kill him, Roger still bursts through a wall right into the Judge's waiting arms. Even though his unwilling human protector, the private detective Eddie Valiant, does little to disguise his contempt for Roger and all toons, Roger remains steadfast in his loyalty to him. Roger, like many cinematic and literary coons, is unable to hold his liquor. We could almost substitute "Roger Rabbit" and "toon" for "Stepin Fetchit" and "coon" in the following summary from Bogle:

> Fetchit's great gift was in rendering his coons as such thoroughly illiterate figures that they did not have to respond when demeaned because they were always unaware of what was being done. When he was kicked in one film, Fetchit merely winked to his audience. When he was shoved in another, he merely moaned "Yessir" and went on his way. By removing his characters' intellects—indeed their psyches—from the real world, Stepin Fetchit's dim wits never had to acknowledge the inhumanity that surrounded them. They were inhabitants of detached, ironic, artistically controlled worlds.[8]

Roger Rabbit did have one thing usually denied to screen coons— a love life. Much of the film's plot is driven by Roger's desire to reconcile with his wife, Jessica. Jessica Rabbit is drawn as a sultry, voluptuous, redheaded white female toon. In spite of her sundry flirtations with human men, her loyalty to Roger is steadfast. The nightclub where Jessica works as a singer bears a strong resemblance to Harlem's infamous Cotton Club where black performers entertained all-white audiences. In *Roger Rabbit*, all of the entertainers are toons while all of the patrons are humans. With the exception of the brown, furry, burly bouncer, all of the toons employed in the club are black, white, or both—the waiters are penguins. In Jessica's opening act, Donald Duck and Daffy Duck play white and black baby grand pianos. Their dueling pianos number is followed by Jessica's sexy torch song. Given this context, it seems plausible to suggest that Jessica's characterization may have been inspired in part by the beautiful fair-skinned women who sang in the original Cotton Club. With her full lips and amply endowed figure, Jessica certainly possesses some of the physical attributes sometimes associated with black female entertainers.

Roger and Jessica's chief antagonist, Judge Doom, turns out to be a toon passing for a human. He has concocted an elaborate plot that includes eliminating the streetcars, the Toons, and Toontown and developing freeways. Just in the nick of time, Eddie Valiant rescues Roger and Jessica. Judge Doom is destroyed by the dip that he had developed to implement toonicide.

However innocently they got started, the filmmakers who devised the human/toon relationship provided glimpses into how the dominant culture would like its subordinate groups to function. Toons are a fantasy minority group. They sing, dance, and make people laugh. They are virtually indestructible. They ask for very little in return for their services. The dominant group can profit from their antics. At night they happily return to Toontown. Their own well-being rests solely on pleasing the dominant group. This configuration underscores the disproportionate appeal of the entertainment dimension of the African-American persona.

Once upon a time, my young son saw a television ad for a newly released feature-length, animated movie. Seduced by the colorful commercial, he cajoled me into taking him to the movie. From my point of view, the movie was a complete failure. The soundtrack was annoyingly cute. The animation was pedestrian. The characters were poorly drawn, one-dimensional, and boring. Needless to say, my son didn't articulate his dissatisfaction in these terms. But he could barely sit through the film until the end. He insisted on several trips to the bathroom. In the days that followed, he didn't ask me to take him to see it again, and he requested no toys or games inspired by its characters.

Disney films generate an entirely different response from both of us. He uses every trick in the book to persuade me to take him to see the same movie over and over again. He sits on the edge of his seat. Through his elementary school grapevine, he discovers what date the movie will be released on video and campaigns tirelessly for a copy. When he gets one, he watches it over and over again. And even as I sit with him charting those aspects of the film that reinforce negative stereotypes, I find myself singing the songs and laughing at the jokes. In short, the Disney people make extraordinarily entertaining films that appeal to children of all ages.

In the half century since *Snow White and the Seven Dwarfs* was released, the Disney studios have surmounted numerous creative challenges. They have seamed together live action and animated footage, creating the illusion of real people talking to cartoon animals. They fashioned individual personalities for each of 101 dalmatians. They made an elephant fly. They created a corpulent blue genie able to do celebrity imitations. The creative family that devised and mastered these techniques ought to channel some of their resources into stories that don't rely on tired conventions. How about some bad guys dressed in white? How about some dark-skinned heroes and heroines complete without European facial features? To be sure, these kinds of films would only partially offset the weight of the fifty plus years' worth of movies that so many of us have watched over and over again. But some change would be preferable to none.

7

In Search of the Young,
Gifted, and Black

*Apart from anything else, I wanted to be able to come here
and speak to you on this afternoon because you are young,
gifted, and black. In the month of May in the year of 1964, I
for one can think of no more dynamic combination that a
young person might be.*

—LORRAINE HANSBERRY, *To Be Young, Gifted, and Black*

Asked to address the three winners of the United Negro College
Fund's annual young writer's contest, the African-American writer
Lorraine Hansberry, best known for her award-winning play *A Raisin
in the Sun,* was optimistic about the futures of the young, gifted, and
black recipients. But in a much different context the celebrated playwright wrote in a piece titled "America as Seen Through the Eye of
the TV Tube" "Negroes do not exist. . . ."[1] Succumbing to cancer at
the age of thirty-four in 1965, the multitalented Hansberry died when
black images on television were still quite few and far between. She
had no doubt seen the *Amos 'n' Andy* Show in the early 1950s, and
she may have caught *The Nat "King" Cole Show* during its brief run
in 1956 and 1957. Three decades later black television actors and
actresses are much more evident than in Hansberry's day. African
Americans now "exist" on television. But are they represented in a

119

fashion that Hansberry would have applauded? In particular, what kinds of portraits has television painted of the young, gifted, and black individuals for whom she had so much hope? How is the public-at-large asked to imagine what a bright, young African American looks like, talks like, walks like?

Representations of young African Americans are now discernible in virtually all modes of popular culture—advertising, music video, film, television, and the stage. But television, in general, and prime-time television, in particular, are the venues where most Americans are exposed to images of young African Americans. Situation comedies and some dramatic series chronicle the lives of fictional young African Americans. The episodic nature of these television series lends itself to an examination of the scope of possibilities constructed for young blacks. Television programs introduce characters and then, over the life of the series, give the audiences sustained contact with them.

Television writers most commonly locate young black characters in either a domestic or an academic environment. Three basic kinds of television families have featured young blacks: white parents/black adopted offspring—*Diff'rent Strokes* (1978–1986), *Webster* (1983–1987); black single parent/black offspring—*Julia* (1968–1971), *What's Happening!!* (1976–1979); black parents/black offspring—*Good Times* (1974–1979), *The Jeffersons* (1975–1985); *227* (1985–1990), *The Cosby Show* (1984–1992), *Family Matters* (1989–present), *Fresh Prince of Bel Air* (1990–present). Academic environments usually focus on an eclectic group of students under the supervision of a particular teacher/coach—*Room 222* (1969–1974), *Fame* (1982–1987), *Head of the Class* (1986–1991), *The White Shadow* (1978–1981), *Welcome Back, Kotter* (1975–1979); or grouped together in the same dormitory setting—*The Facts of Life* (1979–1988), *A Different World* (1987–present).[2] In deciding which series to analyze, I considered several factors. Because they command the largest audiences, I limited myself to programs that were originated on the three major networks as opposed to offerings designed for cable or syndication. In order to examine how characters are developed over time, I also confine my discussion to programs that were aired for more than one season. As a result of that decision, I did not consider any programs that debuted after the 1991 fall season.

The dates of the series listed indicate a rather obvious omission.

Although television came into American homes in the 1950s, programs containing sustained images of young blacks did not surface until the late 1960s. A very few adult images of blacks were featured in 1950s television, and a brief discussion of these will illuminate the characterizations of youth/intelligence that emerged in the series listed above.

The Jones, the Bakers, and the Thomases

In their initial efforts to bring African-American characters to the little screen, television producers faced objections from both black and white audiences—objections that transformed or threatened to be transformed into consumer boycotts and formal legal actions. Television's Amos and Andy, like their radio counterparts, embodied a familiar set of antiblack stereotypes rooted in the nineteenth-century era of blackface entertainment. From the minstrel stages of the 1830s to the television screens of the 1950s, black males were portrayed as raucous, loud, lazy n'er-do-wells. Their language was replete with conspicuously mispronounced multisyllabic words. Referred to alternately as coons and Sambos, these characters frequently lacked any redeeming qualities—save their ability to prompt laughter. Twentieth-century incarnations of the minstrel characters were portrayed as particularly ill-suited to urban, industrial life. To many blacks who felt that African-American industrial ingenuity had been aptly demonstrated by black efforts in the Northern-based defense industry during World War II, these characterizations were insulting and demeaning.

Based on the hit radio series of the same name, CBS's *Amos 'n' Andy* show (1951–1953) highlighted the collisions with urban life experienced by Amos, Andy, and their cohorts from the Mystic Knights of the Sea. Although the Jones family, consisting of Amos (Alvin Childress), Ruby, and their daughter Arbadella, were the first black family to be depicted in a prime-time television series, episodes seldom chronicled the Joneses' family life. Most episodes dwelled on the outrageous misadventures into which Amos, Andy, Kingfish, and their friends found themselves and the malapropisms with which they expressed their frustrations.

The only child "regular" on the series, young Arbadella Jones, appeared so rarely that it is difficult to extrapolate what conclusions the audience might have drawn about blacks, youth, and intelligence from her character. In all fairness, I grant that the producers did not succumb to any temptation to depict her in a pickanninny fashion. Her hair and clothes were always neat, and she spoke in standard English. One of the most well-loved episodes of the series was the Christmas show in which her godfather, the usually inept and clown-ish Andy Brown (Spenser Williams, Jr.), spends a day as a department store Santa Claus to earn the money to buy her a beautiful black doll. In the final scene her father, Amos, is shown reading the Lord's Prayer by her bedside.

Unfortunately, most episodes were much more like the "Vacation Show." In this episode, Kingfish (Tim Moore) has twittered away all of the money his wife, Sapphire (Ernestine Wade), has entrusted to him for their family vacation. After selling the family car to recoup the misspent vacation funds, Kingfish discovers that Sapphire and her mother have bought a trailer, the kind that has to be hitched to a car, for a cross-country sightseeing trip. In order to save himself from Sapphire's ire, Kingfish dupes Andy into paying him to coordinate a cross-country camping trip for him. Then he takes Andy to Central Park and for several days convinces his gullible friend they are really traversing the United States.

By making episodes such as "The Christmas Story" the exception and the "Vacation Show" the rule, the producers paved the path to the legal offices of the National Association for the Advancement of Colored People (NAACP), the most powerful of several civil rights organizations that were eager to get CBS to take the series off the air. Roy Wilkins explained the NAACP's objections to the series: "The visual impact is infinitely worse than the radio version. . . . The television brings these people to life—they are no longer merely voices and they say to millions of white Americans who know nothing about Negroes, and to millions of white children who are learning about life, that this is the way Negroes are."[3] Although the NAACP protest may not have been the raison d'être for the cancellation of the *Amos 'n' Andy* show, it did make other producers leery of casting African Americans, particularly African-American men, in television series.

Five years after the cancellation of this show, the possibility of a boycott was raised in connection with another African-American male television figure. Only this time network sponsors were afraid of the reaction of *white* viewers to a black male depicted in a position of authority. Suave, debonair, intelligent, and talented, entertainer Nat King Cole was the polar opposite of Amos, Andy, Kingfish, and their friends. Cole's sophisticated posture so aggravated white Southern viewers that advertisers refused to sponsor the NBC variety show that had been developed for him.

By the end of the 1950s television producers had faced a damned-if-you-do dilemma in terms of their handling of black male representations. Comic characters such as Amos and Andy were intensely disliked by some black viewers, while intelligent African Americans such as Nat King Cole were reviled by some white viewers.[4] The safe route, then, was to avoid blacks, particularly black men, altogether.

Oddly enough, it was Roy Wilkins who led the anti-*Amos 'n' Andy* campaign, and it was Wilkins who inspired one of its former writers to develop a television series laudable for its more benign portrayal of blacks. After hearing Wilkins implore the Hollywood establishment to improve its representations of the black experience, Hal Kanter, a former writer for *Amos 'n' Andy*, penned a pilot about a very small black family consisting only of a widowed nurse Julia Baker (Diahann Carroll) and her six-year-old son Corey (Marc Copage).[5] Kanter and his team made careful decisions about the characters of Julia and Corey, and the plots they developed were colored by their sense of what audiences did and did not want to see in its first black family of the 1960s. Aware that the eyes of the civil rights establishment were upon them, *Julia*'s producers made a conscious effort to stay as far away as possible from any of the conventional black caricatures. In moving away from any of the familiar negative stereotypes of African Americans, Kanter and his colleagues developed characters whose only discernible black feature was their complexions.

As even Diahann Carroll acknowledges, the characters of Julia and Corey were developed with white viewers in mind. She confessed, "I'd like a couple of million of them [white Americans] to watch and say, 'Hey, so that's what they do when they go home at night.' "[6] Yet for Kanter and his colleagues, getting a show with a black cast—even a show as saccharine and unthreatening as *Julia*—on a major network was no easy chore. His mail reflected the response that some viewers had. " 'How dare you put a black woman on and shove them down our throats.' You'd be surprised how many letters like that I received personally."[7] To many television critics as well as African-American observers, the desire to prove to white viewers that blacks returned to the same kind of homes as whites trivialized very real class and cultural distinctions between the races.

Knowing that the portrayal of African-American single mothers could lead to charges of stereotyping, television producers have stayed away from such characters. By making Julia Baker a widow whose husband died in Vietnam while on active duty, Kanter sought to deflect any negative associations that might be inspired in viewers. Young Corey is so obviously well adjusted that viewers can't help but conclude that Julia is succeeding in both maternal and paternal roles.

Julia Baker emerges as one of television's first superwomen. She is depicted as a very capable nurse and a near-perfect mother. Perfect mothers produce perfect children, and Corey emerges as a well-behaved child and an exemplary student. The unspoken message implicit throughout the run of *Julia* was that by working with whites, going to school with whites, and living with whites, African Americans could and would excel. The intelligence Corey demonstrated was meant to be attributed to his white environs. Carroll points out that just breaking some ground was important. She implies that after these initial barriers were broken, future series would be free to present more realistic portrayals of the black American experience.[8] As we shall see, most subsequent portrayals of young African-American male intelligence resonate with attributes discernible in Corey Baker. Academic success and a white-identified lifestyle/persona remain strongly linked.

In 1976 the producers of *What's Happening!!*, a series based loosely on the movie *Cooley High* (1975), presented the Thomas family, including the divorced mother Mabel "Mama" Thomas (Mabel King), her son Roger "Raj" Thomas (Ernest Thomas), and her daughter Dee Thomas (Danielle Spencer). From time to time, Mama's ex-husband would appear, reminding the audience that Mrs. Thomas had been married to Raj and Dee's father, and the brother and sister still had some paternal influences in their lives. Overweight and overbearing, Mama Thomas is just the kind of caricatured black matriarch that the producers of *Julia* had endeavored to erase.

With his oversized glasses and introspective ways, Raj is consistently overshadowed by his smart-mouthed little sister and his domineering mother. Raj comes across as a bright, academically oriented young African American. Yet, like his two closest friends—the overweight, jolly Rerun and the shy, slender Dwayne—Raj is a social misfit. His academic acumen ostracizes him from the mainstream. Raj was the first, but certainly not the last, bespectacled, skinny, nerdy adolescent African-American male on television.

The producers of *Julia* and *What's Happening!!* made sure that black single mothers were portrayed as capable of raising schoolsmart black sons. But Corey's intelligence is rooted in his lily-white environment, while Raj's abilities are *in spite of* his urban, black environs. Both characterizations suggest that some aspect of blackness must be sacrificed in order to achieve academic success.

Diminutive Black Darlings—From Arnold to Webster

Both *Diff'rent Strokes* and *Webster* belong to the white parents/black adopted offspring classification. The two highly successful programs have more in common than this basic formula. In both series, the white parents are fairly affluent, successful, and well educated. And in both series the mixed-race adoptions were justified on the grounds that the children's parents had extracted a promise that should they die, the white friends/employers would assume responsibility for the black children. Thus neither *Diff'rent Strokes'* widower Philip Drummond (Conrad Bain) nor *Webster*'s George and Katherine Papadapolis (Alex Karras and Susan Clark) went out looking for African-American children to adopt; rather they inherited graciously the obligations implicit in their promises to their late friends. These are not noble do-gooders, just ordinary, everyday prosperous whites willing to open their homes and hearts to orphaned black males. Last, but certainly not least, both series featured black actors who were particularly fetching and particularly short. And they stayed short. Fans of *Diff'rent Strokes* star Gary Coleman and *Webster*'s Emmanuel Lewis didn't really get to watch their young leading men "grow up" over the life of their respective situation comedies. Due to a serious kidney disorder, Gary Coleman was only slightly taller at the end of the program's final season than he was at the beginning. Similarly, Emmanuel Lewis did not outgrow many clothes during his four-year run as *Webster*.

Inclusion in the Drummond and Papadapolis households came with a handsome benefits package. After crossing these thresholds, the boys were guaranteed access to all of the trappings of upper-middle-class life. Good schools, posh clothes, well-appointed rooms, and excellent health care were all included in the package. The writers took some pains to suggest that the boys were not asked to sacrifice very much in exchange for these benefits. All of the children kept their family names and, after several seasons, Arnold and Willis (the "normal-size" big brother to Arnold) even returned to worship in their mother's church in Harlem.

Everyday situational conflict and likable, albeit marginally eccentric, personalities gathered under one roof, the fuels that propel successful domestic situation comedies, were generated from storylines highlighting the trials and tribulations of the youngsters as they learned how to adapt survival skills honed in other settings to their new environs and the disruptions their presence created in the households. In some episodes these clashes were clearly rooted in the racial and social distance between the boys and their new guardians. In others, the mundane challenges of everyday life were the fodder for the story.

Arnold, Willis, and Webster demonstrate the same kind of ambivalence toward school that is evident in so many of the children featured in situation comedies. When plots take them outside of their designer-decorated bedrooms and into the classroom, conflict must emerge from forces within the academic setting. Consequently, school and the accoutrements of formal education—substitute teachers, science projects, book reports—function as obstacles that the children must tackle. Since a child who does his reports in a timely and diligent manner doesn't lend itself to creating an entertaining half hour, episodes tend to feature good-natured deviousness as the children attempt to invest minimal time and effort in schoolwork while trying to earn the highest grades. Arnold, Willis, and Webster are depicted as fundamentally smart kids easily capable of doing the work assigned to them in school. An early episode of *Diff'rent Strokes* did depict Willis as having some academic problems in his new school. Philip Drummond immediately hires a tutor to help Willis catch up and, in standard situation comedy fashion, the boy's problems are resolved within the allotted half hour of screen time. Drummond (assisted by his series of competent but daffy housekeepers), and George and Katherine Papadapolis are shown as concerned guardians eager to make all the necessary efforts to educate the children who have been entrusted to them. Under their care and with access to their financial resources, these young white-identified black males are shown as fully capable of academic achievement.

Like most people who have pondered the images of African-American youth in popular culture, I have spent a great deal of time wondering why in the world television viewers have so much affection for pint-size, cherubic black males. What purpose is served by centering both of these programs on a particularly short young African American? One answer resides in the essentially copycat nature of network television programming. Media critic Todd Gitlin's extensive interviews with television insiders confirms the truism that a successful television program usually spawns one or more thinly veiled imitations. Given this fact of television life, the placement of *Webster* on the air in 1983 can be explained as a predictable attempt by ABC programmers to duplicate the success of NBC's *Diff'rent Strokes*. According to Gitlin, after three successful seasons of *Diff'rent Strokes* the diminutive Gary Coleman was so valued by his home network that "[his] lawyer got him a guarantee of movies and pilots, then worked out a money deal to swap his commitments to Twentieth Century Fox."[9] When ABC executive Lew Erlich saw another under-size black male child actor, Emmanuel Lewis, in a Burger King commercial, he may well have surmised that young Lewis would prove to be the kind of young, short black goldmine Gary Coleman had proved to be for NBC.[10] But this reasoning does not explain why *Diff'rent Strokes* caught on in the first place and why both series enjoyed such successful prime-time runs.

> Wanted immediately a negro boy. He must be of a deep black complexion, and a lively humane disposition, with good features, and not above 15, nor under 12 years of age.[11]

The juxtaposition of cute black children with conspicuously patrician white benefactors was not invented by the creators of *Diff'rent Strokes*. As this advertisement and others suggest, upper-crust eigh-

teenth-century households once actively sought diminutive black darlings. The desire to strip young black men of the garments they wore
in Africa and dress them in the raiments of the master class was
evident among a select few of the highest classes of European whites.
The standard uniforms of domestic servants were not good enough for
this class of servant. These ebony-faced young men would be dressed
in the very best clothing, matching ensembles with ruffles around the
cuffs, and fashioned from plush fabrics. The presence of such a young
man in a household signaled to all the world the extent of the family's
wealth. During a time when most whites used Africans as New World
tools to increase their fortunes, only the richest of the rich could take
a slave who could fetch high prices for his labor potential, dress him
in velvet and lace finery, then put him to work handling sugar with a
silver service.

     Fine art paintings from this era offer ample evidence of this trend.
Here we see amid scenes of opulent decadence, lace-cuffed, velvet
pantalooned ebony black male bodies and faces. Too old to be children but too young to be men, they inhabit the corners and shadows
of the paintings of Hogarth, Van Dyck, and other artists. The paintings verify the demand implicit in the advertisements—dark skin and
youth were the desired attributes of these servants. Some advertisements sought young females, but males fetched a much higher price.
At the onset of puberty, however, the servants' value diminished. The
more benevolent families would merely relegate the no longer aes-
thetically pleasing servants to the less visible and more arduous
household tasks. The more callous families implemented another
plan. They took these pampered servants, individuals whose most
taxing chore had been filling a sugar bowl, and sold them into New
World slavery where the back-breaking labor of working in cane
fields hastened the deaths of even the strongest field hands.

     What has all this to do with Webster, Arnold, and the other di-
minutive dark darlings of the twentieth century? For starters, it suggests that the juxtaposition of diminutive black males and privileged
white families is not an isolated phenomenon. It is also worth noting
that none of the black actors who commanded such attention in their
youth have been able to make solid acting careers in their
postpubescent years. Just as the aristocracy removed from visibility
its young black boys after they matured into black men, so has the
twentieth-century public shelved formerly popular actors.[12] Two pos-

sible explanations for this persistent fascination with wholesomely cunning boys can be offered. On the one hand, it could be argued that to the whites who embraced this image of black male children being kept by white benefactors, the children functioned somewhere above the realm of pet but below the level of white child. This could certainly be the case with the seventeenth- and eighteenth-century impulse. In some instances during this era, masters and mistresses actually had collars crafted for those servants they wanted to discourage from running away. The collars could be removed by the owners but not by the individuals wearing them. On more than one occasion one of my students has likened this trend to the one in which well-to-do people keep fancy-breed little dogs within close proximity.

Hogarth's paintings remind us that these diminutive dark darlings are not rendered alone either in the seventeenth- and eighteenth-century art works or the twentieth-century television programs. The artists and television producers position the dark boys with white elders. From an aesthetic perspective, it is obvious that these images are rife with oppositions—white is contrasted with black, age and wisdom are contrasted with youth and ignorance, wealth is contrasted with relative poverty. From a structuralist perspective, the appeal of *Diff'rent Strokes* and *Webster* stems from the audience's eternal fascination with polarities.

Neither Willis and Arnold Jackson nor Webster Long are forced to wear jeweled collars. Any unwanted chains tethering them are invisible. The audience is not supposed to seriously challenge the premise that their birth parents had no capable black friends or families to function as godparents to their children. The storylines of both series include episodes in which the boys are seen rejecting the overtures of African-American adults who might exert some custodial claim on them. No doubt these episodes reinforced negative stereotypes about the ability of black families to take care of the members of their own kinship groups.

The black children as "pet" thesis does not adequately speak to the gender issue implicit in this phenomenon. Again, images of blacks in popular culture lend credence to the presence of sexual tension between the races. The image of African-American males sharing the same household with whites is still more of a taboo than the image of black females in such settings. The depiction of cute, prepubescent African-American males juxtaposed with benevolent white adults offers a mild dose of tame titillation. Whites are seen in close proximity to black male youngsters who are just on the verge of catapulting into sexual maturity. Before their voices deepen and their need for jock-straps develops, these young men can be embraced and coddled. Such depictions apparently please and ever-so-mildly excite the eye and the imagination.

Webster and *Diff'rent Strokes* imply that black male youngsters are capable of intellectual achievement. Because the programs are situated in privileged white households and the physical contrasts between the boys and their guardians is so extreme, the message is a conditional one. The audience is led to see the intelligence of these young men as linked to the support and guidance of their benevolent surrogate families, not to any innate capability on the boys' part.

Two Black Parents: From J.J. to Urkel

Education is ostensibly an important theme in those prime-time television programs featuring black adolescents cared for by two-parent black families. However, when we look at the ways African-American television families are constructed, some rather disturbing patterns are evident. In order to see how pernicious these patterns are, we must examine the characteristics assigned to all of the principal family members in a given series.

The first television situation comedy to promote a two-parent family was the now-notorious *Good Times*, a spin-off from Norman Lear's *Maude* (itself a spin-off from *All in the Family*). Set in a Chicago inner-city housing project, the characters include Florida Evans (Esther Rolle) as a tough but tender mother and James Evans (John Amos) as her hard-working husband. Their three children include Thelma (BernNadette Stanis), usually shown as a "good" girl and a fine student. Michael (Ralph Carter) is the younger brother, a very bright boy, fond of spouting quasi-radical sentiments. Early in the series, Michael's efforts to extract the best possible education out of his inner-city school are the subject of episodes in which he faces suspension after pointing out that George Washington owned slaves and one in which he intentionally does poorly on an IQ test in order to protest a fundamental unfairness in the test. For most of its five-year run, the show highlighted the antics of the oldest son, James Junior, aka J.J. (Jimmie Walker). Plots or subplots that acknowledge Michael or Thelma's commitment to education are consistently overshadowed by J.J.'s coonfoolery. Like a classic minstrel dandy, J.J. Evans is depicted with garish clothes, an unswerving commitment to the pleasure principle, and a propensity to misuse the English language. School is little more than a holding cell for J.J., whose only redeeming qualities are his affection for his family and some talent as a painter. Even series creator and producer Norman Lear has acknowledged that "we erred by giving the audience too much of him."[13] Just as the audience has a chance to get involved in matters important to Thelma and Michael, J.J. literally jumps into camera range and utters "Dy-No-Mite," successfully deflecting attention from his siblings and his parents and placing it all on himself.

The next prime-time situation comedy to feature a two-parent African-American family was also a Norman Lear product—*The Jeffersons*, a spin-off of the highly controversial *All in the Family*. Following the economic and social progress of George (Sherman Helmsley), Louise (Isabel Sanford), and Lionel Jefferson as they moved up from their blue-collar Queens home next door to the Bunkers' own 704 Houser Street to a *"de*-luxe apartment in the sky," *The Jeffersons* offers a decidedly different view of black urban life. For the Jeffersons, the struggle to achieve financial security has been won.

During their sojourn as the Bunkers' neighbors, the Jeffersons served as mirrors against which Archie's racism and Edith's benevolence could be reflected. As Archie vociferously described his opinions of African-American inferiority, the Jeffersons stood as exemplars of the ignorance of Archie's views. When Archie claimed that blacks were intrinsically lazy, George's devotion to his dry-cleaning business stood as evidence to the contrary. Archie's insipid generalizations about African-American fertility were disproved by the fact that George and Louise, like he and Edith, had only one child. And George and Louise's son Lionel, the first member of the Jeffersons to be seen in *All in the Family*, was an articulate, hard-working, intelligent young man—the exact opposite of what Archie believed to be the norm for blacks.

Within the context of their own series, the attributes of the Jeffersons, particularly George and Lionel, are modified. As Archie's hard-working, no-nonsense neighbor, George was portrayed as a man who might well possess the business acumen necessary to build a success-ful fleet of dry-cleaning stores. The audience does get to see his biases, but his loyalty to his family and devotion to his business are para-mount. But this side of him is all but absent when he gets his own series. In some episodes his loud, impulsive, foolish behavior is so insipid that the viewer is hard-pressed to imagine he ever possessed the ingenuity and drive necessary to build a successful business.

The move uptown dilutes the intensity of Lionel's drive. Although he is still portrayed as an intelligent young African-American man, he lacks the ambition and determination he possessed on Houser Street. Plots and subplots focus much more on his relationship with his pretty upstairs neighbor than on his studies. Lionel's new love interest is Jenny, the mixed-race daughter of Tom and Helen Willis, the bira-cial couple forced to endure countless barbs from George. In one epi-sode, Lionel seriously considers submitting a term paper George has bought for him, and in another it is Jenny who receives a coveted scholarship to the prestigious Oxford University. Unfortunately, this development suggests that individuals with white ancestry are likely to outperform blacks academically.

Although the Evans of *Good Times* and the Jeffersons ostensibly share little more than ethnicity and urbanity, the composition of both families is much the same. In both series somewhat overweight but attractive matriarchal figures act as human buffers, perpetually pol-ishing and smoothing over the rough edges of their coarser family members. Both families have resident coons in constant need of such grooming. For most of its run, *Good Times'* Florida was compelled to check J.J.'s outrageous behavior and rescue him and the family from his poorly thought out schemes. In *The Jeffersons*, Louise Sanford consistently helps George extract himself from the silly predicaments in which his greed and haste entangle him. The ridiculous behavior of J.J. Evans and George Jefferson steer attention from the more realisti-cally drawn characters. The other family members drift into the background, and the shows keep coming back to the havoc that a resident clown can generate.

With the premiere of *The Cosby Show* on Thursday, Septem-ber 20, 1984, NBC introduced to the American public the most suc-cessful black prime-time two-parent family in television history. We met Cliff (Bill Cosby), Clair (Phylicia Rashad), Denise (Lisa Bonet), Vanessa (Tempestt Bledsoe), Theo (Malcolm-Jamal Warner), and

Rudy Huxtable (Keisha Knight Pulliam), and for the next eight years, the Thursday night "family hour" belonged to NBC. The other networks eventually abandoned any thought of beating Bill Cosby in the ratings race. When enough episodes of the series had been completed to qualify it for syndication, Cosby cut the most financially lucrative deal in television history. Regularly at or near the top of the Nielson ratings, *The Cosby Show* has to be one of the most familiar, popular, and beloved programs ever broadcast.

Eager to prove that a television situation comedy about an African-American family could be popular without relying on the antics of a resident coon, Cosby and the producers demonstrated that a program about a black family could keep the audience laughing *with* rather than *at* the situations in which modern American families find themselves. By contemporary standards, the Cosby family was a large one. With five children, the producers ran a slight risk of reinforcing the stereotype of overly fertile black women, but the obvious fact that the Huxtables could easily handle feeding, clothing, educating, and loving these children diverted attention from any negative aspects of the family's size. Before long, the family expanded beyond the six principals featured in that first program. By the last season the family members consisted of: Cliff Huxtable, a well-to-do obstetrician; his wife, Clair, an equally capable attorney; their eldest daughter, Sondra, a Princeton graduate married to another Princeton alum, Elvin Tibideaux, and their twin children Nelson and Winnie (named after South African freedom fighters Nelson and Winnie Mandela); Denise Huxtable and her husband career navy man Martin Kendall, and Olivia, his daughter from an earlier marriage; Vanessa Huxtable and her fiancée, a university groundskeeper; their only son Theo Huxtable; their youngest daughter Rudy, who had an occasional boyfriend, Kenny; and Clair's niece, Pam Tucker, the streetwise adolescent.

The education of all of Cliff and Clair's children, their significant others, and their grandchildren was a consistent theme throughout the series. Bill Cosby himself earned an Ed.D at the University of Massachusetts–Amherst, and he insisted that scripts for each episode be reviewed by the eminent Harvard psychologist Alvin Poussaint in order to ensure that no insidious negative stereotypes had slipped into the pages. Thanks to their diligence, the program remained free of the caricatures that plagued so many other situation comedies. For eight years *The Cosby Show* remained coon-free, mammy-free, pickaninny-free, buck-free—in short, no stock black character types found their way into the programs.

But Cosby and the show's writers developed traits for the characters of the Cosby kids—traits that could contribute to the perpetuation of negative stereotypes about African-American youth and their academic abilities. Like so many of the successful black students featured on television, the most successful Cosby kids are the most white-identified. The eldest daughter, Sondra, is portrayed as a very bright Princeton student. Although she temporarily abandons her ambition to pursue a career in law in order to open an outdoor goods store with her husband, she is portrayed as one of the family's more solid and reliable members.

Denise, the second oldest daughter, is also very intelligent, but she is definitely drawn as the family's loosest cannon. More so than any of her siblings, Denise is intrigued by African and African-American culture. After being accepted by several fine universities, she ultimately chooses to attend her parents' and grandparents' alma mater, the mythical black college Hillmann. Denise's character "spins off" for a season during which she is largely absent from *The Cosby Show* but very much in evidence on *A Different World.* In order to move her back onto *The Cosby Show*, the writers have her take a leave from Hillmann, and she embarks on a series of escapades that reinforce the by now well-established flightiness of her personality. Soon she wears her hair in a "dredlock" style, and she goes to Africa.

Interested in sports, girls, and prodigious quantities of junk food, Theo, the Huxtable's only son, is ascribed with the characteristics commonly associated with most television teenage males. The first episode featured an enormously funny exchange between Cliff Huxtable and then fourteen-year-old Theo over the subject of the latter's less-than-stellar grades. Trying to convince his father that the Huxtable academic standards were higher than he could ever meet, Theo pleads with his father to love him in spite of his poor academic record. Cliff responds swiftly that Theo's problem is not that he is incapable of better work, but rather that he is refusing to put in the effort necessary to get better grades. For the next several seasons, Theo's struggle with academics resurface from time to time as he and his best friend, Cockroach, chart an uncertain path toward high school graduation. Finally Theo is enrolled in college where he is diagnosed with dyslexia. After this diagnosis, he develops studying strategies that enable him to master his coursework. For the first time Theo can actually enjoy learning. The final episode of the series brings Theo's story full circle as he triumphantly graduates from college. Vanessa and Rudy, the two youngest girls, are portrayed as bright, competent students who seem destined to follow paths similar to Sondra's.

At first glance, the range of scholastic aptitudes exhibited by the Huxtable kids appears thoroughly in keeping with those that might be found in any family of five children. However, by making the one male the learning disabled individual and characterizing the daughter who shows the most interest in black culture as the family misfit, the producers of *The Cosby Show* are perpetuating two common stereotypes. First, "normal" African-American teenage males raised by their own families are rarely allowed to be smart. Seemingly, the kinds of guys who play basketball, wear trendy clothes, and make jumbo hero sandwiches can never be portrayed as individuals fully capable of earning academic honors. Talent on the basketball court is irreconcilable with talent in the classroom. Second, the children who assimilate into the dominant culture most successfully (attend respected white schools, straighten their hair, choose safe careers) are the ones most favorably portrayed. All of the Huxtables pledge allegiance to at least the superficial trappings of black culture. The house is replete with paintings by black artists, and the show has featured some truly fine black music. But some African Americans want to do more than decorate with black culture. Denise's desire to go to Africa is presented as just another of her misguided infatuations. The possibility that a young black woman might choose to spend a year abroad, perhaps attending an African university, is never contemplated as a legitimate or praiseworthy decision.

The Huxtable parents measure their children's success in narrow, conventional fashion. In an episode near the end of the series run that reveals a great deal about the whole family's values, Cliff and Clair respond very negatively to Vanessa's announcement of her engagement to a landscaper she met at college. Cliff can barely endure a meal with the young man who has won his daughter's heart. But his attitude changes completely when he learns that the young man is a homeowner. Within minutes Cliff becomes enamored of the young man, and his earlier objections to the age and class differences that separate his young daughter and her older lover evaporate. His son-in-law-to-be's financial security compensates for any of the flaws Cliff has previously enumerated.

Just as the appearance of *Webster* is most probably connected to the success of *Diff'rent Strokes,* so too is it likely that the several situation comedies featuring black family life in the late 1980s and early 1990s owe their existence to the long reign of *The Cosby Show.* Audiences were particularly enthusiastic about *Family Matters,* an ABC series spun off from *Perfect Strangers* centering on the humorous comings and goings of an extended black family trying to live harmoniously under one roof. The primary family includes a typical television patriarch, a rotund gruff but lovable police officer father, Carl Winslow (Reginald VelJohnson); a quick-witted and loyal mother, Harriette (JoMarie Payton-France); their two just-cute-enough children, Laura (Kellie Shanygne Williams) and Eddie (Darius McCrary); a salty but charming grandmother; Harriette's earthy single-mother sister, Rachel (Telma Hopkins), and her adorable toddler son, Richie. An early episode revolves around the antics of a neighbor boy infatuated with Laura. Intended to appear in only one episode, the character of Steve Urkel (Jaleel White) became a star of the series. Urkel's look and demeanor place him squarely within the domain of classic nerdom. His nerd uniform never varies: oversize tortoiseshell glasses, saddle shoes, high-water (too short) pants held up by suspenders, and white socks. He plays the accordion. Despite her constant protestations, he pursues the lovely Laura with unswerving gusto.

Of the three young people featured on the show, Steve Urkel is far and away the most academically successful. Whereas most families—black or white—would be proud of a son with Steve's academic credentials, the Urkels show little support for their talented son's endeavors. Episode after episode finds Steve seeking the Winslows for the familial support his own family refuses to supply. The Winslows tolerate his constant interruptions and reluctantly incorporate him into their extended family.

Laura Winslow is portrayed as a strong student, but she is not a superstar like her unwanted suitor. Her brother Eddie, a regular-looking African-American teenager usually dressed in the standard jeans and sweatshirts expected of his age group, comes in a distant third in the academic races. Like Theo Huxtable, Eddie Winslow likes sports, parties, and girls. Eddie is not depicted as learning disabled, but rather as a young man inclined to take academic shortcuts. He can do the work when he applies himself, but chasing girls and having a good time with his friends all too often takes precedence over hitting the books. Several episodes have focused on Steve and Laura's attempts to rescue Eddie from academic doom. Popularity and scholastic prowess are once again represented as irreconcilable.

Fresh Prince of Bel Air includes a duo similar to Steve and Eddie. Will Smith, played by a real-life Will Smith, is the street-savvy, hip cousin who comes from a deteriorating neighborhood to live in Bel Air with his prosperous relatives. There he meets his buppie (black upwardly mobile urban professional) cousin, Carlton Banks (Alfonso Ribeiro), whose clothes, while not as hyperbolically nerdy as Urkel's, are still remarkably conservative for a teenager. Argyle socks and vests, blue blazers, and penny loafers are his standard uniform. With his baseball caps and "fresh" short sets (matching baggy T-shirts and knee-length shorts), the streetwise Will is portrayed as a fundamentally bright kid who, like Theo and Eddie, suffers from time management problems. He can always find the time to pursue a pretty neighbor or go to a party, but he often runs out of time to complete his academic obligations. Carlton, always looking ready for an L. L. Bean fashion shoot, takes academic achievement much more seriously. Will is actually credited with possessing more potential than Carlton, although the latter character is seen as the one more willing to apply himself. This fact is revealed in an episode where Will outscores his cousin on a standardized intelligence test. Carlton is disgruntled because he has prepared himself for the test, while Will, without any preparation, earns a higher score.

Carlton's sisters Hilary (Karyn Parsons) and Ashley (Tatyana M. Ali) are the two females on the series. With her shallow personality and narcissistic leanings, Hilary is the consummate black valley girl, a character who could easily be the West Coast cousin to *A Different World*'s Whitley Gilbert (Jasmine Guy), the original African-American self-absorbed clotheshorse. Ashley, the younger sister, is the most academically and personally responsible of the four young people on the show.

227 took its viewers into an apartment building in Washington, D.C., where several series regulars comprised a pseudoextended family. The focal family is the Jenkins family, consisting of Lester (Hal Williams), Mary (Marla Gibbs), and their one daughter Brenda (Regina King). Smart and cute, Brenda is portrayed as a youngster easily able to balance a conventional teen's social life with serious attention to her academic responsibilities. With her pungent wit and killer sidelong glances, an elderly but earthy neighbor Pearl Shay (Helen Martin) serves as a matriarch for the building's residents—a sort of black golden girl. Landlady Rose Lee Holloway (Alaina Reed-Hall) plays a kind of nice aunt to the Jenkins children, while upstairs neighbor Sandra Clark (Jackee) is clearly the naughty aunt. Wearing tight clothes and spewing off innuendoes, Sandra's overt sensuality soon usurped attention from the more mundane goings-on of the rest of the "family."

According to these television programs, most two-parent African-American families produce very popular and bright adolescent girls. Thelma Evans; Sondra, Vanessa, and Rudy Huxtable; Laura Winslow; Ashley Banks; and Brenda Jenkins excelled in school and enjoyed satisfying social lives. The two exceptions are Denise Huxtable, the least white-identified character of the group, who is depicted as ethnoeccentric—misguided and off center. Spoiled Hilary Banks is the other extreme; she is completely enamored of the comforts of the material world and has obviously never let any academic obligations interfere with her shopping.

According to the television moguls who brought us these programs, the young men raised in two-parent African-American households fall into two basic categories—street smart and school smart. Only occasionally do the two converge. Those rare characters who are simultaneously school and street smart include only Lionel Jefferson (more so in his *All in the Family* days than in *The Jeffersons*) and Michael Evans. For the most part, these characters are able to move as easily through their social milieu as they do through the school library. Street-smart young men include J.J. Evans, Theo Huxtable, Eddie Winslow, and Will Smith. Steve Urkel and Carlton Banks are school smart. Both are completely white-identified characters within whom even symbolic ethnicity rarely emerges. Urkel with his nerdy uniform and Carlton with his preppie togs contribute to the notion that black male intelligence must be framed by white values.

From Home to School:
From *Room 222* to IHP

Several television series have been set in academic environs. Familylike relations develop among the cast members and bond the individual classmates to one another. Before long the classmates begin to relate to each other like siblings, and often several academic authority figures assume parental and avuncular roles within the school settings. These programs offer viewers access to the classrooms, cafeterias, and gymnasiums where young people spend the part of the day they don't spend at home watching television. Theoretically, we are seeing behind the gates and the walls into the classrooms.

The familylike relationships that develop between the characters are in contrast with the fact that the core cast members always look very different from each other. In any series with a large cast, the writers must develop distinctive personalities and physical appearances for their main characters within the first couple of episodes. Producers of these programs are eager to give the viewers a conspicuously eclectic cross-cultural mix of students. Height, weight, complexion, hair color, skin color, and wardrobe are combined in order to give each student a distinctive look. The personality traits assigned to the young people are also rarely duplicated on the same show. No series is going to feature two shy kids, two loudmouths, two bullies, two Lolitas, two class clowns; producers are much more likely to present one of each of these rather stock types. In many instances the matching of physical looks with personality traits emerges in a very predictable manner. Overweight kids are funny; smart kids are skinny and wear glasses; flirtatious students have long, straight hair; and students who push school authorities to the edge and test their prowess as teachers tend to be black males.

The first of these students was Jason Allen (Heshimu), the most prominent young black male in the late 1960s–early 1970s series *Room 222.* By contemporary standards, Jason resembles a black choir boy, but during the show's run, his clean, neat, well-pressed dashikis, his carefully groomed Afro, and his somber facial expression spelled black rebel. Of all of the regularly appearing students, Jason is the one who poses the most challenges to the school's administrators. He shoplifts a coat, contemplates dropping out to get married, and is usually just on the edge of some kind of trouble. His academic work is so-so. Thanks to interventions by the authority figures in the series, usually teacher Pete Dixon (Lloyd Haynes), Jason is rescued from his frequent dilemmas. Because of their ability to rescue Jason from his predicaments, the skill and compassion of the adult characters is verified. Mr. Dixon's talent as a teacher, Liz McIntyre's (Denise Nicholas) adroitness as a counselor, Alice Johnson's (Karen Valentine) potential to be a skilled teacher, and Seymour Kaufman's (Michael Constantine) abilities as a principal are all demonstrated through their ability to keep Jason, and by implication other black male students, in school and off the street.

Unlike so many series in television history, *Room 222* does at least contribute some positive images of blackness and intelligence. Both Pete Dixon and Liz McIntyre are portrayed as caring, competent professional African-American educators willing to devote themselves to the well-being of their students. Dixon's looks and demeanor are as extraordinarily mainstream as Jason's were exotic. In Jason, the audience sees a rebellious black youth, always on the edge of trouble. But at least he is ushered out of that trouble by another black male. The series owes much of its popularity to Dixon's nonthreatening but nonetheless principled ethos. Few television series since *Room 222* have granted African-American males even this much autonomy.

Given that all of the students in the class are juvenile delinquents, it may seem unfair to critique *Welcome Back, Kotter*. Because its premise is based on the antics of an academically marginal class, the students who comprise the core clique of this series all share one fundamental characteristic: They are misguided screw-ups. Beyond that common link, they are individualized largely in terms of conspicuous ethnicity. Vinnie Barbarino (John Travolta) is an Italian Catholic, Juan Epstein (Robert Hegyes) identifies himself as a Puerto Rican Jew, and Freddie "Boom Boom" Washington (Lawrence-Hilton Jacobs) is black. Known as the sweathogs, the students are grouped in one class under the tutelage of former-sweathog-gone-straight Gabe Kotter (Gabriel Kaplan). In spite of the fact that the very premise of the series rules out academic excellence, the program is worth mentioning briefly because it reinforces two trends that run through this chapter. First, Washington's identity as a former juvenile delinquent contributes to the negative stereotype of young black males as ill-suited for academic success. And second, the fact that a white teacher manages to help Washington solve so many of his problems feeds the notion that, under the guidance of white benefactors, some black youths will be able to resist real trouble.

It may seem equally inappropriate to consider the critically acclaimed *Fame* within the context of a discussion of intelligence/blackness/youth. This series also established a group of students connected by one particular attribute that governed the kind of educational environment in which they were placed. As students who had passed the highly competitive auditions requisite for New York's prestigious High School for the Performing Arts, these teens are certifiably talented. Their individual distinctiveness stems from their ethnic/regional identity and the artistic endeavors to which they are committed. Bruno Martelli (Lee Curreri) is the Italian songwriter/pianist; Doris Schwartz (Valerie Landsburg) is the Jewish actress/comic; Julie Miller (Lori Singer) is the midwestern cello player; and, representing the underclass, Leroy Johnson (Gene Anthony Ray) is the black inner-city-born dancer. In the tradition of *Room 222*'s Jason Allen, Leroy Johnson is the student most likely to test his teachers' stamina. It takes all of Elizabeth Sherwood's (Carole Mayo Jenkins) considerable talents as an English teacher to move Leroy forward, and he is often at odds with his dance teacher, Lydia Grant (Debbie Allen). Miss Grant succeeds quite well and Leroy emerges as a talent so bright that, after his graduation, the school hires him as an assistant dance instructor. The ultimate message is a mixed one. On the one hand, the audience is permitted to witness the nurturing of a wonderful talent in an African-American male. On the down side, the talent is dance, a talent many believe to be "natural" to African Americans —if a young African-American male is going to be seen succeeding at anything, it will be dance.

Or basketball. In an unprecedented casting decision, the producers of *The White Shadow* assembled an inner-city cluster of students in which the black students outnumbered the nonblack ones. For the first time, race was the common denominator, and television writers confronted the task of individualizing several characters who shared poverty, race, youth, and an affection for basketball. The producers also deserve kudos for using so many African-American cast members in an hour-long dramatic program. At the time of this writing, no comparable attempt to delve into the lives of several young African Americans in any format other than situation comedy has even been attempted. Easygoing Warren Coolidge (Byron Stewart) is distinguished by his height and the implication that he has the best chance of earning a basketball scholarship; good-looking James Haywood (Thomas Carter) is the even-tempered ladies' man; bespectacled Morris Thorpe (Kevin Hooks) is the smart-mouthed know-it-all; and Curtis Jackson (Eric Kilpatrick) is the most troubled of a basically trouble-laden team. Many viewers were offended by the series' raison d'être—the premise that an aging white ex-professional NBA player recruited to take over as the Carver High basketball coach succeeds in simultaneously building a better team and better black men. For the most part, whatever predicament ails a given team member is usually remedied with the assistance of the tough-but-tender coach, Ken Reeves (Ken Howard). The series did allow for some failures. The coach's inability to save all of his students from the very real dangers of inner-city life was illustrated when Curtis Jackson, finally coming into his own, is an innocent victim in a convenience store robbery.

Intelligence is the connection between the members of the accelerated IHP (Individual Honors Program) class at Millard Fillmore High in the series *Head of the Class*. Laid-back teacher Charlie Moore (Howard Hesseman) confronted a class of students who were academic overachievers and, outside their own clique, social underachievers. For the first several seasons only one member of the IHP was black. With her impeccably straightened hair, her cashmere sweaters, and plaid wool skirts, Darlene Merriman (Robin Givens) exudes buppie wealth, poise, and arrogance. Eventually two other African Americans join the class. One was T.J. Jones (Rain Pryor), whose acceptance is provisional. She lacks the demonstrated ability to earn the high grades of the other IHP students, but shows the potential to blossom into a young scholar. Aristotle McKenzie (De Voreaux White), the male, is actually a fairly hip, streetwise character, who wears fashionable clothes and sports a baby-dreds hairstyle. Of course, he has a slight build. According to the creators of television series, smart, young black men are thin. But here the television audience gets a rare chance to see that coolness and smartness can be compatible.

Television series set in schools echo the messages of those set in family households. Once again, young black males are presented as particularly "needy" in terms of the academic world. Jason Allen, "Boom-Boom" Washington, Leroy Johnson, and the entire Carver High basketball team stay in school by the skins of their pearly white teeth. Blessed with caring teachers/mentors who go above and beyond the call of pedagogical duty, the young black male characters on these programs stumble toward graduation.

Dormitory Dilemmas: Eastland to Hillmann

Domestic and academic spheres are wedded in those programs that place young characters in dormitory settings. Writers and producers can develop storylines that play on family conflicts—such as bathroom domination, sloppiness, and the like—or they can speak to academic dilemmas—for example, losing a library book or waiting until the last minute to start a long paper. These kinds of situations emerged in the popular series *The Facts of Life.* Spun off from *Diff'rent Strokes*, the series featured only one continuing African-American character. "Tootie" Ramsey (Kim Fields) is the youngest of a clique of adolescent women who, for nine seasons, remain roommates/suitemates/housemates. As teenagers who have been sent to live at a posh boarding school, the young women grow to depend on each other for family-style loyalty. In spite of their widely divergent backgrounds and the range in their ages, Blair, Jo, Natalie, and "Tootie" develop close ties that see them through their long separations from their parents.

"Tootie," whose parents are lawyers, exhibits no real longing for connections with other African-American young people. From time to time the writers would find an ingenous way of introducing a black male teenager into the sphere so that "Tootie" could have an occasional boyfriend. She is depicted as a good student who, much to the dismay of her professional parents, aspires to be an actress. This series reinforces the notion that when entrusted to a white school and peer group, a young black female will hold her own.

But the producers of *A Different World* moved away from stereotypes in successive seasons. They brought together a group of students, attending a fictional traditional black college. Originally designed as a spin-off vehicle for *The Cosby Show*'s Denise Huxtable, the series' cast has always included more female students than male. Like so many situation comedies, the series was visibly altered within the first few seasons on the air; characters who reigned supreme in the first season were modified and sometimes removed. Other characters joined the remaining cast members and the overall feel of the series became quite different. However, the producers of *A Different World* broke new ground after the first season by stripping conventional black stereotypes from several of their characters and endowing them with more fully rounded personas.

In many of the series featuring black life, the shows increased their dependency upon negative stereotypes. For example, when *Good Times* first aired in 1974, the Evans household included two parents. By 1976 the father was written out of the series when John Amos resigned and the Evans household became a single-parent one headed by Florida Evans (Esther Rolle). In the following season, Esther Rolle resigned, and rather than cast another actress as Florida, the producers made the Evans offspring, by now young adults, responsible for themselves. *Good Times* went from chronicling the challenges of a family as it endeavored to maintain its integrity within the confines of an inner-city housing project to highlighting the buffoonish antics of the family's most outrageous member. By the same token, *The Jeffersons* focused increasingly on George's unmitigated arrogance and obnoxiousness. *227* shifted attention from Mary Jenkins and her immediate family and placed it on the flirtatious adventures of the tight-skirted, pouty-lipped Sandra Clark.

The modifications made to Dwayne Wayne (Kadeem Hardison) became the most significant character change in the transformation of *A Different World*. In the first season, Dwayne is a tall, pencil-thin, bookwormish math wiz who is hopelessly infatuated with Denise Huxtable. His unsuccessful attempts to be cool and his attempts to win her affection function as the butt of the jokes of her dormitory mates. Try as he might, Dwayne Wayne can never get himself taken seriously by his peers. He is, however, taken seriously in the classroom, where his intelligence and, in particular his mathematics prowess keep him at the top of the class. Once again the message is imparted that those black men in black environments who possess academic know-how lack the social skills of their peers. To their credit, the producers of *A Different World* reshaped Dwayne. In the second season he was reinvented as a tall, pencil-thin, bookwormish math wiz who is able to move as comfortably outside of the classroom as he does within it. He was given more stylish clothes and glasses and changed from being a character intended for ridicule to one deserving of respect.

From *Amos 'n' Andy*'s Arbadella to *Fresh Prince of Bel Air*'s Will, young black characters have been confined to a rigid, uncomfortably finite range of attributes. Tally up the characters from the 1950s to the early 1990s and the same sets of qualities stand out. It is almost as if a rule book of African-American dos and don'ts circulates among television show producers. The rules go like this. Black females are more apt to be smart than black males, unless, of course, the males are placed in the household of white surrogate parents. The more assimilated or white-identified the character, the more likely she or he is to be intelligent. School smarts separates black young people from their peers. Smart black males are very skinny and wear unique eyeglasses (Raj—*What's Happening!!*; Dwayne Wayne—*A Different World*; Steve Urkel—*Family Matters*). "Cool" middle- to upper-middle-class black males get into academic trouble (Theo—*The Cosby Show*; Will—*Fresh Prince of Bel Air*; Eddie—*Family Matters*). Dark-skinned black youths from underclass environments are often on the edge of real trouble (whole team—*The White Shadow*; Jason—*Room 222*; "Boom-Boom"—*Welcome Back, Kotter*; Leroy—*Fame*). Rarely are young African-American males depicted as possessing both street smarts and school smarts.

I am perfectly willing to concede that television producers have been less than flattering in their representations of whites, youth, and intelligence. The anti-intellectual thrust of American culture is all too obvious on network television. The teen years, according to television, are intended for sleepovers, learner's permits, dating dilemmas, surfing, sneaking out, malt shops, and young people who take their studying seriously while maintaining popularity and a regular social life are outnumbered by those who don't. Black nerds are, after all, modeled on white nerds—quirky adolescents whose fondness for knowledge stigmatizes them and ostracizes them from the mainstream of their peer groups.

The implications of portraying young people as cavalier about their studies has, I think, more negative consequences for social attitudes about blacks than about whites. Because white young people

are featured so much more often on television (and in other mainstream popular culture outlets), there are ultimately more positive
portrayals of smart young white people than black. A number of
simultaneously popular and smart white teenagers have crept onto
the screen over the years. *Leave It to Beaver*'s Wally Cleaver, *The
Waltons*' John Boy, and *Life Goes On*'s "Becca"—even *Doogie How-
ser, M.D.*'s Doogie manage to enjoy the societal rewards of adolescence while recognizing the importance of applying themselves to
their studies.

Situation comedies have dominated this discussion, largely because these are the only series in which black families are presented
within a continuous format. But young blacks do appear in other
programs. In dramatic shows that highlight some aspect of the law
enforcement community, young blacks play very significant roles—as
suspects, prisoners, and victims. News programming also emphasizes
blacks who have gotten into trouble with the law much more than
blacks who have gotten into law school.

It is very likely that the limitations of these images have a delete-
rious impact on black youngsters. If whites aren't seeing high-achiev-
ing blacks on television, then neither are blacks. Academic achievement seems to be reserved for skinny, bespectacled nerds, not guys
who like to play basketball.

Social scientists and public policymakers perpetually debate the
"plight of African-American youth." While enumerating the plethora
of economic and social reasons for black underachievement, they
should seriously consider the role television has played in shaping
black and white consciousness about the profile of those blacks who
can excel in academic environments and those who cannot.

8

Ethnic Aliens

In the mid-1960s folklorists Alan Dundes and Roger D. Abrahams noted a marked increase in the circulation of elephant jokes.[1] They surveyed a few dozen assorted texts in order to see if any patterns emerged. Several aspects of the joke cycle became apparent. Many of the jokes portrayed the elephant as sexually aggressive.

Q: Why do elephants climb trees?
A: To rape squirrels.

Q: Why do elephants wear springs on their feet?
A: So they can rape flying monkeys.

Others focused on the elephant's frustration with fitting into a natural environment:

Q: Why do elephants wear green tennis shoes?
A: To hide in the tall grass.

The question-and-answer format in which so many of the elephant jokes were delivered was reminiscent of the style in which many antiblack jokes are structured.

Q: What's dangerous, lives in a tree, and is black?
A: A crow with a machine gun.

To Dundes and Abrahams, the timing of these joke cycles was the key to understanding the circulation of these texts. In the 1960s, sharing patently racist jokes and slurs had fallen into disfavor in most polite circles. But the negative stereotypes associated with blacks were still very much alive, and indeed intensified, as African Americans became increasingly assertive in their demands for equal treatment. In elephant jokes, the tellers were able to articulate their antiblack prejudices and fears in a socially acceptable fashion. The folklorists hypothesize, "The two disparate cultural phenomena [elephant jokes and the civil rights movement] appear to be intimately related, and, in fact, one might say that the elephant is a reflection of the American Negro as the white sees him and that the political and social assertion by the Negro has caused primal fears to be reactivated."[2]

In teaching this hypothesis, I have encountered many students who find it untenable. They fail to understand how the collective unconscious could have substituted elephants for blacks in the manner just described. Yet other examples of antiblack characteristics being attributed to animals or nonhuman creatures can be used to reinforce the validity of Dundes and Abrahams's perspective.

Potent Plots

Filmmakers have constructed "elephants" of their own. Without realizing it, they have brought to the screen stories in which an antiblack message is implicitly conveyed through situations and characters in which race is not an apparent issue. *Gremlins* (1984) and *The Little Shop of Horrors* (1986) exemplify this phenomenon.

In *Gremlins*, a charmingly inept, middle-class white father, Rand Peltzer (Hoyt Axton) purchases a furry little "Mogwi" to give to his teenage son. The mysterious Chinese vendor who reluctantly parts with the Mogwi gives the father very specific instructions on how to take care of the creature. The father then passes these prohibitions along to his son: (1) Don't expose the Mogwi to light, (2) don't get the Mogwi wet, and (3) don't feed the Mogwi after dark.

Inadvertently, Billy Peltzer (Zach Galligan), the befuddled teenager, preoccupied with thoughts of his job, his dog, and his pretty
coworker, violates all three of the interdictions. As a result of Billy's
carelessness, the Mogwi, named Gizmo, initiates asexual reproduction. Gizmo's offspring bear little resemblance to their benevolent
parent. They gleefully begin to destroy the Peltzer home. After attack-
ing Billy's mother, they set about trashing the idyllic community of
Kingston Falls and terrorize many of its residents. Together with his
girlfriend, Kate (Phoebe Cates), and Gizmo, Billy manages to rescue
the town from the clutches of the evil gremlins. The film concludes
when the mysterious Chinese gentleman reclaims the original Mogwi
and removes him from the household.

The basic plot of the musical *Little Shop of Horrors* is more difficult to summarize. The time is the early 1960s, the setting is Skid
Row, and the primary characters are a young pair of poor, white,
well-meaning employees of an unsuccessful Jewish flower store owner.
Unnoticed by any of these characters, a trio of talented black singers
(Krystal, Chiffon, and Ronette) serenade the audience with terse observations on the action throughout the film. Seymour Krelborn (Rick
Moranis), the male hero, is eager to help his employer and unofficial
adoptive father, Mr. Mushnik, save his unpopular shop. Why
Mushnik ever thought the impoverished, blighted Skid Row community would support a flower shop is a question left unanswered.
Mushnik's other employee is the voluptuous blond Audrey whose misguided affections are directed toward a mean-spirited dentist rather
than the bespectacled Seymour who worships her from his secluded
cubbyhole in the dilapidated florist shop.

One day Seymour is plant shopping in the general vicinity of an
old Chinese wholesale flower vendor. Unexpectedly, a total eclipse of
the sun occurs. Following the eclipse, Seymour discovers a new be-
nign-looking potted plant in front of the vendor's storefront. After
paying the merchant $1.95, Seymour cheerfully takes the flytrap like
plant back to Mushnik's. This incident sets off a chain of events that
changes the lives of all of the characters.

The plant, named Audrey II, of course, is more than just a little
"strange and interesting." At first, none of Seymour's horticultural
skills stimulate the plant. One day he accidentally drips blood on it
and discovers that if fed with human blood, or better yet, human
parts, it thrives and attracts multitudes of customers. In order to

satisfy Audrey II's unorthodox appetite, Seymour is forced to the brink of personal anemia as well as to body-snatching and finally homicide. The film climaxes as Seymour rescues Audrey I from the protruding lips of Audrey II and succeeds in blowing up the now-humongous plant. In the closing scene, the camera follows Seymour and Audrey I as they walk into the yard of a model suburban home and then pans from their happy faces to the garden where the audience can see a seemingly nondescript little Audrey II nestled in among the blooming flowers.

Aliens Afoot

At first glance, the plots of these movies seem to lack any references to white attitudes about minority groups. However, the seemingly innocuous stories of both *Gremlins* and *Little Shop* reinforce controversial, negative ethnic stereotypes. Let's start with the exotic elderly Chinese men who are the sources of the plant in *Little Shop* and the equally malicious Mogwi in *Gremlins*. The well-meaning whites have laudable motives for doing business with the Chinese gentlemen. In *Gremlins* an eager-to-please father is merely looking for a special Christmas gift for his teenage son. In *Little Shop* Seymour seeks plants that will attract customers to his surrogate father's struggling florist shop. In both films the Chinese gentlemen seem reluctant to part with their otherworldly commodities, but allow their greed for the white man's hard-earned money to sway them. In both films an exotic, nonwhite man serves as the original source of the marauding creatures. Hence, no one in the dominant culture is to blame for the havoc wrecked by the unruly aliens.

Kingston Falls, the setting of *Gremlins*, is just the kind of pristine, upper-middle-class suburban community that *Little Shop*'s Audrey I daydreams about while reading *Better Homes and Gardens* in her dingy Skid Row apartment. Audrey and Seymour long to escape the turgid atmosphere of Skid Row. When Audrey dreams of her idealized Tupperware party, her guests are all white women; Krystal, Ronette, and Chiffon, the black trio who have tried to encourage her to part from her abusive boyfriend, have no place in her ideal future. The racial and ethnic mix of Skid Row is completely missing from the future of her fantasies.

The first human victim of the man-eating Audrey II is the previously benevolent Mr. Mushnik. Content to carry Audrey and Seymour
on the payroll when his business was dying, the merchant becomes
unexpectedly greedy when he realizes how much money can be made
from Audrey II. While trying to run Seymour out of Skid Row, the
florist unwittingly becomes plant food for the now-mammoth Audrey
II. In *Gremlins* the first victim of Gizmo's malicious offspring is also
an ethnic minority, the only one prominent in the entire movie. Determined to learn all he can about the mysterious gremlins, Billy's African-American high school science teacher prods and pokes until the
gremlin in his laboratory destroys him. On the surface level, the
teacher is being punished for investigating matters he had no business
pursuing. On a deeper level, the punishment may be for pursuing a
place in a predominantly white society.

Nowhere are the negative ethnic messages clearer than in the actual depiction of the unearthly beings in the two films. Audrey II and
Gizmo's offspring embody the full range of negative stereotypes associated with blacks. Audrey II is supposed to resemble a flytrap-styled
plant. Another way of describing the plant would be to say that it
resembles a watermelon with thick, oversized lips. As its need for
human blood is met, its lips become larger and more exaggerated. In
inflection, tonal quality, and vocabulary, Audrey II's voice is conspicuously black. Her words are spoken and sung by Levi Stubbs, a member of Motown's popular Four Tops singing group. Audrey II tries to
placate Seymour with promises of a "Cadillac car." Her grammar is
typified by comments such as "Don't do me no favors" and "You sho'
do drive a hard bargain." Audrey II's songs include such lines as
"Feed me, Seymour, Feed me all night long, / cause if you feed me
Seymour, I'll grow up big and strong." Or, from a tune nominated for
an Academy Award, "I'm a mean, green mother from outer space and
I'm bad." Audrey II also yearns for white women, as can be seen in an
early scene where a still-small plant pursues the well-rounded derri-
ere of a radio station secretary or the climactic scene where it lures the
blond Audrey dressed in a white wedding gown into the booby-
trapped florist shop.

Both Audrey II and the gremlins "punish" their victims by
procreating in abundance. Miniature Audrey IIs burst out from every
corner of the enormous plant. When Gizmo is mistreated, he also
generates countless offspring. These malevolent miniature Mogwi are

the most destructive and reflect negative African-American stereotypes. Soon after their unexpected birth, the pesky gremlins are de-
vouring fried chicken with their hands. Their first target is Billy's
kind, overburdened mother, and they are soon pursuing the hero's
girlfriend at Dorry's Tavern. In some unexplained way, several of
them have managed to acquire shades and caps that cover their eyes.
Cigarettes droop from the corners of their mouths. They make haste
to a tavern where they cannot get enough to drink. Here we see their
love of music and their ability to break-dance.

Black Dragons

Narratives in which an unassuming male protagonist must "slay a
dragon" in order to win the pretty girl and save his village are as old
as taxes. What is interesting about the 1980s releases is that the
"dragon" is a thinly disguised black male. In both films, the climax
pits marginally pubescent white males against soulfully destructive
creatures. Before they can consummate their relationships with their
respective love interests, Seymour and Billy must subdue the foreign
creatures. Saving their women and their communities from the threat
posed by Audrey II and the gremlins becomes a rite of passage for the
white heroes. Before they reach genuine maturity they must prove
their mettle by destroying the "dark" forces that threaten their place
in the world.

While this analysis may explain *what* is happening in these two
films, it does not tell us *why* the intruders are blacks in disguise. The
notoriously antiblack film *Birth of a Nation* had been produced in
1915. In those days the white moviemaking community and its audiences could easily rationalize and applaud a film in which white heroes aggressively pursue a supposedly undeserving but doggedly
usurping black population. In the 1980s, however—when *Gremlins*
and *Little Shop* were produced—the white filmmaking community
and its audiences ostensibly accept the African American's right to
share in America's wealth. Perhaps the impulse to assign black characteristics to otherworldly creatures reflects a subconscious belief that
blacks are still intruders whose demands for equality have escalated
into a desire for dominance. Seymour and Billy start out trying to

treat Audrey II and the gremlins fairly, but the ungrateful creatures don't want to stay in their place—they want control over their former masters and their women. They want to take over any available turf. When they get a root or a foot in a white environment, they start randomly destroying it.

Of Elephants, Gremlins, and Mogwi

Just as the elephant jokes coincided with the emerging black power movement, these films were produced during an era in which the advisability of integration was being challenged. Many white Americans were still reluctant to embrace blacks in their neighborhoods. The battles waged by Seymour and Billy allow the audience to cheer for white underdogs as they square off against the loathsome intruders. Until they have rid their worlds of these menaces, the white heroes cannot truly be men.

Gremlins and *Little Shop of Horrors* are very likable films. The former is a rather charming love story, and the latter is one of the most originally rendered musicals ever produced. Indeed, it is the entertaining veneer of the films that makes their underlying message so insidious. Fortunately, the final twist common to both films can give solace to the viewer who would like to see the disguised blacks triumph. At the end of *Gremlins*, the original Mogwi is still alive, albeit back in the capable hands of the mysterious Chinese gentleman. In *Little Shop*, the audience sees a baby Audrey II hiding in Seymour and Audrey's garden. Temporarily subdued by the white heroes, the blacks in disguise might triumph in the future.

9

Distorted Soundtracks

Like most of my colleagues engaged in film studies rather than moviemaking, I occasionally allow myself to fantasize about making my
own films. At least two of the films I envision would rely very heavily
on music. *White* music. I envision one of these films being set in the
recent past, say the last thirty or so years. The second would focus on
the more distant past, that is to say, within the first couple of decades
of the twentieth century. Several commercial films popular in the past
few decades have inspired in me a bare-bones scenario for the former
film. This one would have an all-black "ensemble" cast. The plot
would be glued by flashbacks tracing the events in the characters'
adolescence that solidified their friendship. These flashbacks would
be punctuated by rhythmless music performed by well-known white
artists. Although no hint of "soul" would be tolerated on my movie's
soundtrack, my African-American characters would enthusiastically
embrace the music as if it were their own. Their recollections of their
rites of passage would be interspersed with innocuous, inane music.
As to the one set in the early twentieth century, its very title would
evoke some subgenre of European music or a linked landmark. I
might try to call it something like *The Birth of Country and Western*
or *The Grand Old Opry*. Its cast would be almost entirely black. I
would feature a couple of talented white performers singing a few

well-placed songs, but for the most part, this film would focus on the pains and pleasures experienced by black Americans in conjunction with the rise of country and western music. I suppose if I went with the title *The Grand Old Opry*, my plot would center on the trials and tribulations of the African-American men and women who built the structure or those who have spent their lives cleaning it.

No Soul

I doubt that either of my films would earn any real commercial success or critical accolades, in spite of the fact that so many recent movies have portrayed the reverse situations. Ever since George Lucas's classic *American Graffiti* broke box office records in 1973, white filmmakers have endeavored to find innovative ways of turning nostalgia for the late 1950s and 1960s into moviemaking success in the 1970s, 1980s, and 1990s. The more notable efforts have included John Landis's raucous view of early 1960s fraternity shenanigans in *National Lampoon's Animal House* (1978), Barry Levinson's *Diner* (1982), Lawrence Kasdan's depiction of a yuppie reunion weekend in *The Big Chill* (1983), Steven Spielberg and Robert Zemeckis's time-travel adventure in *Back to the Future* (1985), Francis Ford Coppola's foray into middle-class fantasy in *Peggy Sue Got Married* (1986), and Rob Reiner's glimpse of male coming of age in *Stand by Me* (1986).

With vintage costumes, period automobiles, and authentic sets, the white writers and producers meticulously re-create the environments of their youth or idealized projections of one. Period music becomes an essential component. Each of these movies boasts a soundtrack true to the era it reflects. Most of the musical selections are, in fact, classic rhythm and blues or early rock and roll. The fraternity brothers and their sorority counterparts in *Animal House* dance to Otis Day and the Nights' rendition of "Shout." The white hero in *Back to the Future* inadvertently "inspires" an unknown Chuck Berry to develop a new sound. The married couple in *Diner* fight over the order of rhythm and blues albums in a record cabinet. Peggy Sue is shocked to discover that her musician husband played with an R and B group in the 1960s. The opening credits in *The Big*

Chill are set against Marvin Gaye's rendition of "I Heard It Through the Grapevine," and *Stand by Me* takes its name from Ben E. King's 1957 hit record.

Although the characters in these films identify black music as a significant reminder of their coming of age, their social groups don't reflect any impulses to integrate. Neither of the competing fraternities in *Animal House* includes any black members. Nonetheless, the members assume that they will be welcome in the all-black jook joint they invade during one of their raucous road trips. While the *Back to the Future* hero momentarily pauses to assure a black floor sweeper and his boss that the post-1950s era will bring about political opportunities for blacks, his own life in the 1980s doesn't reflect any interracial friendships. The cliques that unite the characters in *Diner*, *Peggy Sue Got Married*, *The Big Chill*, and *Stand by Me* are all white.

I strongly suspect that the talented filmmakers who produced these films would protest any accusations of racism. After all, if their young lives were influenced by black music but not by black people, then they are correct to portray that phenomenon in their films. However, the filmmakers may not be aware that their films can be used to study much more than adolescent rites of passage. Whether they realize it or not, their films have little applicability to the black experience. Although many blacks wish that civil rights issues could be as popular with 1990s whites as they were with some 1960s whites, most blacks don't share in any of this reverence for the past. Black coming of age was rarely as idyllic as white. References to hypocrisy and broken promises are likely to emerge in present-day black discussions about the 1960s and 1970s. By focusing on the good old days when blacks could be relied upon to supply good dance music without intruding into the social milieu, the filmmakers are inadvertently chronicling a very fundamental difference in black and white perceptions of the past and the myth of integration.

Kasdan's 1983 hit *The Big Chill* blatantly exemplifies this pattern. Set in a rambling vacation home following the suicide of a 1960s radical, the movie focuses on the group of old college friends who gather for the funeral and end up spending the weekend together. Reminiscing about the 1960s social crises that originally brought them together, the friends recall protesting the war in Vietnam and working for the civil rights movement during their student days at the

University of Michigan at Ann Arbor. One long-defunct couple remembers making love on the night before the March on Washington. Sipping white wine and smoking pot on overstuffed couches, they fondly recall the days when Huey and Bobby (referring to black activists Huey Newton and Bobby Seales) were their heroes. Their recollections are often triggered by a never-ending supply of oldies their host puts on the turntable. The film did trigger renewed interest in Motown music. A subtle tension emerges as this all-white assemblage listens and dances to lively black music while bringing each other up to date on the paths they have taken from their college years to the present.

At least two of the characters had intended to work for social change following graduation. Michael (Jeff Goldblum), now a writer for *People* magazine, began his career by teaching in Harlem. Meg (Mary Kay Place), now a real estate lawyer in Atlanta, began her law career as public advocate in Philadelphia. She categorizes her former clients as "scum," while he reduces his students to "those kids in Harlem." They acknowledge that they had been ill-equipped to cope with the demands of their original, more idealistic vocations. With a moderate amount of guilt, they review their decisions to pursue more lucrative ventures. In the end, the justifications for career choices that limit their contact with nonwhites prevail. Their postgraduation ventures into public service work emerge as trials by fire they survived prior to finding their true, conveniently capitalistic callings.

Meg and Michael agree that their original motivation for altruistic efforts was inspired by the self-sacrificing spirit of the college group of friends currently reassembled. The casting of this group is particularly intriguing. In spite of their alleged concern with the civil rights movement and social change, this all-white clique never seems to have incorporated any black friends into their inner circle. Given this casting, the audience can only assume that their college days' contact with African Americans was completely superficial. These white characters danced to the beat of Temptations' hits, made love to Aretha Franklin ballads, and stylishly affiliated themselves with all of the right causes, but they limited their contact with black people. It is no wonder that Meg and Michael were so nonplussed by the communities they tried to serve; apparently their previous relationships were limited to individuals like themselves.

Like the other nostalgia films, *The Big Chill* enjoins the audience to share in a celebration of the "good old days." But what exactly made these times so special? Most of these films foreground the tenacity of interpersonal relationships. The implied complexity of contemporary life is contrasted to the simplicity of the earlier times. Race relations were less perplexing in those times. Blacks had been encouraged to cross over in the music world, but other white environments were still restricted. The proliferation and popularity of these nostalgia films suggest that they offer a genuine view of contemporary white attitudes toward the present and the past. If this is the case, then it seems reasonable to assume that whites are voicing a preference for an era in which they could guiltlessly exclude blacks from their social and occupational circles while enjoying the music made by black artists.

The Birth of Country and Western

Another group of filmmakers has invoked the classifications of African-American music or landmarks associated with it. In African-American cultural history, the term crossroads has a very specific meaning. It refers to a junction of two roads in the Mississippi Delta. As restless African-American men abandoned agricultural occupations and took to the road to make their music their livelihood, they invariably traversed the crossroads where Highways 49 and 61 intersect. According to several legends, the crossroads was where a man could swap his soul for musical endowments. The infamous Cotton Club, a preeminent Harlem nightspot, is an African-American urban equivalent to the crossroads. The Cotton Club was a significant stopping point for many African-American musicians eager to increase their visibility. "Ragtime" refers to a style of African-American music that began to cross over into mainstream American musical traditions at the end of the nineteenth and beginning of the twentieth century. Either one of these terms could be used as a foundation for a fine film about African-American culture. But the movies that have been produced with these titles minimize and trivialize the black experience.

No Ragtime in Ragtime

While teaching a class in African-American vernacular music, I found it difficult to explain and define ragtime music. I decided that I would rent the film *Ragtime*, which I had seen shortly after its release in 1981. My goal was to find one sequence in which the camera rests on the hands of the black piano player, Coalhouse Walker (Howard E. Rollins, Jr.) long enough for me to show the class that a ragtime piano player's left hand establishes a beat while his right moves in at a different pace. Much to my dismay, in the entire 155-minute film there are few sequences in which the camera shows the piano player's hands on the piano, and these never occur in an example that illustrates the manual dexterity demanded by ragtime music. White composer Randy Newman was charged with scoring the film. In the film, the scenes with Walker playing piano are outnumbered by scenes with his hands on weapons. Since my students have seen more than enough screen images of black men holding guns, I opted not to show them the movie.

Based on E. L. Doctorow's best-selling novel of the same name, *Ragtime* contains several subplots chronicling the fortunes and misfortunes of a seemingly unrelated group of people whose lives intersect during the turbulent first decade of the twentieth century. Much of the film foregrounds the misguided and ill-fated romances pursued by the white characters. Aside from a compelling cameo by Booker T. Washington (Moses Gunn), only two of the principal characters are black. They are Sarah (Debbie Allen), a new mother taken in by a well-heeled suburban family, and her lover, the father of her young child, an aspiring piano player, Coalhouse Walker. As Walker becomes increasingly successful, he makes arrangements for them to marry. His plans go awry one afternoon when he encounters a cadre of bored, racist volunteer firemen who deface his spanking new automobile. Sarah is killed when she tries to present his case to President Theodore Roosevelt. An infuriated Walker gives up on bringing the men to justice through regular channels and takes the law into his own hands, by orchestrating a takeover of the J. Pierpont Morgan Library.

Rollins delivers a first-rate performance. Even during violent confrontations, Rollins infuses his character with integrity and intelligence. It is because of Rollins's stellar performance as well as those of

Moses Gunn and Debbie Allen that I'm ultimately disappointed by *Ragtime*. It teases the audience by giving fascinating snippets of information about black/white relations in the first decade of this century. Since black life is so rarely documented on screen, I would have liked to have seen much more character development. Except when she goes to plead Walker's case to Roosevelt, we never see Sarah outside of the white family's home. No members of her family or Walker's come forward after her funeral to care for her young son. If I knew that some other film might take up the complexities of early twentieth-century urban black life hinted at by *Ragtime*, I might not hold it to such a standard. At the time of this writing, however, the film is ten years old and no other such film has been released.

No Blues in Crossroads

The hard-living Delta bluesmen whose raw lyrics and assaultive guitar playing anticipated the birth of rock and roll serve as offbeat background for *Crossroads* (1986), essentially a standard buddy/coming-of-age film. The buddies are Eugene Martone (Ralph Macchio), a white, Long Island–born, seventeen-year-old Julliard student, and Willie Brown, aka Blind Dog Fulton (Joe Seneca), a Delta-born, harmonica-playing senior citizen. Eugene's Julliard studies are devoted to classical guitar, but his passion is to play blues guitar in the style of Robert Johnson or Charley Patton. His room is a makeshift blues archive crammed with sheet music, cassettes, posters, and books on the Delta blues. He seeks Willie out because he believes the still-sharp senior citizen might recall a song Johnson wrote but never recorded. His reverence is tempered with stark ambition. He dreams about recording the lost song and establishing himself as a rock guitarist in the same vein as Eric Clapton, the rock-and-roller who covered Johnson's "Crossroads Blues."

Willie recognizes Eugene as "just one more white boy ripping off our music." Anxious to return to the Delta, Willie promises to share the song if Eugene will help him get back to Mississippi. Just as the teams who comprise most pairs in buddy films begin with acrimonious relationships, Eugene and Willie (or Lightning and Blind Dog in their stage incarnations) get off to a bumpy start. In the vein of all good-buddy pictures, assorted obstacles keep emerging to prevent the pair from reaching their destination. Lack of traveling money is the ostensible reason they are forced to hitch and steal a car during their trek. Yet the plot signals Willie's subtly growing affection for Eugene by showing the two of them pawning the latter's $1,100 watch to buy Eugene a $400 electric guitar and portable amplifier. Given Willie's purported eagerness to return to the Delta, it seems farfetched that they would spend that sum on musical instruments rather than bus tickets. Of course, a bus ride would not provide the same kind of provocative obstacles they encounter as they "hobo it." Such obstacles compel the buddies to rely on each other, therefore ensuring that they will bond.

Crossroads also contains an essential ingredient in any male coming-of-age film. Early in their travels, Eugene and Willie stumble upon the obligatory tough-but-tender, beautiful, worldly teenage girl, Frances (Jami Gertz), who is eager to escape a lecherous stepfather. After joining Eugene and Willie for a few adventures, she slips away. Pining after her, Eugene's blues-playing skills intensify. Although Willie boasts about his past status as a ladies' man, he has no liaisons during the film. This is typical of white/black buddy films. Such films generally spend more time on the white buddy's romantic adventures.

The filmmakers sprinkle authentic tidbits about blues history throughout the film. *Crossroads* correctly identifies Legba as the trickster figure who purportedly makes deals with musicians for their souls. The names of all the right Delta bluesmen are dropped throughout the movie; Eugene and Willie banter about Robert Johnson, Charley Patton, Son House, and Muddy Waters. They also wear the right dark suits, and when they buy Eugene his electric guitar and amp, they get him the right hat. Willie shares his Mojo hand—the preferred good-luck charm of all leading bluesmen—with Willie prior to his climactic performance.

As is often the case with black/white buddy films, the white buddy is called upon to save the black one. Although Willie helps Eugene out of a few scrapes along the way, the climax comes in a surreal scene where Willie asks Legba to release him from the Faustian deal that they had made at the crossroads fifty years earlier. Initially Legba refuses. But Eugene offers himself (his soul, presumably) instead. Legba says he will release Willie if Eugene can outplay another white guitarist to the satisfaction of an audience. If Willie doesn't win, Legba can keep Willie's soul and add Eugene's to his roster. Of course, Willie wins—he plays Mozart on an electric guitar in a fashion that mesmerizes his audience and that his hard-rocking

opponent can't match. Thus a film titled *Crossroads* tells the story of
how a selfish white Julliard student uses Mozart to save an elderly
black bluesman from the devil.

No Jazz in the Cotton Club

In *Ragtime* one of the main characters, a black man, is a professional musician. Yet the audience rarely sees his hands play his piano
—he certainly never plays one entire song from start to finish. In
Crossroads two of the principal characters are musicians. The audience does get to see Willie, the black character, play his harp. Yet
more screen time is devoted to Eugene, the aspiring white guitarist.
Given its very name, *The Cotton Club* should exalt black music. True,
several scenes are devoted to Sandman's dancing and Lila's singing,
but significant attention is placed on the solo played by the white
lead, Dixie Dwyer (Richard Gere), backed by the Cotton Club orches-
tra.

To tell the story of the Cotton Club, the film's producers opted to
move back and forth between stories about the nightspot's white patrons and black performers. The patrons' stories dominate the film.
Their love triangles and turf wars are foregrounded. After innocently
saving the life of a mob boss, cornet player Dixie Dwyer and his
brother become tied to organized crime. Dixie falls in love with a
mobster's teenage girlfriend, Vera Cicero (Diane Lane), and his
brother's involvement in the gang war threatens their whole family's
well-being. The film boasts several scenes in which the mobsters
strategize over the politicians they can control, kidnap each other,
and assault one another. Talented white actors, including Fred
Gwynne, Bob Hoskins, and Nicholas Cage, ensure that the audience
will be able to distinguish the individuality of each mobster.

The story of the Cotton Club's performers starts in a similar fashion. The audience quickly realizes that two talented brothers will be
the focal point of the black story as well. A warm scene even takes
place in their home. Sandman Williams (Gregory Hines), Dixie's
black counterpart, also falls for a woman with divided loyalties. His
affections are stirred by Lila (Lonette McKee), and their romance is
thwarted by her ambitions. A beautiful light-skinned woman (a concrete job requirement for several years at the Cotton Club), she is
willing to leave everything behind for a singing career. She passes for

white and gets a singing gig at a club Vera's mobster boyfriend buys
her. Before long Sandman also has a feud with his brother, but this
rift seems to be orchestrated so that they can reconcile in the middle
of a tap-dance number. The black story also features a small contin-
gent of black mobsters, but their presence is dwarfed by the powerful
white gang leaders. African-American actor Larry Fishburne, not
particularly well known at the time of the film's release, is the only
distinguishable character in this group. Aside from a couple of scenes
with the black gangsters and a few scenes between Sandman and
Lila, the only other scenes in which the black characters figure are
those where they are performing on the Cotton Club's stage.

In the montage at the film's end, the audience sees that both Dixie
and Vera and Sandman and Lila overcome the various obstacles to
their respective relationships. They board a train, presumably going
off to live happily ever after.

Lillian's Cotton Club

When I was a child, one of my favorite grown-ups was a friend of
my parents who had been a Cotton Club dancer in the mid-1920s.
When I knew her, Lillian was a domestic worker in the employ of a
wealthy white widow. She dressed in crisp uniforms with elaborate
costume jewelry or intricately folded floral handkerchiefs pinned to
the bodice. Although she never looked tawdry, she wore lots of
makeup and perfume. She entertained me for hours with stories
about the beautiful women and handsome men she had known in the
Harlem of her youth. She talked of parties and vacations. She taught
me the steps to some of the dances she remembered. She created
G-rated stories of her love affairs. She still bore a grudge against a
good-looking beau who left her in pursuit of Nina Mae McKinney,
star of several all-black films of the 1930s. She said she had known
Lena Horne and Duke Ellington. None of these names meant a
whole lot to me at the time, but the adults were impressed so I
was too.

In all of Lillian's stories of her Harlem adventures, never once did
she mention organized crime or anything to do with the white pa-

trons/owners of the nightspot. If she was still alive, I would have a ton of questions for her. How well did Duke Ellington and Cab Calloway get along? Was Ellington jealous when Calloway was so successful when he filled in while Ellington and his Washingtonians took a leave to appear in a Hollywood film? Was Ellington as much of a ladies' man as they say? What kinds of relationships developed among the women, such as Josephine Baker, Lena Horne, and Ethel Waters, backstage? How did it feel to perform on a stage in a club where your own parents couldn't get in to see you?

It is unlikely that any of these stories will reach the big screen. Since a movie entitled *The Cotton Club* has already been made, producers will be hesitant to underwrite another film on this cultural landmark. I suppose this is my biggest problem with all of these films. The stories of Delta bluesmen, the Cotton Club performers, and the early ragtime pianists will not get told, at least by filmmakers. These films, which sandwich the accomplishments of black musicians into stories about the very people who exploited them, will prevent the real stories from being presented to a mass audience.

Since the centuries during which slavers forced their west African captives to sing and dance during the Middle Passage—the interval on board slave ships en route from Africa to the New World—in order to maintain their physical fitness aboard slave ships, the dominant culture has exploited and commodified the music of Americans of African descent for purposes lucrative and beneficial to itself. During slavery, traders forced their chattel to sing on the auction block so as to raise their selling price. In the aftermath of slavery, African Americans were forced to "blacken up" to compete with white minstrels. Groups such as the Fisk Jubilee singers kept their college running on the money they made by selling polished versions of spirituals. At every juncture in our history it has seemed as if the dominant culture appreciates us mainly for our music. Wouldn't it be nice if fledgling adolescent white musicians could redeem the souls of elderly black men, all the while enhancing their rock careers, as is the case in *Crossroads?* Wouldn't it be nice if, as is the case in *The Big Chill*, whites could just dance to the music without ever encountering real African Americans? The people who make these films probably don't perceive themselves as belonging to the same category as those who cracked the whip on the slave ships. Our responses may not be as visceral as those of our ancestors. Yet when film after film, commercial after commercial, episode after episode hinge on the music and lyrics of our hearts and souls, we feel a decided kinship with our ancestors. It's the same old song, but with a different meaning to those of us compelled to sing it.

10

From Real Blacks
to Reel Blacks

Robert Townsend's wickedly funny 1987 film *Hollywood Shuffle* stands as the best cinematic testimony to the obstacles faced by African-American actors trying to break into commercial Hollywood films. While living in a tidy home with his mother, grandmother, and younger brother, the hero is forced to confront a film community that refuses to acknowledge any but a stereotypical role for a black man. Forced to compete for parts as a pimp, drug dealer, or oversexed slave, the hero fantasizes about Black Acting School where white teachers teach Shakespearean trained African-American actors in the subtleties of jive and Blackspeak. Indeed Townsend's myth-shattering film highlights virtually every fictional stereotype black male actors encounter.

In addition to the limited range of fictional characters depicted in *Hollywood Shuffle*, real African-American film actors are semiregularly pursued for one other type of film role: nonfictional or real-life characters. One of the clearest indications of Hollywood's lack of imagination in the use of African-American actors can be seen in the fact that "true stories" in which real black people have been participants make up a disproportionate number of the films featuring black actors. The recent career of actor Morgan Freeman reflects this pattern. Following his riveting performance (as a criminal, of course) in

Street Smart (1987), after which *New Yorker* magazine's reviewer Pauline Kael asked the question, "Is Morgan Freeman America's greatest living actor?" Freeman was featured in three very successful films. *Lean on Me* (1989) and *Glory* (1989) were both based on true stories, and even *Driving Miss Daisy* (1989) was inspired by a series of incidents that occurred in the life of the screenwriter. Numerous other examples can be cited, but it seems safe to assert that filmmakers are nearly incapable of constructing viable, nonstereotypical African-American characters, so when they do stray from the safety of stereotypes, they rely on adaptations of real-life stories as vehicles through which to portray blacks on screen.

This chapter considers several of the films in which nonfictional persons and events are depicted. My purpose here is to draw certain conclusions about the patterns that emerge when nonfiction stories based on real incidents in African-American history are prepared for the big screen. My interest is in what the majority of the white and African-American viewing public sees when it goes to the movies or rents a video for home entertainment. Therefore I have limited myself to the standard type of commercially released film that plays in the suburban movie house for a respectable length of time and is several months later prominently displayed in the new releases section of the typical video rental shop. I realize, of course, that third world and noncommercially oriented filmmakers are producing excellent movies that challenge the conventional portrayals of blacks on screen. Unfortunately, only a small portion of the movie-viewing public sees these films.

Real Life to Reel Life

The process of adapting any real-life story into a script for a successful film always requires certain kinds of cinematic compromises. Real stories have a nasty tendency to be slightly more untidy than the fictional ones usually found on the big screen. Filmmakers have devised a series of strategies to reshape a nonfiction story into one suitable for the movies. When too many individuals are connected to the true story, filmmakers often take the traits and actions of many real people and attribute them to a few. These are referred to as "composite" characters. Sometimes the events of the real story are not as dramatic as the filmmakers would like. In order to increase story tension, they might employ some sort of hyperbole, thereby exaggerating the impact of the real events. Filmmakers tend to manipulate romance as well. If they feel the story needs a little spice, they might add a romantic encounter; if they prefer to avoid digressions, they might eliminate the love interest. In some instances filmmakers may choose to alter the physical appearance of the real-life person whose life they are chronicling. Real heroes are rarely as glamorous as the actors who portray them on screen. The textile mill union organizer whose experiences inspired *Norma Rae* bears little resemblance to Sally Field.

The abbreviations and deletions often made ostensibly in the name of time yield the greatest potential for distortion. Few whole stories can be told in two hours or so. Most require the filmmakers to abbreviate or even omit incidents and individuals in order to get the story told.

In my study of the late 1980s and early 1990s films based on real-life occurrences among African Americans, I noted a rather persistent pattern in the kinds of modifications filmmakers used to tell these stories. When the story that emerges on the screen is compared with what is known about the real-life events, we can see that all of the alterations result in a film that minimizes the role African Americans have played in shaping their own destiny and exaggerates the role whites have played in fighting racial hostility.

The Media Goes to Mississippi

The 1988 film *Mississippi Burning*, based on the 1964 investigation of the disappearance and deaths of civil rights workers James Chaney, Andrew Goodman, and Michael Schwerner, exhibits this pattern quite concretely. *Mississippi Burning* promotes itself as a reasonably accurate account of the events of 1964 in Neshoba County, Mississippi, when local Klansmen killed two white and one black civil rights workers. Information about this incident is extraordinarily accessible to anyone with a library card. Excellent, detailed accounts are contained in several books, including *Racial Matters* by Kenneth

O'Reilly and *We Are Not Afraid* by Seth Cagin and Philip Dray.[1] Reporters were as plentiful and persistent as mosquitoes during that hot Mississippi summer. And a segment of Henry Hampton's twelve-episode documentary series for public television, *Eyes on the Prize*, entitled "Mississippi: Is This America?" focused on the relationship between these events and the emergence of the Mississippi Freedom Democratic Party. Thus in taking this story to the big screen, the filmmakers were not unearthing some obscure, unknown, poorly chronicled segment of distant history. Indeed as Hampton's series and "Why Was Mississippi Burning and Who Put Out the Fire" by documentary filmmaker Ron Bailey demonstrate, many of those involved in the incidents were alive and well when the commercial film was being made. Almost as soon as the movie was released in early 1988, two competing bodies of commentary emerged.

Critics opposed to the film responded that the inaccuracies were so heinous that they resulted in a complete whitewash of this era. A *Time* magazine writer referred to it as "A version of history so distorted that it amounts to a cinematic lynching of the truth."[2] Although numerous minor details are inaccurate, three major ones provoked the most consternation. Few aspects of the civil rights history generate more pride in African Americans than the fact that activists trained in nonviolent resistance overcame enormous obstacles to racial equality. Alan Parker's decision to exaggerate the drama of this summer by inventing scenarios in which the FBI agents use force to topple the Klan demeans the legacy of hundreds of civil rights workers whose repertoire of anti-Klan measures never included dirty tricks. Pauline Kael notes that, "This cheap gimmick undercuts the whole civil rights subject; it validates the terrorist methods of the Klan. . . . Parker uses the civil-rights movement to make a wham-bam Charles Bronson movie, and, from his blithe public statements, he seems unaware that this could be thought morally repugnant."[3] The second and third flaws reinforce the historical damage incurred by each other and the first. Although the slew of FBI agents originally assigned to the case carried out their tasks in a methodical, albeit reluctant, fashion, the filmmakers develop two composite characters and embody them with the kind of conflicting traits requisite for a standard "buddy" picture. They become the film's heroes; their tempestuous relationship overshadows what little attention was given to African Americans in the film. Rewriting the FBI's attitude toward the civil rights movement as positive is nearly tantamount to describing the Nazis as pro-Jewish. Historians can easily document that J. Edgar Hoover, then director of the FBI, and his operatives felt coerced into investigating the deaths of Chaney, Goodman, and Schwerner. Whereas in the film, the murderers' identity is realized when the wife of a Klansmen/policeman decides that she can no longer condone his brand of racism, in reality the FBI paid a still-unknown informant for this information. And the FBI is wrongly portrayed as overly enthusiastic in its quest to bring the evil Klansmen to justice; the African-American community is depicted even more inaccurately. The film's landscape includes only local, ostensibly terrified blacks who mutely accept the dictates of the white supremacist regime that controls the town while rejecting the assistance proffered by the FBI. And while the process of adapting real stories into scripts often results in the omission of some of the people involved, the makers of *Mississippi Burning* managed to leave out the entire civil rights movement. As journalist Brent Staples indicates, "Conspicuously absent are black civil rights giants who were astride the land then, real live heroes—Robert Moses, John Lewis, Fannie Lou Hamer—who daily risked their lives for changes that inevitably altered the way most Americans live."[4]

The film implies that the FBI was diligent in its efforts to seek justice for the civil rights workers. In reality, however an organized, courageous group of activists, largely African Americans, was responsible for demanding that the FBI do the job that Hoover never wanted it to do. At great personal risk these activists stayed in Mississippi and kept the pressure on the law enforcement community to protect civil rights workers. Because of the efforts of these activists, the FBI was compelled to investigate the deaths or risk considerable embarrassment from the public at large. The screenplay for *Mississippi Burning* completely silences the role that African Americans took in exposing the virulent racism of the South. Instead, two composite characters represent the white FBI agents, and their reluctance to investigate the incident is transformed into enthusiasm. Moviegoers leave the theater with the erroneous impression that impassioned white law enforcement agents were the heroes of the civil rights movement.

In those accounts favorable to the film—which was nominated for Best Picture in the 1989 Academy Awards—reviewers claimed that any inaccuracies did not distort its power and potential for educating a viewing audience unfamiliar with the extent of racial violence in recent American history. After acknowledging that ". . . it is wrong to make heroes out of fictional FBI agents," Mike Royko of the Chicago *Tribune* maintained, "You don't go in the movie theater expecting to see and hear facts. The best you can hope for is a sense of reality and that's what *Mississippi Burning* provided."[5] Royko rationalized that since documentaries do not snare large profits, critics should not demand accuracy from moviemakers—"But if they insist on facts only on the screen, they should get together with some investors, come up with about $20 million, make such a documentary and put it in the theaters."[6] Writing for the *New York Times*, film critic Vincent Canby echoed Royko's sentiments: "It is the fate of most documentary films to be seen almost exclusively by audiences who want to be reassured about what they already believe. The chances are that *Mississippi Burning* will be seen by a lot of people who haven't the foggiest notion of what went on in the 1960s in Mississippi and throughout the rest of the South."[7] For Canby, like Royko, the fact that moviegoers will leave this film with only a foggy notion of this era is outweighed by the filmmakers' skill in adapting the story to the big screen. "Most of the conventions are used with discretion, and to good dramatic effect. They aren't enough to condemn the film to the junk heap of sleaze."[8] After claiming that the film's critics are merely upset by the racial violence depicted, Canby reasons, "The easiest way to do this [condemn the film] is to find reasons not to believe the film, to seize on historical inaccuracies and what seem to be (and in a couple of cases are) clichés. . . . the movie's triumphant ending is inaccurate, but it doesn't send one out of the theater looking to emulate Charles Bronson."[9]

Some film critics believe that the film lost the Best Picture Oscar due to the revelation of these and other inaccuracies. However, in spite of the attention given to the gross factual distortions that characterize the film, Roger Ebert, a Pulitzer Prize–winning film critic, listed it as among the best ten films of the *decade*. It was also a very hot rental during its first month on videocassette. The permanence and accessibility of popular movies on videocassette makes the flaws inherent in films of such concern.

Glorious Inaccuracies

Unlike their counterparts at the helm of *Mississippi Burning*, the producers of the 1989 film *Glory* could at least partially blame the historical distortions on the fact that they were dealing with a body of fairly anonymous African Americans who lived during an era when chronicling the experiences of African Americans was undervalued. Whereas scores of individuals whose lives served as contradictions to the content of *Mississippi Burning* emerged following that film's release, actual members of the Massachusetts 54th Regiment, established in the 1860s—the purported inspiration for the film—were obviously unavailable for comment. While several books and documentaries have focused on the civil rights movement, precious little has been written about blacks in the Civil War.

It should come as no surprise that the bulk of available information on the Massachusetts 54th—the first free black Civil War regiment—focuses on the life of its young white leader, Robert Gould Shaw. And most of the point of view in the film is his: The audience sees the events play out through his eyes, from his perspective. One marvelous exception to this pattern is in an early sequence following the Battle of Antietam when the camera shifts from the point of view of Shaw (played by Matthew Broderick), wounded in battle, to the view of Rawlins, the black gravedigger (played by Morgan Freeman), as he peers down on the wounded young white character who looks like little more than a boy.

Like all of the battle scenes, the Antietam battle scene is meticulously filmed, as is the chilling hospital scene in which Shaw is bandaged. The details of Shaw's life are, for the most part, meticulously recorded. As the producers acknowledge in the film credits, they relied on the young colonel's letters, now in the possession of Harvard University.

Unfortunately, the producers seem to have made little effort to consult the extant primary sources that would have offered the African-American point of view. To be sure, some if this material is rare, but trained scholars could have unearthed it. For example, few African-American lives have been better documented than that of Frederick Douglass, the abolitionist leader who, in reality, played a significant role in the formation of the 54th, but whose contributions are reduced to a cameo in the film. Even a cursory examination of the biographies of Douglass would have revealed accurate examples of how he looked in the Civil War years. Perhaps the filmmakers chose to age Douglass for theatrical purposes. The scene in which Shaw and the audience is introduced to Douglass turns on the visual contrast between the adolescent-looking, young white man in uniform and the venerable-looking black man in starched collar. Of course, perhaps this distortion disturbs only those viewers with a mental picture of Douglass in the 1860s. After all, one can imagine the filmmakers arguing, Douglass did look like that *eventually*.

Other character modifications involved changes much more significant than ages. Attention to detail is severely lacking in the scenes that focus on the African-American characters. As mentioned, Douglass's role in the film is limited, while in fact his role in the actual events that precipitated the formation of the 54th was extensive. He and African-American religious leaders were involved with the recruitment of Northern freemen for the company. His sons served as drill sergeants.

In order to tell the story of the men in the 54th, the filmmakers employed a time-honored cinematic device of highlighting a core group of individuals whose experiences are meant to be representative of the whole. These four tent mates include Rawlins (Morgan Freeman), the Southern gravedigger; Trip, played superbly by Denzel Washington; Sharts (Jihimy Kennedy), a runaway from Tennessee, and even more conspicuously a Southern ex-slave; and, as the sole Northern African American, Searles (Andre Braugher), ostensibly a boyhood friend of Shaw's and Forbes's (another white officer) whose "white" education has ill-prepared him for the demands of army life. With his tasteful suit, his glasses, and essays by transcendentalists, he is seen as having more in common with the white officers than with his fellow black soldiers. None of these characters is based on actual African-American soldiers who made up the 54th, even though the details of their lives could have been incorporated. The filmmakers offered the standard justification for using composite characters—they argue that these four characters can better portray the breadth of the 54th's communal personality than would have been possible by sticking to four genuine accounts. The major flaw in this line of reasoning can be seen in the decision to make of these characters three recent slaves and the fourth an inept Northerner. The rank-and-file members of the 54th do not match that profile. Many were the sons or grandsons of ex-slaves who had spent their whole lives in the North. They were not all illiterate; we have letters and diaries that prove it.[10] They were not as rough as the Trip, Rawlins, and Sharts characters suggest, nor were they polished to the point of ineffectiveness as the Searles character indicates. To use the much-quoted but very appropriate adage coined by Ralph Ellison, the real men of the 54th are *invisible* in this film.

In a series of fictionalized incidents, Colonel Shaw is depicted as the agent of positive change for all of the black characters. First, when he demonstrates that the sharp-shooting techniques that Sharts has developed for hunting won't guarantee him success on the battlefield, the fugitive slave learns how to pack his musket, aim, and shoot under fire. The validity of such an encounter is particularly weak when we consider that few slaves would have been permitted the kind of access to guns that would have allowed a real-life Sharts, had there been one, to develop skills as a marksman. Next, Shaw's supposed African-American boyhood companion, Searles, ostensibly one of the few Northern-born Blacks in the regiment, matures through the colonel's consistent refusal to intervene as the highly literate black recruit struggles to adopt to the rigors of camp life. Since the audience is led to believe that Shaw, the other white officer Forbes, and the African-American Searles have had the same education, why are the two white men able to prove their military mettle in spite of their privileged backgrounds while the genteel Searles falters throughout his training? Of course, Shaw is only ignoring his friend "for his own good." This indifference is seen as paying off when Searles performs admirably under fire and refuses to return home after he is injured. During at least part of the film the dignified gravedigger, Rawlins, is permitted to play teacher to Shaw as the white colonel seeks advice on how to best understand the men of his black regiment. With great flourish, Shaw recognizes Rawlins's quiet leadership abilities and rewards them by finding a loophole through which he can appoint him as a noncommissioned officer. This new rank intensifies Rawlins's already unswerving commitment. In actuality, noncommissioned officers, notably Frederick Douglass's sons, were appointed much sooner in the history of the regiment. And finally, Trip, the recruit with the roughest edges, has a series of confrontations with his young commanding officer. Each one, including a whipping, seems to bring the two closer to an understanding. (I know of no references in the historical records to substantiate the whipping of a 54th recruit.) Before the final battle, Shaw seems to have earned Trip's respect. Following Shaw's courageous but fatal charge into enemy fire at Fort Wagner, Trip and his comrades, knowing that they are outnumbered and outmaneuvered, bravely pursue the Confederate enemies who have killed their leader.

Probably the most well-known African American of the 54th was William Carney, incorrectly identified in the Tri-Star Pictures *Glory* press kit as John Carney. The first black recipient of the Congressional Medal of Honor, Carney was from the New Bedford area. To use his words:

> In rising to see if I could determine my course to the rear, the bullet I now carry in my body came whizzing like a mosquito, and I was shot. Not being prostrated by the shot, I continued my course, yet had not gone far before I was struck by a second shot. Soon after I saw a man coming toward me, and when within hailing distance I asked him who he was. He replied, "I belong to the 100th New York," and then inquired if I were wounded. Upon my replying in the affirmative, he came to my assistance and helped me to the rear. "Now then," said he, "let me take the colors and carry them for you." My reply was that I would not give them to any man unless he belonged to the 54th Regiment. So we pressed on but did not go far before I was wounded in the head. We came at length within hailing distance of the rear guard, who caused us to halt, and upon asking who we were, and finding I was wounded, took us to the rear through the guard. An officer came, and after taking my name and regiment, put us in the charge of the hospital corps, telling them to find my regiment. When we finally reached the latter the men cheered me and the flag. My reply was "Boys, I only did my duty. The old flag never touched the ground."[11]

In the film it is the illiterate, angry Trip who picks up the flag. At the end of the battle the audience sees his body being dumped in the mass grave on top of Shaw's. The audience may not realize that Civil War custom dictated the return of officers' corpses to their side, but because the Confederates were so insulted by the concept of a white officer commanding a regiment of black soldiers, they mutilated Shaw's body (not shown in the film) before burying him with his men. To their credit, the Shaw family responded to this news by claiming that he would have wanted to have been interred with his soldiers. Returning to the discussion of the Trip/Carney character, aside from the act of retrieving the flag, the "composite" character Trip exhibits nothing of the real-life Carney. The fact that Carney survived and Trip dies is, I think, telling. Congress rewarded Carney's bravery with its highest honor—the Congressional Medal of Honor. The rest of his life was not without interest. But, in keeping with the movie world's reluctance to depict black men as participants in the dismantling of oppressive forces against their people, the filmmakers kill off the character that so feebly represents him.

Principal Problems

One Hollywood film that at least partially depicts a black individual as a participant in an attempt to bring about change for his people is the 1989 film *Lean on Me.* Starring Morgan Freeman as Joe Clark, the no-nonsense principal of Eastside High, the film traces the career of this controversial African-American educator whose unorthodox tactics drew national attention to a neglected and deteriorated high school in Paterson, New Jersey. Clark became an instant celebrity when he locked unruly students out of the school and patrolled the halls with a bullhorn and a Louisville slugger in his hand. As the academic performance of Eastside's student body increased, so did attention to Clark.

The film posits Clark in a hero-versus-the-rest-of-the-world scenario. In the opening scene we are introduced to a dashiki-clad Clark of the 1960s lashing out against his fellow teachers as they swap higher salaries for the curriculum control that Clark believes is essential. After his fellow teachers agree to a compromise with the school board that will force the dedicated young teacher into another school, we see the Eastside of the 1980s. The clean, quiet, wholesome-looking school on screen moments before is now filthy, loud, and unsafe. Four minutes into the film the audience is led to believe that this urban school's enormous problems were instigated by the actions of a selfish group of teachers in the 1960s. Unable to find a suitable principal to accept the charge, a savvy but spineless white mayor and his pragmatic African-American superintendent transfer Clark from an elementary school post to Eastside. Finding a school building in which hard-nosed "miscreants" are virtually holding their teachers and the more well-meaning students hostage, Clark assembles a security force to expel these hoodlums. One of his first official acts is to herd those students labeled by their teachers as troublemakers onto the stage, while the docile students retain their seats in the audience. The film leaves the viewer with the impression that there were two types of Eastside student—violence-prone, lewd, n'er-do-wells escorted off the stage by Clark's security force and neglected, intimidated underachievers who remain to clean up the mess left by their nefarious former classmates. Conflicts in the film result as Clark almost immediately runs afoul of the teaching staff and the parents. The teachers are seen as unwilling to take the necessary steps to regain control of the school and return to the task of teaching, while the parents, led by Mrs. Elliot (Robin Bartlett), a loud, militant black woman, defend the expelled students' access to education. As she hurls profanities at everyone from the assistant principal to the fire chief, Mrs. Elliot is depicted as possessing little more civility than the expelled students. The audience will not take seriously her conviction that Clark has unfairly forced deserving students out of school because her character is rendered so unsympathetically.

Clark's challenges require him to win over these four constituencies. The first group is the students themselves, the earnest group that remained after the exodus of the drug dealers. Perceiving Clark as a gruff but loving, strict but supportive, demanding but willing-to-reward authoritarian, most of the students embrace the father figure. Among the second group, the teachers, some welcome Clark's changes, while many others are outraged by his disrespect for them. Within minutes he suspends two competent teachers whose only faults seem to be that they don't bow and scrape to him. The unfairness of these acts is diffused as Clark invites one of the teachers to return and replaces the other, a white music teacher who was preparing the students to sing Mozart at Lincoln Center, with an African-American one who teaches them a soulful version of the school song. The third and toughest constituency is represented by the community groups, inexplicably anxious to return drug dealers to the classroom. Of course, the fourth group, the politicians, is the most fickle of Clark's constituencies; the politicians will clearly abandon him if he doesn't win the support of the other groups, but will stand squarely behind him if he does. As is customary in narratives depicting heroes, *Lean on Me* hinges on a test that the hero must pass. In this film the test is a real one—a standardized basic skills test that the school's students must master in order to validate the success of Clark's regime. Success on this test will satisfy or at least silence the four constituencies.

Inspired by their paternalistic principal, the students master the exam. The community groups retreat; the teachers celebrate; the politicians take the credit; and the students walk down the aisles at graduation with a renewed sense of self-esteem. A black man is seen in a film as participating in the liberation of his people. But whom is he liberating them from? Now, given the premise of this chapter, that commercial Hollywood filmmakers distort the historical record in order to avoid depicting blacks as leaders in the liberation of their people, I suppose I should embrace *Lean on Me*. The problem is that this film distorts the record so that a black hero is defined as an individual who subdues other black people in order to save a black silent majority. This scenario is no more accurate than those of the first two films discussed in which the filmmakers overlooked the accomplishments of real African Americans.

Lean on Me casts their own people as Clark's and the students' enemies. The villains are represented by a strident, humorless parent and the omnipresent drug dealers. No real indictment is leveled at the indifferent political system that allowed Eastside to decay in the first place. Mysteriously absent from Clark's problems are the budgetary woes that beset most urban schools. The film does not tell the audience that in 1987 Paterson allocated $2,691 per student, ranking it 572nd among 591 school districts in New Jersey. The film does not highlight the fact that funds insufficient for running a school of that size preordained the subsequent problems. In one scene, when Clark is forced to defend chaining the doors of the school in order to keep the drug addicts out and thus risking catastrophe in the event of fire, he does note that if Eastside could purchase the fire doors that the white schools are allotted, the whole issue would be moot. But the film never explores the ramifications of this comment, nor of the one in which Clark tells the school superintendent that Eastside's fate is the result of economic disparities that no one wants to address. The miseducation of the largely minority student population is seen almost entirely as an in-group problem. The school was supposedly fine until its student and faculty population shifted to a predominantly African-American and Hispanic one. They ran the school down and lowered its academic standards. Then one of their own returns wielding academic tough love to decimate the evil minority peoples who have been preventing the good ones from excelling. The audience is cajoled into believing that if just the right person is put in charge, he or she can undo the damage incurred by decades of neglect. By removing Eastside's erosion from its context and grossly oversimplifying the environment the real Joe Clark had to face, the filmmakers distort the historical record.

Although *Lean on Me* attempts to capture some of Clark's more brazen moments, there is no doubt that he is meant to be seen as a hero. The records of Eastside High certainly suggest that the real Joe Clark and the world he operated in was much more complex than they appear on screen. The film depicts the expelled students as drug-crazed vermin; yet the profiles of those students locked out by Clark throughout the early 1980s suggest that many were educationally disabled, not sociopathic morons. The parents who opposed his efforts were not trying to force the school system into housing drug peddlers but rather to hold it accountable for the large numbers of high school students who were underserved at each level of their education. The complaints of the teachers who worked under Clark were more concrete than those registered in the film. Finally, the problems that beset Eastside High did not end when the students improved their scores on the basic skills test. Singing the school song in doo-wop harmony did not remedy the ills that had plagued their education.

Coincidence or Conspiracy?

After hearing me lecture on this topic, an African colleague asked if I thought that Hollywood filmmakers were involved in a conspiracy to keep the stories of black leaders out of the movie theaters. Coming from a nonwestern background, he was startled to learn that true stories would be consistently reshaped to minimize black activism. *Mississippi Burning*'s white producers created white composite characters to function as heroes while eliminating real black ones from consideration in the film; *Glory*'s producers created composite black characters that are killed off, denying the audience the opportunity to witness the scope of their heroism. Anyone inclined to subscribe to conspiracy theories could make a case by examining these films and other films. Chapter 11 includes an extended consideration of *Cry Freedom* (1987), based on the book of the same name by white South African writer Donald Woods. Although the film may have been quite true to the story of black South African Steve Biko, the filmmakers minimize his life by starting the film when he meets Donald Woods and then soon killing Biko off. As a result it is much more about the education of Woods in the evils of apartheid than about Steve Biko, lifelong opponent of the regime.

As compelling as the evidence is, I do not believe that Hollywood writers and producers are engaged in a clandestine pact to keep audiences from seeing blacks successfully fighting for their liberation. Rather, like movie critics and everyone else, filmmakers are a product of the American popular culture. They want to believe the familiar, comfortable notion that whites have led the movements that have improved black status. They subscribe unquestioningly to a Eurocentric view of the world, accepting that what is really important in the matters of racial equality is what whites have contributed to it. But besides being products of their culture and education, they are producers of it. They produce films that reinforce their worldview and perpetuate the racism they claim to want to reveal. The core storylines beneath the surface of these films are strikingly consistent. Film critic Clyde Taylor, discussing this phenomenon as it relates to older films, has applied the term "master narrative" to describe the core storyline that reemerges in movies featuring black/white relations. He notes that in film after film in which African-American characters have any stature at all, the circumstances of the plots always subordinate their role in order to highlight and applaud the white characters who are noble enough to engage themselves in racial matters. I can't think of one successful commercial film in which a black hero is allowed to be the successful agent of change in any aspect of the oppression of his or her people. Such a story would contradict the master narrative, the prevailing worldview subscribed to by the filmmakers and the white audience members. This theory explains why so many film critics refuse to attack a film on the grounds that it is historically inaccurate; these films fit the critics' worldview as much as they do the filmmakers'.

This indictment would be less damaging if we could assume that people would not accept these film visions as accurate. Unfortunately, we live in a society in which people are much more likely to see the film than read the book. Even after the fairly public backlash to *Mississippi Burning*, I encountered college students who accepted it as gospel. Video distributors don't put negative criticisms on the boxes we get when we rent or purchase a tape. We can only hope that eventually the influence of black studies on education will "trickle down" to the makers of the movies and that filmmakers of color who have not internalized the dominant master narrative will infiltrate the commercial film industry.[12]

11

Of Primates, Porters, and Potables: Images of Africa on Screen

The mountains, rivers, deserts, jungles, and plains of Africa have always provided enticing landscapes for American and British filmmakers. African wildlife—the apes, elephants, cheetahs, gazelles, and a pantheon of other exotic animals—have also beckoned moviemakers throughout the years. But considerably less cinematic invention has been inspired by the indigenous peoples who inhabit the sub-Saharan regions of the "dark continent." Commonly portrayed as porters for white adventurers or the savages who assault well-meaning non-Africans, on the big screen the black African is rarely treated as much more than a narrative prop. Although a small cadre of struggling African filmmakers have been trying to cultivate a western audience for film projects that redress this imbalance, their efforts are not the ones that reach the mainstream American film-going public. This chapter focuses on a selection of those stories that commercial filmmakers have marketed for that mainstream audience. In the films past and present, the apes, elephants, and other species of wildlife of Africa are depicted much more sympathetically than its peoples. Movies in this tradition humanize the continent's wildlife while objectifying and depersonalizing African people.

Movies tell stories, and the stories that movies tell are always connected to the narratives that come to comprise the history of a culture. When western filmmakers take their cameras and their imaginations to Africa, they carry with them all of the cultural lore developed and handed down over several generations. Since African peoples have been afforded second-class citizenship in the New World, it is not surprising that they are depicted with so little dignity in American movies. Since western scientists have been searching for connections between primates and human beings, it is not surprising that movies anthropomorphize apes and gorillas. Since white men and women have sought unfamiliar environments in which to test the strength of western values and spiritual systems, it is not surprising that films located in Africa so often focus on the maturation and success of a white hero or heroine.

In her extraordinarily compelling study of the nexus between the history of primate studies and common attitudes about race and gender, culture critic Donna Haraway examines a wealth of popular and "scientific" data in order to demonstrate that the stories that get told about man and nature are those that reinforce a white, male-dominated worldview.[1] Although she speaks of popular film only peripherally, it is clear that the charges she levels are discernible in the commercial movies that use Africa as a backdrop. Just as Haraway sees the trappings of colonialism in the impulse to marshal knowledge about primates, so too can we see that filmmakers have opted to tell stories of Africa that convey messages of entitled white dominance and black African inferiority. In the filmmakers' taxonomy, white men and women are at the top, followed by animals, especially primates, with African peoples at the bottom.

The Apes and Tarzan

Since the success of *Tarzan of the Apes* (1918), an adventure film based on the popular novel by Edgar Rice Burroughs, the formula for movie success has dictated that Africa function on the screen as a lush, exotic background against which the mettle of white European and/or American rugged individuals can be examined and tested. This theme was commonplace in "high" literature as well. Joseph Conrad's *Heart of Darkness* remains the quintessential examination of the white man's need to come to grips with the "dark" side of his soul by confronting the unfamiliar interiors of the dark continent. The perennially popular Tarzan series positions the white male in the African jungle from birth. Raised by nurturing apes, the displaced white hero is more at home with these primates than with the human kind. Whereas Kurtz, the hero in Conrad's novel, is an adult—complete with the blemishes of his western upbringing—Burroughs and the films based on his stories construct an unsullied hero who at once manifests complete physical maturity and complete intellectual and social innocence. And he is white.

These seemingly contradictory characteristics, along with numerous plot lines implicit in the volatile environment, have continued to capture the imagination of moviemakers. This is a story they love to tell and retell. Since the first Tarzan movie was issued in 1918, there have been over three dozen films with "Tarzan" in the title. While many of these are of the potboiler "B" film variety, the tenacious appeal of this story is undeniable. The Tarzan films are a fairly easy target for those of us interested in the perpetuation of antiblack stereotypes. Critic James R. Nesteby sums up the cultural impact that the Tarzan films from 1918 to 1954 had by stating

> The Tarzan films are the most important representatives of the jungle film genre, for no other series has been so popular and led to so many imitators. The positive attributes of the "white ape myth" and the negative attributes of the "black ape myth" in a film like the original *Tarzan of the Apes* represent an interpretation and an ordering of experience in American culture. This film is an example of the mythic golden age as well, even to the extreme of re-creating the timeless Adam and Eve in Eden through Tarzan and Jane in the jungle of the Dark Continent.[2]

Nesteby's 1954 cut-off date should not be construed as evidence that the Tarzan appeal has eroded. During the 1960s a popular television series was devoted to the king of the apes. The various Tarzan movies that Nesteby chronicled continue to appear regularly on television. Most of them are available on videocassette. Writing in the 1980s, film critic Roger Ebert maintains that "The story of Tarzan is one of the most durable myths of the twentieth century."[3] Thus today's young generation is just as apt to be influenced by them as earlier ones.

Since 1980 two Tarzan films have secured the considerable financial backing now necessary to bring a movie to the theaters. In 1981 *Tarzan, the Ape Man*, an examination of the sexual exploits of Tarzan and Jane, was released to fairly poor reviews, and in 1984 the big-budget *Greystoke: The Legend of Tarzan, Lord of the Apes*, a study of Tarzan's aristocratic roots, was released to mixed reviews.

Greystoke was billed as the most authentic film version ever produced of the original Burroughs novel. In keeping with its forty-odd predecessors, it offers a much more sympathetic examination of the apes who raise the "white ape" than it does the African peoples. After the birth of their son in a treehouse constructed in the midst of the African jungle where they have been shipwrecked, John Clayton and his wife, aka Lord and Lady Greystoke, are attacked by a group of ostensibly hostile apes. Given the Claytons' decision to fashion a domicile out of a cluster of trees, it is perhaps with good reason that the apes felt justified in forcibly evicting the uninvited trespassers. After all, the apes were unaccustomed to having to share the trees. Although Lord and Lady Greystoke don't survive the ape attack, the innocent white male infant who is dangling in a makeshift cradle is unharmed. A female ape whose own offspring has just died adopts the boy and proceeds to nurse him and raise him as her own. The film humanizes her and affords her all of the dignity that would be bestowed on any human (white) mother on screen. This portion of the film contains numerous scenes of the small boy playing gleefully among a group of apes that consider him just one of the gang. Numerous close-ups of the apes show facial expressions that seem loving and kind. The camera lingers on the gentle, soft fingers and hands that embrace the child. As the boy matures, he reciprocates the affection he receives from the group. The filmmaker has given the audience a family to care about, albeit a nonhuman one.

The apes, which appeared so threatening when they first attacked the treehouse, are portrayed more sympathetically as they are shown as the victims of other ape groups, a panther, and a hostile group of Africans who maliciously attack them. With spears and bows and arrows, these ostensibly barbaric Africans pursue the apes. Since the Africans attack without reason, the audience is expected to conclude that the blacks are "savage" and "uncivilized." The film offers no clues about the motives of the African ape attackers. There is no evidence that they are poaching for profit. They don't seem to be hunting for food because after the kill they just leave the carcasses in the jungle. *They* are the animals who wantonly intrude upon the sanctity of the extended ape family that the film has constructed as if it were human. In a particularly poignant scene, the now-adolescent white male tries unsuccessfully to nurse his surrogate mother ape back to health. Through a series of daring escapades, the young man (in *Greystoke* the Tarzan name is not used) finesses his way to the top of the hierarchy where he becomes the leader of his ape group.

The next Africans the audience sees are those employed by the motley crew of white hunters and explorers who are collecting "specimens" for the British Museum. Whereas the "jungle" Africans who pursue the innocent apes are depicted in garish revealing costumes, complete with full tribal makeup and jewelry, the African servants on the expedition wear turbans and long overshirts and pantaloons that connote Islamic influences. The latter group's docility offers only a partial contrast to their distant brethren of the jungle. Both groups are muted by the cinematic circumstances in which they are couched. No African face gets a benevolent frame from the camera. More "humanistic" attributes are allotted to the apes that raise young Lord Greystoke than the Africans who also share the jungle with him.

In the Tarzan films, as well as in numerous other movies set in Africa, the primates are depicted in their own environs and in family units. Since a pair of apes "adopt" Tarzan, the filmmakers have plenty of opportunities to highlight the nurturing, protective roles associated with family units. But no Africans in the Tarzan films are shown in relation to family members. The audience never gets to see the Africans as capable of love, sorrow, fear, or other human emotions granted to the primates.

The producers of the 1984 film might well argue that their *Greystoke* is much less overtly racist than the earlier films in the Tarzan roster. At least these Africans don't throw Tarzan, Jane, and her family into a pit with a hungry ape (the climactic scene in *Tarzan, the Ape Man*, the Johnny Weissmuller/Maureen O'Sullivan 1932 version). Nonetheless, *Greystoke* is true to the Tarzan tradition of privileging the purportedly "civilizing" aspects of ape culture over the "uncivilized" ways of the Africans.

The producers of the 1981 film *Tarzan, the Ape Man* were committed to giving a different point of view to the familiar story. But they didn't choose to look at Tarzan through the eyes of the Africans. (Now, that would be an interesting premise for a movie.) Instead, they focused on his love interest in this softly pornographic exploration of the physical attraction that develops between the nubile Jane (Bo Derek) and the muscular, albeit chaste, white ape-man. Most of the film is dull cinematic foreplay designed to give some credibility to a plot that will bring the two together as lovers to cavort in the water with Cheetah. Kidnapped by a tribe of dirt-coated Africans, Jane is just about to be sacrificed when Tarzan commands the local elephants to stampede the evil Africans. In this Tarzan flick, as in many of the earlier ones, a pack of well-trained pachyderms, as well as the apes, triumph over the African humans. Jane's virginity becomes Tarzan's reward for having rescued her from the snares of the evil Africans.

In the final scene of the movie, it is clear that Jane and Tarzan have consummated their relationship. In a mildly erotic sequence, the two white humans frolic on the shore and allow Cheetah the chimp to participate in their sex play. Cheetah is allowed and encouraged to paw the bare-breasted Jane. It is difficult to imagine that a male African would have been permitted the liberties granted to Cheetah in this ostensibly wholesome menage à trois.

These two 1980s Tarzan films adhere to the taxonomy established by the earlier ones. The Tarzans, Janes, and other white upper-crust Europeans reign supreme. The animals, while sometimes shown as hostile, are ultimately depicted in a balanced fashion, worthy of the respect of and near-equal footing with the white humans. Whereas some animal death scenes are poignant enough to bring tears to the eyes of the sensitive viewer, no African characters are well developed enough to prompt such emotions. At the bottom of the totem pole we find the African peoples. Shown as savages or servants, they are depicted either as the intractable enemies of the white humans and the animals or as placid porters for the former.

White Africans

By examining the movies that get made about Africa, it is easy to
see that filmmakers are comfortable telling a finite number of stories.
The Tarzan formula worked so well that it has been told over forty
times. Makers of non-Tarzan African films also concentrate on the
experiences of whites in Africa. The list of white Hollywood stars who
have battled the elements to make movies in Africa is a long and
distinguished one—Katherine Hepburn, Humphrey Bogart, Meryl
Streep, Robert Redford, Kevin Kline, Donald Sutherland, Barbara
Hershey, Susan Sarandon, and Marlon Brando have all trekked to the
dark continent. Yet only a few well-known black actors—for example,
Denzel Washington, Morgan Freeman, and Whoopi Goldberg—have
been featured in films about Africa, and they rarely get top billing.
Most of the black actors featured in these films are unknowns—Linda
Mvusi, Zakes Mokae, John Omirah Miluwi. Now, there are two ways
to write a story about whites in Africa. The first, as seen in the Tarzan
series, is to write scripts in which European or American whites journey to Africa. The other, as this section will show, is to delve into the
lives of white Africans. And what better place to look for white Africans than the now-notorious nation of South Africa? In the past few
decades more commercial Hollywood films have been made about the
country of South Africa than have been produced about all of the
other nations of sub-Saharan Africa combined.

Dramatic potential abounds in the peoples and policies of South
Africa. Economic, social, and political power has resided with the
white minority population. Consisting of the descendants of English,
Dutch, German, and French colonizers, present-day whites still enjoy
an uneasy alliance. Likewise, the black majority is made up of members of various indigenous nations who don't always share the same
political philosophy. "Apartheid"—the name given for the code of
strict racial segregation in South Africa—has caught the attention of
the western world. By the mid-1970s American and European corporations, politicians, athletes, and college officials had been asked to
take sides. In the 1980s "divestment" gained a niche in many vocab-
ularies. Many individuals who had given little thought to South Africa

before were debating whether it was moral or wise to participate in any venture in which the white South African minority would directly or indirectly benefit. All of this attention was not lost on moviemakers. Stories about apartheid allow filmmakers to craft stories about contemporary individuals confronted by very tangible social injustice.

The movies on South Africa were preceded by books, and several of the filmmakers credit books on the country as their inspiration. Among the most successful of these books was *Biko*, published in 1978 by white South African journalist Donald Woods. Woods begins by giving the reader background on South Africa and then describes the history of South Africa's black activist tradition and how antiapartheid leader Bantu Stephen Biko rose to prominence. The book is a standard biography. The reader learns about Biko's family, his philosophy, and his political strategies. The latter half of the book focuses on Biko's arrest, his historic trial, and his subsequent incarceration. Biko dies as a result of horrific police brutality implicitly sanctioned by the white South African government. Woods, his wife, Wendy, and other antiapartheid activists succeed in forcing the government to hold an inquest. The book ends with Woods's searing indictment of the Nationalist government that then ruled his homeland. The success of *Biko* led Woods to pen a second book two years later entitled *Asking for Trouble: Autobiography of a Banned Journalist*. Here Woods, a fifth-generation South African, discusses his own life and the impact his relationship with Steve Biko had upon him and his family. A standard autobiography, Woods's family, philosophy, and political inclinations are the meat of this story. Detailing the escapades of the Woods family as they struggle to leave South Africa in order to get the first book published, this story has a strong adventure component.

Although movie producer Richard Attenborough identifies both books as sources for his 1987 film *Cry Freedom*, he clearly favors the autobiography of the white South African Donald Woods over the biography of black leader Steve Biko. One of the first clues comes from the billing given to the actors who play the roles in the movie. Top billing goes to Kevin Kline, the actor who portrays Donald Woods. Kline's name is followed by Penelope Winton's, the actress who portrays Donald's wife. Third place goes to Denzel Washington, the African-American actor who plays Steve Biko.

In many respects, *Cry Freedom* is a character study. The character being scrutinized is white newspaperman Donald Woods. At the beginning of the film he is seen as only partially sympathetic to the struggles of black South Africans. After meeting Biko and observing black life in the squalid townships firsthand, Woods's stance begins to change. At great risk to himself and his family, he becomes more and more involved in the struggle for freedom. Aside from the fact that he is alive at the beginning of the film and dead about a third of the way through it, Steve Biko changes hardly at all through the film. His character is stagnant. He is consistently wise, funny, and heroic. After Biko's death, the whole Woods family becomes more involved in the struggle. The audience rarely sees what life is like for Steve Biko's family. The day-to-day hardships that the black South African family endured are not chronicled. But the film shows Woods as he is confined to house arrest, as his children are mailed T-shirts laced with a severe irritant, as the family makes the decision to leave their beautiful home and possessions with very little money in order to make sure that Donald's biography of Steve will be published. Woods and his family embark on a treacherous journey across the nation in order to smuggle the manuscript out of the country. He and his family are the heroes of the film.

Apartheid's impact on whites is also the focus of *A World Apart* (1988). Once again audiences are given a view of one white South African family's ordeal as a result of the political convictions of its members. Like *Cry Freedom*, *A World Apart* is based on the lives of real individuals. The script was written by Shawn Slovo, whose mother, journalist Ruth First, was the first white South African imprisoned under the ninety-day detention act. Slovo was twelve when her mother's political activity disrupted their family's existence and caused the adolescent great personal pain as her friends ostracized her. To the bereft child, her parents' decision to disrupt their household in order to fight apartheid seemed inexplicably harsh.

In the introduction to the published version of the script for *A World Apart*, Shawn Slovo acknowledges, "Set against a backdrop of increasingly violent repression, it [the script] chronicles the effects of the break-up of the family. Above all, it is about the child's attempts to come to terms with the political choices her parents made."[4] Slovo had a hard time selling the story. Production companies balked at the idea of doing a period piece about South Africa (the film takes place in 1963) and were also hesitant because two other films were being made about apartheid. Apparently no one objected on the grounds that audiences might prefer to see a film about the impact of apartheid on a black South African family.

Shawn Slovo had every right to tell her story, and the film is quite compelling. But, like the other films on apartheid, the film tells the audience much more about the impact of white minority rule on whites than on blacks. The preference filmmakers have shown for the stories of white South African experiences should not be attributed to a lack of good stories by and about blacks. Black South African writer Mark Mathabane's autobiography, *Kaffir Boy*, offers an excellent study of the impact of apartheid on a young black and his family. Although the film rights to the book have been purchased by Harpo Productions (Oprah Winfrey's company), at the time of this writing no movie version has been started.

Only one black director has been able to make a major film about South Africa. And even *A Dry White Season* (1989) focuses more on whites in South Africa than on blacks. It was directed by Euzhan Palcy, a Martinique-born director whose *Sugar Cane Alley* (1984) was a shining example of a deftly told story from the black point of view. But Palcy was unable to secure the kind of financing needed to make a film about South Africa from that point of view. As she says, "It's a hell of a problem to get a film made with black characters in Hollywood. I had a story with black characters but nobody would produce that, so if I wanted to make a film about apartheid, I had to find another solution."[5] Palcy adapted a novel by Afrikaans author Andre Brink. She assembled a stellar cast, including Donald Sutherland, Susan Sarandon, and, in a quasi-cameo appearance, Marlon Brando. Once again the black actors do not receive top billing. The film foregrounds the story of white school teacher Ben du Toit who opposes the South African government only after a gardener and his son are killed in the aftermath of the 1976 Soweto uprisings.

A prominent subplot, at least by apartheid film standards, concentrates on the life of the gardener and his family. Palcy allows the audience to see the Ngubenes' home and to get to know the members of the family. The father, Gordon (Winston Ntshona), is not an educated, articulate antiapartheid activist. Because the movie allows him a greater range of emotion, he is in many ways a much more interesting character than *Cry Freedom*'s Steve Biko. He is a father, trying to make the best life possible for his family. His struggle with government begins when he asks simple questions about his son's death in prison and the disposition of the corpse. He, too, dies at the hands of his captors. Because she is now a widow, his wife, Emily (Thoko Ntshinga), is forcibly removed from her home and transported to a "homeland" to which she has no affiliation. By telling the Ngubenes' story, Palcy has given the audience a rare chance to develop a relationship with black South African characters—to see, albeit briefly, the devastating impact of apartheid on the rank-and-file black South African.

The du Toit family disintegrates as a result of the father and his son's involvement with the Ngubenes. Ben's wife and daughter aren't moved by the fate of a "kaffir" gardener and his family. Indeed, these female characters are so self-centered, the audience will likely perceive Ben and his son as better off without them. Near the end of the film Ben du Toit is killed by the law enforcement officer who has been responsible for so much of the Ngubenes' pain. Not long after that, the black lawyer (Zakes Mokae) who has tried to struggle within the system for change shoots du Toit's killer. Palcy allows a black character to make the film's final statement.

The producers of *The Power of One* (1992) pull out all of the stops in their efforts to generate sympathy for the young white English hero. As the film unfolds, the audience sees that the child's father has died a few months before his son is born. The child, known as PK, is sent to a pro-Nazi boarding school where both teachers and classmates torment him. After the boy develops a bedwetting problem (due perhaps to his classmates' propensity to urinate on him at regular intervals), his mother dies. A charming and talented grandfather shows up, but he is sent to prison. While visiting his grandfather in prison, the boy is befriended by a black inmate, Pete (Morgan Freeman), who teaches him to box. At Pete's request, PK teaches the inmates to sing. On the night of the big concert, a guard beats Pete to death. After his release from prison, PK's grandfather leaves him to return to Europe. PK's boxing coach is beaten up by the police and carted off to jail. PK falls in love with a beautiful young woman who comes to share his liberal views about teaching black Africans to read. The girl is killed when police catch them teaching in a church. The misfortunes of no African in the movie can possibly compete with those endured by PK.

In spite of the fact that individuals to whom PK becomes attached keep dying or being sent to jail, he has a knack for inspiring awe in blacks wherever he goes. His nanny nurses him before she takes her own child to her breast. The inmates give him the nickname "Rain-maker" after a mythological character who is purported to have the power to bring all of the African tribes together. When he begins to pursue boxing, an African youth seeks him out for a match in Alexandria. After PK knocks the youth out in front of the entire township, the youth gets up and embraces his blond competitor and encourages the eager crowd to cheer for him. The two become buddies, and the black youth urges him to decline a full scholarship to Oxford University in order to travel surreptitiously from township to township teaching the blacks to read and write.

The Power of One gives the audience the impression that South Africa consists of two kinds of whites: the noble English and the dastardly German. The former are all in favor of racial equality, but the latter are completely opposed. Recognizing them as saviors, the black Africans worship the good English South Africans and solicit their help in fighting back against the oppressive regime established by the pro-Nazi majority.

There is a perverse irony in the fact that the films that get made about South Africa have emphasized the struggles of whites. The only good apartheid stories—the only ones worth telling, according to Hollywood—are the ones that foreground the heroism of the whites who confront the system. Most of the films are intended to be critiques of apartheid and a system of government that oppresses the black majority population. However, in their efforts to tell the story of black oppression, western filmmakers have indulged in cinematic apartheid. Just as they are in South Africa, the voices of blacks are silenced in the story of their country.

African Queens

Filmmakers have showed a particular fondness for films that juxtapose white women against Africa and its inhabitants, human and animal. This trend may have been inspired by the success and popularity of John Huston's *The African Queen* (1951). Never has the continent of Africa been more successfully used as a background for the concerns of nonnative peoples than in this classic movie starring Katherine Hepburn and Humphrey Bogart. "Africa" is important to the film only in so far as it presents challenges for the characters to overcome.[6] The filmmakers include precious few reminders that the indigenous peoples might have cared very little about trading their British colonizers for German ones.

Set in World War I, it is the saga of the Englishwoman Rose Sayer, the Canadian Charlie Allnutt, and their trusty vessel, the *African Queen*. In their pursuit of the German enemy, the unlikely two are forced to tackle African nature in the form of a rough river, slimy leeches, and swarms of mosquitoes. The film is appealing because the inept missionary woman and the slovenly machinist find love while waging their Davidian attack on the German Goliath. Neither African peoples nor African animals play any real role in their adventure.

The African Queen contains a scene familiar to anyone who has watched more than a couple of films set in Africa with British men and women as characters. I call it the obligatory fine-dining-in-the-jungle scene. In the middle of the African interior, British characters, in this case Miss Rose Sayer and her brother, the Reverend Sayer, have tea with all of the lavish trappings of an English countryside manor. No detail of this social ritual is omitted. No apparent concessions are made to the uniqueness of the environment. In *The African Queen* the scene sets up the enormous gulf between Charlie Allnutt and Miss Rose Sayer. She is dressed impeccably in one of those omnipresent white cotton high-necked outfits that English women of that era were born to wear. She conducts the tea ritual with confidence and, like a good hostess, remembers how Mr. Allnutt has taken his tea on past visits. He, on the other hand, is clearly ill at ease. His clothes are soiled, and his unseemly stomach churnings serenade the threesome. He makes no secret of the fact that his usual daily libations are of the alcoholic variety. As Rose and Charlie embark on their adventure and begin to fall in love, the compromises they make in their beverage consumption signals the growing warmth between them. Charlie eventually forgives Rosie for throwing all of his gin overboard and joins her in drinking tea, which she must get used to drinking from a plain mug after the water has been heated on the ship's stove.

The film's title ostensibly refers to the clunky but intrepid vessel that is eventually sacrificed to destroy a marauding German warship.

Yet the title could be construed as having a double meaning. Rose Sayer is the character who exercises the most control over the situation at hand. The indefatigable white spinster learns to navigate the boat over the rough waters and devises the plan to transform the innocent ship into a deadly torpedo. Her influence inspires Charlie to shake an obviously long-term drinking problem and renews his flagging self-esteem. In short, she too is depicted as an African queen.

Perhaps moviemakers are compelled to tell stories of white women as authority figures in Africa because such power is permissible only outside of the white male–dominated western world. No other fictional treatment of World War I offers the possibility of a woman engineering a successful military maneuver. In films set in Africa, white women can be shown with much more autonomy than is usually afforded them. Of course, they need something to exercise their authority over. In the films that followed *The African Queen*, it is African people who must succumb to the will of these white mistresses.

Although *The African Queen* is based on a novel by C. S. Forester, the really provocative books to consider in light of it are those that were inspired by the making of the film. Indeed the first of these, Peter Viertel's *White Hunter, Black Heart*, was itself made into a film directed by and starring Clint Eastwood. First published in 1953, the text of the book is preceded by the standard disclaimer: "The characters and the incidents in this book are entirely the product of the author's imagination and have no relation to any person or event in real life." But Viertel was clearly motivated by his experiences as a screenwriter on location in Africa with the cast and crew of *The African Queen*. Viertel's protagonist is a self-centered, hard-drinking, contentious, talented movie director who chooses to direct a film in Africa because he wants a chance to shoot an elephant. John Huston, director of *The African Queen*, was a self-centered, hard-drinking, contentious, talented movie director whose desire to hunt was at least equal to his desire to make the film. Because they focus on the behind-the-scenes world of making a Hollywood movie about Africa, the novel and the film provide unique glimpses of the concerns that shape the image of Africa on screen. Although the director in Viertel's book is depicted as more interested in the lives of the Africans who will serve as extras in the film, his utter selfishness results in the death of the African who has served as his scout. In the film version, East-

wood adds a chilling touch to the ending. After returning from the
hunt that has resulted in Kivu's death, the director does not go over to
the man's family. Instead, he walks to the director's chair and begins
to shoot a scene obviously meant to evoke *The African Queen.* The
individual who had claimed to want to do justice to the African people refuses to accept accountability for the life that has been lost on
his behalf.

In her 1987 memoir *The Making of the African Queen: Or How I
Went to Africa with Bogart, Bacall and Huston and Almost Lost My
Mind*, Katherine Hepburn offers only a few clues about the ways in
which the filmmakers perceived the Africans. After describing the
devotion to her showed by her personal servant, Tahili, Hepburn concludes:

> It is hard to say anything about the natives and whether they
> work hard and how they were treated and what was their
> situation here or there. It goes from good to bad. As we go—
> they go. There are tremendous problems of which we have not
> the vaguest comprehension. Then or now. A real lack of
> education is a tough thing to combat. And the country is so big
> and transportation is so difficult. It's tough too on the whites
> who moved out there to supposedly earn a fortune on coffee.
> They had paid a tremendous price and lost. The country is like
> a great sponge—it finally absorbs you. Eventually you will get
> malaria or you will get dysentery and whatever you do, if you
> don't keep doing it, the jungle will grow over you. Black or
> white, you've got to fight it every minute of the day.[7]

Hepburn never questions the legitimacy of the imperialistic regime
that wrested the land from Tahili and his people and placed it in the
hands of the white coffee growers. To her, the problems of the colonizers and the colonized were comparable.

Produced thirty-four years after *The African Queen*, *Out of Africa*
(1985) documents the life of individuals who did come to make their
fortune in coffee. Focusing on a woman who is eager to embrace the
privileges of royalty, it too testifies to the sacredness of European
accoutrements for foods and beverages. As the soon to be Baroness
Karen Blixen, aka Isak Dinesen (Meryl Streep), arrives from Denmark, she chastises the first African she meets for haphazardly han-

dling the boxes that contain her precious crystal and Limoges china. Throughout the first two-thirds of the film, her conspicuous attitudes of superiority are foregrounded. One favorite house servant is forced to wear gloves when handling her things. She repeatedly refers to the local population as "my Kikuyu." In defending her decision to build a school on the plantation, she describes them all as children.

On the other hand, her lover, Denys Finch-Hatton (Robert Redford), is depicted as an exemplar of a nonpatronizing, egalitarian white European. Whereas she patronizes the Kikuyu, he has earned the respect of the much feared Masai. His gentle jabs at Blixen's expense remind the viewer that he is the character most sensitive to the conditions of life for the Africans. Yet, like so many other whites depicted in African films, he has no problem employing large numbers of Africans to tote the niceties of western living about for him. When he and Blixen make a trip in search of safari locales, they bring with them, among other things, an enormous gramophone so that their evening meals can be followed by dancing. African servants haul all of these encumbrances about for them. Finch-Hatton's hypocrisy is much more evident in his speechlessness when he learns that his longtime partner and close friend has kept a Somali woman as a lover for many years. Nonetheless, the clear message of the film is that Finch-Hatton's relationship with the Africans was a praiseworthy one. The Masai stand respectfully at his funeral, and in a voice-over Blixen claims to have heard that his grave has become a resting spot for a lion and lioness.

The baroness's absorption with material things is one of the obstacles she supposedly overcomes in the film. At the end she must face two unpleasant tasks. First, she must part with virtually all of the possessions she has accumulated over the years. She is remarkably indifferent as she witnesses the elaborate tag sale where her white neighbors purchase her once-indispensable belongings. Her other task is to try to insure that the African workers who have served her can remain together after she leaves Africa. In a dramatic scene, she humbles herself by dropping to her knees in the presence of the new colonial governor who has the power to tell the Kikuyu where they can or cannot live. Touched by Blixen's willingness to humiliate herself to speak for these natives, the governor's wife assures her that her request will be honored. The audience then is supposed to conclude that Blixen's values have shifted, that she has come to understand

that men and women are more important than flatware and champagne glasses. The viewer can walk away from the film knowing that
she took care of *"her* Kikuyu." This act is intended to minimize her
role in the perpetuation of colonial oppression and, indeed, give the
audience the impression that she is on the side of the Africans.

Out of Africa's treatment of Africans and animals is somewhat
more complex than the films in the Tarzan compendium. Clearly the
white Danish and English characters are intended to be perceived as
civilization personified. Animals and Africans in the film represent
tests to their western-style humanity. Blixen's maturation in the film
is linked to the increase in sensitivity she shows to the plight of "her
Kikuyu" and the other African peoples (Somali, Masai) with whom
she has contact. The Kikuyu make up the large labor force that will
raise coffee on her plantation. Since her philandering husband wants
to avoid all responsibility for the success of this endeavor, she is the
one who must negotiate with the "natives." The female Danish aristo-
crat encounters no real problems in convincing the Kikuyu to follow
her instructions. The umbrella-toting Kikuyu chief willingly grants
permission for his tribespeople to work for this African queen. Language and vocational training problems are minimal. Their reverence
for her is apparent at many junctures in the film. Several scenes show
her favored house servant in Africa replacing fresh flowers in a vase
on her dressing table while she is in Denmark trying to conquer the
syphilis she has contracted from her husband. Legions of loyal workers greet her as she returns to the plantation. The filmmakers send the
message that since these Kikuyu people clearly appreciated her, the
audience should not question the validity of the colonial occupation of
African lands.

As a result of the need to depict Finch-Hatton and Blixen in a
positive light, the Africans in *Out of Africa* are infanticized. They pose
no threat to the goals of the whites who are capriciously colonizing
Kenya. When the white men leave for war, Blixen shrugs off the
possibility that the native men might attempt to take sexual advantage of the white women who are left behind. When she undertakes
her trek to bring supplies to the white men at the front, she travels
with African men and puts her sleeping bag adjacent to theirs in front
of the campfire. By depicting her as a courageous, all-knowing, maternal, dominant figure whenever she is in the company of Africans,
the film emasculates the African men.

Although the film gives the impression that the Africans offered very little resistance to white attempts to domesticate them, it celebrates the freedom and majesty of the wildlife. Finch-Hatton refuses to shoot the lion that Blixen stumbles upon in the brush. The sequences devoted to their safarilike vacation are punctuated with captivating scenes of herds of animals traversing open spaces. The white government eventually enforces regulations that will prohibit white hunters from pursuing the elephant's ivory tusks, presumably in an effort to forestall the senseless deaths of these animals. But the same government originally refuses to take seriously Blixen's request that the Kikuyu, the original inhabitants of the land, be allowed to remain together on a choice piece.

The filmmakers could easily defend the great white father and mother posture assumed in *Out of Africa* by claiming that they were in fact working with biographies and autobiographies of real people, Denys Finch-Hatton and Isak Dinesen (Karen Blixen), and that the film was merely reporting their interpretation of childlike Africans.

The reality angle of the recently published accounts of Dinesen and Finch-Hatton's lives are the ones that attracted filmmakers to them in the first place. The "right" kinds of films about Africa are based on stories with well-meaning white heroes and heroines, complacent African natives, and a few wild animals thrown in for sport. Filmmakers looking for viable projects identify those that conform to their western expectations about what a "good" story about Africa is. They have not, for example, been attracted to the stories of African colonialism told from the point of view of the Africans, such as Chinua Achebe's remarkable novel, *Things Fall Apart*.

Africans in the Mist

Just as filmmakers had long been eager to bring the right story of Isak Dinesen's African sojourn to the big screen, so was there great enthusiasm in the filmmaking community for making the autobiography of primatologist Dian Fossey into a movie. With an endangered primate species, merciless poachers, a love affair abandoned in favor of a gorilla census, and a devoted heroine who is killed for protecting animals, Fossey's life and death contained most of the narrative components needed to create a satisfying modern screen tale of a noble

white member of the "weaker sex" versus the heathen morals and
mores of postcolonial Africans. The filmmakers could easily manipulate those elements not present in Fossey's and others' accounts of her
life in order to shape a story suitable for mass consumption.

In writing her memoirs, Fossey, like all people motivated to assume the posture of autobiographer, had an agenda. She had a story
of her life in Zaire and Rwanda she felt compelled to share. I will not
argue that her story is the right or truthful one against which the film
version should be judged. Nonetheless, it seems reasonable to assume
that her autobiography and other texts about her can be used as a
partial basis from which the veracity of certain aspects of the film can
be evaluated. Attracted to Dinesen's story because it conformed to
and reinforced prevailing romantic notions about Africa, filmmakers
were seduced by Fossey's story because it also conjured familiar African vistas as seen through western eyes.

Gorillas in the Mist (1988) features Sigourney Weaver as Fossey,
the headstrong self-taught primatologist, and the film is told from her
point of view. Anyone who has read Fossey's autobiography or any of
the other accounts of her experiences will immediately recognize some
of the liberties the filmmakers take. Some are apparently an attempt
to simplify the complexities of real life in order to move the story in
the film. The movie collapses Fossey's initial relationship with Louis
B. Leakey, her mentor, into a couple of scenes. These sequences leave
the viewer with the false impression that after showing up late for one
of Leakey's fund-raising lectures, Fossey charmed the elder scientist
into sponsoring her, a woman lacking prior experience with animals
or Africa, to count gorillas at the top of a mountain in the Congo. In
the next scene Leakey meets her at the African airport, marginally
oversees the outfitting of her expedition, and sends her off with un-
tested African porters. From the filmmakers' perspective, these short
scenes get the Fossey character to the primary setting of the film (the
mountain) and establish her headstrong character along with
Leakey's self-righteous pomposity. In reality, Fossey had visited Africa and had preliminary exposure to the area in which she would be
working. Her relationship with Leakey was cultivated over several
encounters prior to her decision to conduct the census. She had published papers about gorillas that he respected. In her autobiography,
Fossey shares an anecdote that is only alluded to on screen but certainly reveals a great deal about her character and Leakey's. After

suggesting that she is the right person to conduct the gorilla census (contrary to the view presented in the film), Leakey tells her she should have her appendix removed before living on an African mountain. After the operation she learns that this was his way of testing the commitment of his disciples.

This kind of distortion of real life is not uncommon in Hollywood productions. One could make the case that such alterations don't significantly undermine the audience's understanding of the motives of Leakey and Fossey. In both the film and the autobiography, Fossey emerges as an individual nearly oblivious to personal inconvenience, and Leakey is portrayed as an almost sadistic authoritarian personality. In shaping Fossey's life for the screen, the filmmakers seem to develop their narrative by omitting those aspects of her life and experience that might distract the viewer from her all-consuming devotion to the mountain gorilla. The film gives the distinct impression that Fossey never left the mountain and its outlying areas after her arrival in 1967. It also suggests that she was thoroughly dissatisfied with the commitment of the students who came to do their research at Karisoke. In reality, she did travel out of Africa from time to time, to complete doctorate work and to raise money for the Digit Fund—a charity she established after the slaughter of her beloved gorilla. Numerous students eventually worked with Fossey at the national park. Although she was apparently quite difficult to work with, her autobiography does acknowledge the efforts of her preferred students.

In *Primate Visions*, Donna Haraway discusses Fossey as one of a sometimes competitive group of white female primatologists prominent in the discipline since the 1960s. In the same chapter she includes a picture from one of the early Tarzan movies. Featuring a provocative nuclear family consisting of Tarzan, Jane, Boy, and Cheetah, the photograph raises an interesting question.[8] Did Fossey and perhaps some of her white female colleagues develop their insensitivity to the plight of the Africans who came to rely on poaching income in part from the jungle movies they had seen in their youth? Did the camera's love affair with primates inspire their own?[9] Did the fact that most of the Africans in these films were rendered more animalistically than the real animals generate indifference to the human needs of the Africans they came to know? In her autobiography Fossey has an incredible way of minimizing the concerns of the Africans who live in Zaire and Rwanda in order to focus all attention on the gorillas.

After noting that Rwanda is both one of the world's most densely populated countries and one of its five poorest, Fossey condemns the minister of agriculture for considering a plan that might alleviate some of the food shortages because it would remove some of the acreage set aside for her precious gorillas.[10] Throughout the book it is painfully apparent that to Fossey, the mountain gorillas' survival is more important than the African humans'. Although her autobiography barely disguises her preference for Africa's animal population over human, she does at least tacitly acknowledge some of the concerns of the African populations with whom she has the most contact.

In transforming Fossey's written narrative into a film, the makers of *Gorillas* handily eclipse any genuine discussion of the African peoples and offer precious little insight into *their* point of view on Fossey's conservation mission. The first Africans the viewers see are semiclad children who swarm around after her arrival in order to beg her for a handout. Like all good film whites in Africa, Fossey requires a large number of Africans to work for her. Unlike Dinesen, she does not need them to carry household niceties and a designer wardrobe; her assignment to conduct a gorilla census necessitates porters to carry prodigious parcels of equipment. Fortunately for Fossey, whose Swahili is weak, one man knows English. (In these movies there is always one African who knows English as well as most of the African languages his white employer will need translated.) Together they hire enough porters to carry her equipment to the mountain where they will establish a campsite. The audience and Fossey soon learn that a civil war is in progress. When Leakey glosses over this news, Fossey doesn't concern herself with it. Eager to begin counting gorillas, she decides that the concerns of the Congolese people are insignificant. Having introduced the audience to the African conflict, the movie returns to its primary subject—Fossey and the gorillas.

In an early scene after she has settled into her first camp, Fossey politely queries her English-speaking tracker about his family. After he responds that his family and indeed his entire tribe was killed while he was tracking, she has no further comment. When the man leaves her tent, she returns to her study of George Schaller's book on the mountain gorilla. Once again an issue of interest to the Africans is introduced, only to be swept out of the tent in favor of primate study.

Eventually Fossey is forced to confront local politics when one military group forcibly evicts her from her campsite. Now the war that has set blacks against each other represents an inconvenience for a white scientist, an obstacle to the successful completion of the gorilla census. The audience isn't burdened with any details about the motives of the Africans.

Much like Blixen's Kikuyu, Fossey's Africans fall into two categories. Those like the porters and camp staff she employs are acceptable because they (usually) do her bidding. Bad Africans are those like the Watusi tribesmen who profit from poaching or the Rwandan civil servants who let them get away with it. Unlike Blixen, Fossey doesn't even bother to coddle the Africans who work for her. The gorillas will be accorded the range of her feminine impulses. Since a significant part of her study is devoted to the familial impulses of the primates, much cinematic attention is given to the gorillas as family members. She sees, and therefore the audience sees, the Africans in clusters, such as hungry children, porters, camp workers, and poachers. The Africans, in contrast to the gorillas, are never shown as members of family units.

An important component of the films that place white women in African environments is the presence of a suitable white male companion or lover. No white African queen is left unattached for very long. After her brother's death, Rose Sayer's relationship with Charlie Allnutt commences. After kicking out her philandering husband, Karen Blixen is wooed by Denys Finch-Hatton. Although Dian Fossey's autobiography does not refer to any romantic relationships, the film seeks to give the heroine a series of suitable mates. On her first evening at the campsite, her chief tracker, Sembagare, queries her about the photograph of a handsome man that is next to her bed. Presumably that engagement is called off when she decides to stay in Africa indefinitely. Since no good film about Africa would be complete without some kind of love story between the white human characters, the film adds a dimension to her relationship with *National Geographic* photographer Bob Campbell that her autobiography leaves unmentioned. After he tries to convince her to spend at least part of the year away from the mountaintop, her devotion to the gorillas, not to the Africans, leads her to terminate their relationship. After their relationship ends, Fossey's attachment to the gorillas intensifies. Just as the apes become baby Tarzan's surrogate family, the gorillas function in a similar fashion for Fossey.

As depicted in the film, the relationship between Fossey and the gorillas is saturated with familial and sexual tension. In scenes almost reminiscent of the closing ones in *Tarzan, the Ape Man*, featuring the nubile Bo Derek and Cheetah, a fully clothed Fossey repeatedly permits the gorillas to climb all over her in a fashion that surely would have been forbidden to any of her African staff members—even the loyalist ones. After her favorite gorilla, Digit, is slaughtered, she goes on a rampage, destroying the poachers' enclave. In the film's final scene an uncharacteristically mellow Fossey with what could be described as a postcoital glow smokes a cigarette and caresses old photographs of Digit immediately before the machete-toting murderer kills her. After her body is buried next to Digit's, Sembagare removes the stones that separate their graves. The viewer knows that Fossey wouldn't have wanted it any other way.

Dian Fossey is usually considered to have been the single most important human force in preventing the extinction of the mountain gorilla species. The conservation of all animal species endangered by human folly is essential to the well-being of the human population. This analysis is not intended to minimize the importance of her tireless efforts and sacrifice. It is a story that merits telling. Because it contains the acceptable components of stories about Africa, it was told.

Hollywood Films/African Reality

In Viertel's *White Hunter, Black Heart*, the screenwriter and the director argue over whether to change the end of the book their movie is taken from in order to create a happier ending. The director wants to stick with the original pessimistic one. The screenwriter fears that such an ending will spell doom for the picture. "Movies aren't like literature," he says, "nor are they like music. They're theatre, and theatre has to play to the people that are currently alive."[11] Perhaps this exchange partially explains why commercial filmmakers insist on changing so many of the books on which they base their films on Africa. Moviemakers are extraordinarily preoccupied with molding projects guaranteed "to play to the people." It is much easier and safer to fashion a film that reinforces the conventional stereotypes about Africa than to risk box office failure by stimulating audience discomfort.

The implications of a persistent Hollywood vision that projects Africans in such a tightly constrained fashion are difficult to measure. Most Africans one meets in the United States can recite a litany of stories about the misunderstandings with which westerners greet them. Many of my African students report that American students are eager to hear about life in the jungle amid the vine-covered trees and treacherous animals. The stories of real African life disappoint those who have misspent their Saturday afternoons watching the celluloid Tarzan. If brought to the screen, however, the stories of real African life might better equip Americans to understand this part of the globe. If the cameras of Hollywood swathed African families with the same warmth and dignity that they afford the landscape and primates, we might be better world neighbors.

12

From Homer to Hoke: A Small Step for African-American Mankind

Hollywood as a rule still doesn't want to portray us as any-thing but butlers, chauffeurs, gardeners or maids.

—SIDNEY POITIER, 1951[1]

In the early 1960s motion picture director Ralph Nelson decided to make a movie out of William E. Barrett's short novel *Lilies of the Field.* He imagined that the talented young Sidney Poitier would be perfectly suited for the lead role of Homer Smith. For the role of the German refugee Mother Superior, he cast a little-known former Viennese stage star, Lilia Scala. Poitier was quite well known at the time. The West Indian–born actor had made a name for himself in films such as *The Defiant Ones, Blackboard Jungle,* and *A Raisin in the Sun.* Nonetheless, Nelson faced enormous obstacles in getting the film financed. A feature film depicting the relationship between an itinerant black carpenter and an order of German nuns was unorthodox, to say the least. After much hesitation, United Artists finally agreed to produce the film. However, Nelson was forced to shoot the film in fourteen and a half days or pay the overtime charges himself. Poitier and the scriptwriter were forced to work for a fraction of their usual salaries and a promise of a percentage of the profits, and the cast and crew worked for minimum wage.[2] The film, of course, was a smashing box office success, and Poitier's performance garnered him the first and only Academy Award ever bestowed upon a black male actor in the top category.

Nearly thirty years later the accomplished team of Richard D. Zanuck and Lili Fini Zanuck wanted to adapt Albert Uhry's popular play *Driving Miss Daisy* to the big screen. For the role of the obstinate Jewish matron, they cast veteran stage and screen actress Jessica Tandy. And in the role of the chauffeur whom she reluctantly admits into her life, they cast Morgan Freeman. In spite of the success of the play and the renown of the actors, the Zanucks faced the same kind of obstacles Nelson had faced in securing financial backing for *Lilies*. Hollywood insiders didn't believe that audiences would support a film about the relationship between a dignified black driver and an aging white woman who needed his professional services more than she cared to admit. It's too bad the Zanucks did not merely remind their prospective financiers of the success of *Lilies*. After all, the two films are fundamentally the same story. In this chapter I explore the common foundation that undergirds these two films. First, I continue to explore the similar circumstances that surrounded the production of the films. A discussion of similarities in the characters, plots, subplots, and symbolism of the two films follows. And finally, the chapter notes the similar ways in which audiences and critics responded to the two films. By identifying the host of similarities between *Lilies of the Field* and *Driving Miss Daisy*, we can better understand the subtitle of this chapter—why the second film represents how little progress black actors have made in Hollywood between the early 1960s and the late 1980s.

The Making of *Lilies* and *Daisy*: Steve McQueen and Eddie Murphy?

The year 1963 was an important one in the history of race relations in the United States. As film historian Edward Mapp points out, it was the year of the march on Washington, the assassinations of Medgar Evers and John F. Kennedy, and the bombing of a Baptist church in Birmingham, which resulted in the deaths of four black children.[3] Although African Americans were assuming prominence and visibility in other venues in the nation, the film industry was sluggish and only marginally committed to expanding the possible characterizations it had established for its black members. The black community in and out of Hollywood was committed to aggressively pursuing more roles for blacks in front of and behind the cameras. The Los Angeles NAACP chapter was persistent in its efforts to secure the support of the motion picture industry. Several conflicts resulted after particular films were released. The NAACP protested the Darryl F. Zanuck film *The Longest Day* because it did not show any involvement by black soldiers in the D-Day assault on Normandy. After first arguing that blacks were not involved, the producers were forced to confront evidence supplied by the army's chief of military history that blacks did participate in the assault.[4] The producer of *Kisses for My President* patted himself on the back for risking the wrath of southern movie-goers by including a scene in which Polly Bergen in her role as first female president shakes the hands of several black actors playing members of the White House domestic staff.[5] In spite of the NAACP's diligent attempts, Hollywood did not respond with any real enthusiasm for casting blacks in prominent roles. Mapp counts only ten American-made motion pictures in 1963 that feature any Negro characters, and most of these were in minor roles exemplifying the familiar stereotypical niches into which black actors had been pigeonholed.[6]

Lilies of the Field was going to be different. Homer Smith defied most of the standard conventions about African-American men familiar to audiences in the 1960s. In explaining the reluctance of the movie industry to finance the film, Ralph Nelson recalled, "It wasn't a provocative title, it wasn't suggestive, it promised neither sex nor violence."[7] While Homer's race was not particularly significant in the novel, Sidney Poitier's race was a liability in gaining support for the film. In recounting some of the challenges he faced, Nelson noted that one colleague suggested he cast Steve McQueen as Homer Smith and turn the Mother Superior character into a novice who had not yet taken her final vows. After negotiating a seemingly inexhaustible list of compromises, Nelson was finally able to secure enough support to get the film made with a black man in the lead role.

Just as Nelson had become entranced by William E. Barrett's novella *Lilies of the Field* in the early 1960s, the Zanucks became enamored of Albert Uhry's play *Driving Miss Daisy* in the mid-1980s. Although nearly thirty years had passed, they had to face an environment still struggling over issues of black representation on screen. Controversies over the limited range of opportunities for black actors in Hollywood were still commonplace. No black actor had received an Academy Award since Poitier, and blacks were still considered box office liabilities. Black filmmaker Spike Lee's *Do the Right Thing* certainly inspired the most heated debates about black images on screen in the 1989 film season (see Chapter 5). Lee's depiction of the events that culminate in a race riot on a hot summer day was so devastating that some movie critics and Hollywood insiders predicted that the film would trigger genuine racial unrest in inner-city locales. *Glory*, like *Driving*, another film featuring Morgan Freeman, was applauded by white critics but lamented by blacks, who recognized the numerous historical flaws contained in the purported story of the role of black soldiers in the Civil War (see Chapter 10).[8]

Raising the funds for a movie with an African-American character in a prominent role was nearly as difficult in the late 1980s as it had been in the early 1960s. Richard and Lili Fini Zanuck were not struggling unknowns when they began to seek money for this project. They had been responsible for box office smashes such as *Jaws* and *Cocoon*. But even after Uhry's play won a Pulitzer Prize they could attract no financial supporters for the project. Their original budget of $12.5 million was not particularly extravagant for a film in the late 1980s. Nevertheless, they were eventually forced to pare it down to $7.5 million. Although they had made commitments to Freeman and Tandy early in the process of putting the project together, their colleagues in the film industry urged them to consider more commercial casting possibilities. "Everywhere we went, we heard the same thing: Look it's going to be a wonderful picture and maybe win an award or two. But who's going to see it? One studio executive asked us, 'Are you locked into that cast? Maybe we could put somebody with more marquee in there. Hey, what about Eddie Murphy?' "[9] After a British investor agreed to commit $3.25 million, Warner Brothers agreed to supply $4.5 million. By the time of the 1990 Academy Award ceremonies, the film had earned over $70 million.

From Homer to Hoke

Indeed, African-American male actors eager to earn an Academy Award nomination would be well advised to commission screenplays in which they portray benevolent, warm, working-class men who go to work for aging, self-righteous, tough-minded white women who can't drive. It also might help to have the name of a flower in the title. Although Morgan Freeman was not driven away from the 1989 awards ceremony with a statuette in the Best Actor category, he was considered a front-runner for his performance in this film. While *Lilies of the Field* and *Driving Miss Daisy* were made over a quarter of a century apart, the common denominators that link them reveal a very clear picture of the type of performance and the type of story that the Academy of Motion Pictures Arts and Sciences deems praiseworthy for its African-American leading men.

The films have much more in common than the circumstances surrounding their development, the characters' first names (Homer and Hoke), and their ethnic/racial identities. At the story level both films feature celibate heroes—lone African-American men—who, after passing minor tests, advance to positions in which they are expected to fulfill the desires of older, chaste, white women. In both films one party is particularly reluctant to enter into what is at first intended as an employer/employee situation (although it evolves into a much more personal, yet always platonic, relationship). The eager character must seduce the reluctant one into grudging participation. The action of the films stems from events and encounters that cement the relationships. In both films the explicitly nonsexual union that forms between the men and women is contradicted on a symbolic plane where courtship and coupling are strongly implied.

In *Lilies of the Field*, Poitier plays a multitalented, itinerant carpenter whose 1959 Plymouth Suburban temporarily fails him in the arid domain of a group of German immigrant nuns in Arizona. Led by a Mother Superior whose marriage to her God is so strong that she refuses to even say thank you to a mortal man, the sisters ask Homer to repair a leaky roof. Satisfied with his execution of this simple task, they then approach him about erecting a chapel for the impoverished

Catholic population. Although he seems unimpressed by their limited financial resources, meager food supply, and gruff leader, Smith allows them to shepherd him into their fold. In *Driving Miss Daisy*, Freeman plays an illiterate chauffeur, Hoke Colburn, who is hired to prevent an aging Jewish widow from hurting herself and the expensive cars her doting son selects for her. Hoke's test comes as he enters her son's warehouse to apply for the chauffeur's position. Work in the factory has come to a standstill because a man and a shipment of goods have become trapped in a stalled elevator. Hoke assesses the situation and tells the trapped worker how to free himself and the boss's valuable cargo. Impressed by the black man's know-how, Miss Daisy's son Boolie Werthan (Dan Akroyd) offers him the job in spite of his mother's stubborn refusal to acknowledge that her deteriorating driving skills pose a real hazard to the pedestrians and vehicles of Atlanta, Georgia.

Confrontations with prejudice and antiethnic biases strengthen the relationships between the two films' main characters. Homer and Hoke, both men of impressive stature, have to cope with white men who refer to them as "boy." These white men represent the "other"— the ambiguously defined white majority—in the films. In *Lilies*, the white Mr. Ashton, owner of the lumberyard, makes disparaging remarks about the German nuns to Homer and racist comments about the black handyman to the nuns. Disturbed by Ashton's assumption that a "boy" lacked the skills to be a chapel contractor, Homer sets out to prove him wrong. Recognizing a solidarity in their second-class status, Homer decides to build the nuns their chapel. He also asks the man who called him boy for a part-time job by saying "I understand. Hey, boy? You need a good man?" He then proves his "manliness" to Ashton by going to work for him.

The ubiquitous "boy" label is also leveled at the even more mature Hoke. When he and Miss Daisy share a picnic lunch en route to a remote birthday party, stereotypical white Southern patrolmen spoil their comfortable sojourn by querying the chauffeur about his access to the expensive car. Unimpressed by her Jewish name, they are only moderately less rude to Miss Daisy. After she and Hoke return to the highway, one officer comments to the other, "An old Jew woman and an old nigger taking off down the road together. What a sorry sight."

The ethnics-versus-whites subtext that emerges in the films

makes the leading nonblack characters allies of Homer and Hoke. In *Lilies* the Mexican workers, the German nun, and the black handyman unite to build the chapel in spite of the skepticism of Mr. Ashton and the Catholic priest. Anti-Semitism and antiblack feelings haunt Hoke and the Werthan family and give them a common ground. Miss Daisy calls frequent attention to her daughter-in-law Florine's (Patti LuPone) obsession with gaining the acceptance of Atlanta's non-Jewish elite and comments that they ". . . wouldn't give her the time of day." Hoke takes the view that white Jewish employers are preferable to their non-Jewish counterparts. As he ascends the stairs for his job interview at Werthan Industries, he asks Boolie Werthan if he is Jewish. After Boolie responds affirmatively, Hoke declares that he prefers to be in the employ of Jewish persons. When Miss Daisy's cook Idella dies, she, Boolie, and Florine all attend the funeral service with Hoke. After Miss Daisy asks Hoke if the police know who is responsible for the bombing of her synagogue, he responds that ". . . you know as good as me, Miss Daisy, it always be the same ones." He then continues with a story of the lynching of a boyhood friend's father. To him, anti-Semitism and racism are connected, as he tells her, ". . . that mess back there put me in mind of it." Like the episode in which the two policemen slur them both, this one gives the audience the notion that an ethnic solidarity is developing between these two members of marginalized groups.

Language skills also become an issue in the two films. When Homer discovers that the sisters are trying to improve their English with dated and arcane language records, he convenes English classes after each evening's meal. *Lilies* contains several humorous scenes that portray the black man as teacher at the head of the dinner table using unorthodox but effective methods to teach the sisters how to use English. This gives the black man some margin of power—he is the one who possesses a command of the English language. However, that power is somewhat diluted because Mother Maria's English is much superior to that of the other sisters. The audience will realize early in the film that she only feigns a lack of comprehension when she doesn't want to discuss the issue at hand. In *Driving*, Miss Daisy is a retired elementary school teacher. She soon discovers that Hoke is illiterate. Although the audience is led to believe that she teaches him to read and write, very little screen time is devoted to the lessons. Hoke progresses from being unable to read the names on a tombstone to being able to read maps and the title of a workbook Miss Daisy gives him. No scenes depict the two engaged in the teaching/learning process. One plausible reason for the presence of such scenes in *Lilies* and their absence in *Driving* may be that in the former film the classes involve a group of students working with the teacher, while in the latter film such scenes would have required one-on-one contact between the teacher and her student. In other words, there is little chance of any sexual tension becoming discernible in the wholesome postdinner scenes in which Homer uses the gospel song "Amen" to teach the group of German sisters English. However, if *Driving* had depicted Miss Daisy and Hoke sitting around a table over a book, the careful distance that usually separates them would be violated.

If the Academy were to offer awards for best supporting vehicles, then Miss Daisy's series of polished, high-priced cars and Homer's reliable Plymouth would have deserved recognition. The cars become the grounds over which the characters struggle to assert their power. Hoke and Homer spend a considerable amount of screen time opening and closing doors for their respective female passengers. None of the women can drive, but they all demand as much control over the cars as the male characters will give them. Not permitted to express their masculinity in more natural ways, Hoke and Homer seem to be channeling their latent sexual impulses into the care and keeping of their cars. Homer refuses to sleep under the same roof as his hostesses in black habits; his decision to spend his nights in his trusty Plymouth is depicted as a mechanism through which he asserts his masculine independence. After the sisters persuade him to stay, they automatically assume that their use of his car is part of the deal. For the central pair in *Lilies*, resolution of their conflict over the car occurs when, prompted by the racist Ashton's cutting remarks, Homer takes the Mother Superior's arm and guides her to the front seat of the wagon, signaling their willingness to join forces in the face of outside opposition.

Hoke's position is much more tenuous since the cars belong to Miss Daisy, a fact she rarely lets him forget. She tells him what streets to use, where to park, how fast to go, and, until he forces a confrontation, she even keeps the keys with her. Predictably the confrontation occurs when his need to "make water" on their road trip interferes with her already aborted timetable. She has been oblivious to the fact that the gas stations that they have passed have not contained rest rooms open to blacks. After forbidding him from stopping the vehicle to perform a natural bodily function that no man can postpone indefinitely, Hoke for the first time verbally asserts himself and, when he leaves her alone in the car, he takes the keys. Hoke even purchases each of Miss Daisy's trade-ins as a way of establishing his own automotive autonomy. He assures Boolie that if Miss Daisy doesn't adjust to her new car, he might let her ride in her former one from time to time. The progress of their relationship can be measured in their eventual willingness to acquiesce vehicular control.

While the films omit physical intimacy, they highlight the bonds that come from sharing food. As anthropologists and other social scientists have illustrated, there are strong symbolic connections between food consumption and sexuality. While these two movies seem to lack any overt sexual tension between the characters, they do manifest symbolic couplings as the male and female characters negotiate the terms through which they will share or not share food.

Although he wants to prepare his own meals, the sisters demand that Homer Smith break bread—and little else—at the end of their table opposite the Mother Superior. In these meals and other scenes Homer and she are depicted as if they are the parents and the remaining sisters are the offspring. Because of their impoverished circumstances, the nuns have little food for themselves or their new male guest. Homer is particularly disturbed by the "Catholic" breakfast they serve him: one egg and a cup of milk. After taking them to "town" on Sunday, Homer opts to buy himself a square breakfast rather than join them in the open-air mass that the itinerant priest is performing. Later, after getting a part-time job from Mr. Ashton, Homer spends his own money on food for the whole lot of them. The Mother Superior's ambivalence about his gifts is palpable; she clearly believes that accepting his food is unseemly. She dislikes yielding to the power that the presentation of these edible gifts gives Homer in their relationship. A more Freudian scholar than myself might make much of the fact that with each grocery delivery, Homer brings lollipops to the nuns.

Although their more pronounced class differences prevent them from sharing inside meals together, nonetheless, changes in their food consumption habits mirror the growing bond between Hoke and Miss Daisy. Although she has far fewer reasons for being parsimonious, Miss Daisy initially provides very stingy meals for Hoke. She even summons Boolie to discharge Hoke for supposedly stealing a can of her salmon. Like Homer, Hoke chooses to purchase his own food, thereby asserting his masculine identity through a refusal to accept the woman's miserly offerings. As she grows to accept Hoke's place in her life, Miss Daisy relaxes her food restrictions. As mentioned earlier, the first meal the audience sees them eat together is a picnic lunch outside where social rules don't forbid such familiarity. For indoor meals, the rules still apply. After the cook dies while shelling peas, Miss Daisy and Hoke struggle together to prepare meals, only to have Hoke eat his portion in the kitchen while Miss Daisy eats hers alone in the formal dining room. Following a rare ice storm Hoke manages to drive to work in order to make sure that Miss Daisy gets her morning coffee. By the time the final scene in the film comes, the audience has been prepared to watch the pair symbolically consummate their relationship. Miss Daisy is in a nursing home, and Hoke can no longer drive so he rides with the now-portly Boolie for a holiday visit. After sending her own son away to converse with the nurses, the unsteady Miss Daisy permits Hoke tenderly to feed her a slice of Thanksgiving pie. The two pairs—Homer and Mother Maria, Hoke and Miss Daisy —grow closer as they learn how to share and sometimes surrender their desires to control the cars and the food in their lives.

Remarkable Achievements

The response of critics and audiences to these films has been largely positive. The best evidence for audience support stems from the fact that both films made enormous amounts of money. *Driving Miss Daisy* and *Lilies of the Field* are inherently likable. Simple stories without violence, they offer warm characters, engaging situations, and comfortable resolutions. Columnist Bob Greene devoted an essay to the accolades about *Driving Miss Daisy* he overheard in the movie theater in which he saw the film. His own praise was without reservation: ". . . I think it is a perfect motion picture. . . . It is funny and it is moving and it is thoughtful and I know that certain moments from it will be on my mind for years."[10]

Most white film critics, and certainly the mainstream of the motion picture industry as represented by the Academy of Motion Picture Arts and Sciences, embraced and saluted both films. Reviewing *Lilies of the Field* for the *New York Times* in 1963, Bosley Crowther concluded that "Sure it's 'Going My Way' with a Negro (and without the songs) in mood and moral. But we can do with a nice chunk of sweetness and optimism in a movie for a change."[11] In a strikingly similar comment Roger Ebert also made reference to other films when praising *Driving Miss Daisy:* "After so many films in which shallow and violent people deny their humanity and ours, what a lesson to see a film that looks into the heart."[12]

Crowther, Ebert, and numerous other critics praise *Lilies of the Field* and *Driving Miss Daisy* because they make viewers with similar sensibilities feel good about the world. Unlike other films produced in these eras, they manage to tell stories that celebrate the potential of human beings to overcome differences. Without violence, sex, or rock and roll, these "little" movies tell a message that many people want to hear—that dignity, hard work, and humor are important tools for life. According to these films, ordinary, albeit high-spirited, individuals can surmount race, class, gender, and religious barriers.

A Small Step

Although white and black came together almost effortlessly in the two films, this hasn't been the case in the critical community. While many black critics share their white counterparts' enthusiasm for the movies, some black scholars concerned with film and/or popular culture are adamant in their objections to the films. They too couch their comments about the films in terms of "other movies." However, the other movies they call their readers' attention to are the ones that depict blacks as innocuous agents of white happiness or those that feature Poitier and Freeman.

Most criticisms of *Lilies* come from commentators who compare the character of Homer Smith to other roles played by Sidney Poitier or other black actors. Black film historian Donald Bogle mentions the 1944 film *Since You Went Away*, in which maid Hattie McDaniel takes a night job in order to contribute to the support of a white family facing hard financial times. "Even in 1944 her character's obvious tom quality seemed ludicrous. Twenty years later, when Poitier took a similar part-time job for similar reasons—to help the white nuns—it seemed to black audiences, if not to white, that he was now leading the black character back in his place as a faithful servant."[13] Some blacks rejected the Homer Smith character because he, like so many of the men portrayed by Poitier and his contemporary black actors, led a sexless existence. Calvin C. Hernton maintained that

> *Lilies of the Field* is a pitiful joke. Picture this—here is a tall, regal, young black man in tight white pants that reveal his every muscle, jumping and running around with a group of nuns. (Incidentally, they are foreigners.) He even shows his naked, bulging chest. He is sexy, nobody can deny that. One need not belabor the twisted psychological subtleties of this movie. Yet I am compelled to point out that white America can let its imagination run wild, secure in the knowledge that nothing can really happen between that sexy black boy and those white nuns.[14]

These same kinds of criticism can be and have been applied to Morgan Freeman and *Driving Miss Daisy*. Many blacks were reluctant or refused to attend the film because they were offended by the prospect of seeing this distinguished actor in the role of a chauffeur who develops a platonic bond with his white female employer. Although Freeman has been featured in many prominent roles in the past few years, he, like Poitier, is rarely depicted as a "love interest."

"Sameness" is a frequent lament for those of us who monitor the roles awarded to black actors in Hollywood. In *Clara's Heart* (1988), Whoopi Goldberg is playing *another* black female domestic who changes the life of her white employers; in *Street Smart* (1987) Morgan Freeman is playing *another* threatening pimp; in *The Color Purple* (1985) Danny Glover is playing *another* brutish black man. As African-American critics before me have noted, the merits of individual performances and films become secondary. The first thought that runs through our heads is: Where and how often have we seen this characterization before? *Driving Miss Daisy* reminds us of *Lilies of the Field*, and *Lilies* reminds us of all of the films where actors with the obvious sexual appeal of Sidney Poitier and Morgan Freeman are cast in roles where their goodness is measured in their kindness to whites.

To be sure, the twenty-six years between the films can be seen most concretely in the more well-rounded character of Hoke. Unlike Homer Smith, Hoke is paid for his services at an apparently fair market rate. Although his family and private life do not figure in the foreground of the film, the audience is at least told that he has a life separate from the world of his employer. Whereas other African-American characters (including Homer Smith) are often presented in isolation, as if the sum of their lives resides in their work for their white bosses, Hoke has children and grandchildren—one who becomes a professor at Spelman College. He learns how to receive his due from Miss Daisy and Boolie and in so doing establishes a dignified life for himself in his "sunset years." Nonetheless, Hoke Colburn is as safe and nonthreatening a character as Homer Smith. The moviemaking community is clearly voicing a pernicious preference for docile, apolitical, nonthreatening black characters. With veiled sexuality as a subtext only, these films allow their audiences to witness interracial unions without having to confront African-American male virility.

Perhaps an even more sobering aspect of this analysis stems from the fact that the producers of *Lilies* and *Driving* had to struggle so diligently to get these movies made. If the people who finance motion pictures are reluctant to put up the money for films with black men as laborers and servants, it seems unlikely that they will support movies in which black leading men are depicted as professional men with, Hollywood forbid, sex lives. In his 1963 Academy Award acceptance speech, Sidney Poitier began by noting "It has been a long journey to this moment."[15] Poitier then went on to deemphasize his personal journey to the stage in favor of comments applicable to the bittersweet journey of black actors in general toward this kind of success. His speech emphasized the past, but little did he know that no other black man honored for a leading role would walk up to the Academy's stage for at least thirty years. And he probably could not have predicted that the next time a black man came even close to walking away with an Oscar in his hand would be for a role remarkably similar to that of Homer Smith. Even given the scope of the roles black actors played between 1963 and 1989, the character of Hoke Colburn represents only a small step forward for black actors. While the success enjoyed by black filmmakers such as Spike Lee, Robert Townsend, and Euzhan Palcy seems to be a positive harbinger, it still seems unlikely that the backers of Hollywood films will be more willing to accept black men in nontraditional roles. Each of these black filmmakers continues to confront financing woes with each new project. Palcy, whose 1984 film *Sugar Cane Alley* was critically acclaimed, met rejection after rejection while pitching scripts with blacks as central characters in films about apartheid. Commenting on the situation she said, "It is a hell of a problem to get a film made with black characters in Hollywood. I had a story with black characters but nobody would produce that, so if I wanted to make a film about apartheid, I had to find another solution."[16] Her solution was to give Hollywood what it thinks the audiences will accept, benevolent whites working with nonthreatening blacks to make the world a better place. Given the nearly intractable resistance of those in power to challenge the status quo in Hollywood, it seems reasonable to assume that the future will offer more of the same.

In defending his decision to accept the role of Hoke, Morgan Freeman noted that the playwright based the character on a real African-American man. And like so many of us, the distinguished actor had family members who worked at service jobs in order to provide for their children. He is right, of course; most black people don't have to go too far back in their history to locate members who have worn the uniforms of domestic service. The problem stems from the movie industry's love affair with a limited number of roles for its black leading men. In the years between the making of *Lilies of the Field* and *Driving Miss Daisy*, African Americans have made giant steps in seeking equality. Ironically, many of Hollywood's white producers, directors, and actors have taken public positions in favor of African-American causes. Although willing to preach publicly on the virtues of guaranteeing blacks access to all areas of American life, they have been reluctant to depict the complexities of the black experience for the post-*Lilies* black generation. Sidney Poitier first commented on Hollywood's tenacious attachment for docile blacks in 1952. As of this writing in 1993, important changes have taken place in the real world, but the reel world hasn't chronicled them.

Notes

Part 1 Introduction

1. Randy Shilts, "Two Black Statues Stir a Tempest in White Tiburon," *San Francisco Chronicle*, 31 July 1984, 2.

2. Bob Hohler, "A Window on Racism," *Boston Globe*, 20 June 1991, 1, 17.

3. Ibid., 17.

Chapter 1: Contemptible Collectibles

1. Letter to Ann Landers, November 3, 1982. To her credit, Landers consulted several experts who confirmed her suspicion that tales of the servant's death were, in fact, legends.

2. Unless otherwise noted, all of the jokes, riddles, rhymes, and other forms of verbally transmitted folklore contained in this book are archived in the University of California—Berkeley Folklore Archives.

3. A representative portion of Janette Faulkner's collection was on display from October to December 1982 at the Berkeley Art Center. Faulkner graciously allowed me to interview her and generously shared her insights.

4. Harriet Beecher Stowe, *Uncle Tom's Cabin* (New York: New American Library, 1966), 258.

5. Robert C. Toll, *Blacking Up: The Minstrel Show in America* (New York: Oxford University Press, 1974), 69.

6. *Ethnic Notions*, Exhibition catalog (Berkeley, CA: Berkeley Art Center, 1982), 23.

7. Douglas Congdon-Martin, *Images in Black: 150 Years of Black Collectibles* (West Chester, PA: Schiffer Publishing Ltd., 1990), 121.

8. Jackie Young, *Black Collectables: Mammy and Her Friends* (West Chester, PA: Schiffer Publishing Ltd., 1988), 5–6.

Chapter 2: Alligator Bait

1. See Elsie Clews Parsons, *Folk-lore of the Sea Islands, South Carolina* (New York: Memoirs of the American Folklore Society, 1923).

2. Jay Mechling, "The Alligator," in Angus K. Gillespie and Jay Mechling, eds., *Symbolic American Wildlife* (Knoxville: University of Tennessee Press, 1987), 90.

3. Robert C. Toll, *Blacking Up: The Minstrel Show in Nineteenth Century America* (New York: Oxford University Press, 1974), 7–8.

4. Charles C. Jones, *Negro Myths From the Georgia Coast* (Boston: Houghton Mifflin and Company, 1888), 149.

5. See Joel Chandler Harris, *Nights With Uncle Remus* (Boston: Houghton Mifflin and Company, 1883), and *The Complete Tales of Uncle Remus* (Boston: Houghton Mifflin and Company, 1955).

6. Florence E. Baer, *Sources and Analogues of the Uncle Remus Tales*, Folklore Fellows Communications, no. 228. 145–146.

7. John Muir, *A Thousand Mile Walk to the Gulf* (Boston: Houghton Mifflin Company, 1981), 96.

8. Robert Farris Thompson, *Flash of the Spirit: African and Afro-American Art and Philosophy* (New York: Vintage Books, 1984), xiv.

9. Personal communication.

10. Daryl C. Dance, *Folklore from Contemporary Jamaicans* (Knoxville: University of Tennessee Press, 1985), 14–15; 16–17; 102–103.

11. Jones, *Negro Myths*, 143–144.

12. Zora Neale Hurston, *Dust Tracks on the Road* (Urbana: University of Illinois Press, 1984), 81.

13. Mahalia Jackson with Evan Mcleod Wylie, *Movin' On Up* (New York: Avon Books, 1969), 27.

14. Roger D. Abrahams, "The Negro Stereotype: Negro Folklore and the Riots," *Journal of American Folklore* (1970), 234.

15. Susan Johnson, folklore archivist at Indiana University, sent me two variants of this joke, including one in which President Jimmy Carter was the "hero."

16. Alan Dundes, "The Curious Case of the Wide-Mouth Frog," in Alan Dundes, ed., *Interpreting Folklore* (Bloomington: Indiana University Press, 1980), 62–69.

17. Mechling, "The Alligator," 8.

18. For further discussion of the alligator-in-the-sewer legend, see Jan Harold Brunvand, *The Vanishing Hitchhiker* (New York: Norton, 1981), 90–101.

19. This story was reprinted from the *San Francisco Chronicle*, 19 May 1984, 1.

Chapter 3: Back to the Kitchen

1. Catherine Clinton, *The Plantation Mistress: Woman's World in the Old South* (New York: Pantheon Books, 1982), 201–202.

2. Robert C. Toll, *Blacking Up: The Minstrel Show in Nineteenth Century America* (New York: Oxford University Press, 1974), 79.

3. Harriet Beecher Stowe, *Uncle Tom's Cabin* (New York: New American Library, 1966), 31.

4. Ibid., 37.

5. Deborah Gray White, *Ar'nt I a Woman?: Female Slaves in the Plantation South* (New York: W.W. Norton, 1987), 14.

6. E. Bruce Kirkham, *The Building of Uncle Tom's Cabin* (Knoxville: University of Tennessee Press, 1977), 190–191.

7. Jackie Young, *Black Collectibles: Mammy and Her Friends* (West Chester, PA: Schiffer Publishing Ltd., 1988), 7.

8. Susan Strasser, *Satisfaction Guaranteed: The Making of the American Mass Market* (New York: Pantheon Books, 1989), 182–183.

9. Ida B. Wells, *Crusade for Justice: The Autobiography of Ida B. Wells* (Chicago: University of Chicago Press, 1970), 117.

10. Daniel J. Leab, *From Sambo to Superspade: The Black Experience in Motion Pictures* (Boston: Houghton Mifflin Company, 1976), 107.

11. White, *Ar'nt I a Woman?*, 165.

12. Jo Ann Gibson Robinson, *The Montgomery Bus Boycott and the Women Who Started It: The Memoir of Jo Ann Gibson Robinson* (Knoxville: University of Tennessee Press, 1987), 107.

13. Trudier Harris, *From Mammies to Militants: Domestics in Black American Literature* (Philadelphia: Temple University Press, 1982).

14. Interview with Hal Kanter in *Color Adjustment*, documentary produced by Marlon Riggs and Vivian Kleiman, 1991.

Part 2 Introduction

1. Winthrop D. Jordan, *White Over Black: American Attitudes Toward the Negro, 1550–1812* (Baltimore: Penguin Books, 1969), 6.

2. Ibid., 7.

Chapter 4: The Troping of Uncle Tom

1. This particular class discussion took place prior to the testimony of Anita Hill.

2. Wilson Jeremiah Moses, *Black Messiahs and Uncle Toms: Social and Literary Manipulations of a Religious Myth* (University Park: The Pennsylvania State University Press, 1993), xii–xiii.

3. Richard Yarborough, "Strategies of Black Characterization in Uncle Tom's Cabin and the Early Afro-American," in Eric J. Sundquist, ed., *New Essays on Uncle Tom's Cabin* (Cambridge: Cambridge University Press, 1986), 46.

4. A component of the Compromise of 1850, the Fugitive Slave Law obligated Northern law enforcement officials to seek out runaway slaves and return them to the South.

5. Quoted in E. Bruce Kirkham, *The Building of Uncle Tom's Cabin* (Knoxville: University of Tennessee Press, 1977), 64.

6. For an excellent discussion of antebellum attitudes about race, see Stephen Jay Gould's *The Mismeasure of Man* (New York: W.W. Norton, 1981).

7. Harriet Beecher Stowe, *Uncle Tom's Cabin or Life Among the Lowly* (New York: New American Library, 1966), 479. All subsequent references will be to this edition.

8. Ibid., 32.

9. Ibid., 164.

10. Ibid., 439.

11. Harry Birdoff, *The World's Greatest Hit: Uncle Tom's Cabin* (New York: S.F. Vanni, 1947), 21.

12. Ibid., 42. Although they are presented as a direct quote in the text, it is unlikely that these are Thurmon's actual words.

13. George Aiken, *Uncle Tom's Cabin in American Melodrama* (New York: Performing Arts Journal Publications, 1983).

14. Birdoff, *World's Greatest Hit*, 225.

15. Quoted in Daniel J. Leab, *From Sambo to Superspade: The Black Experience in Motion Pictures* (Boston: Houghton Mifflin and Company, 1976), 13.

16. Donald Bogle, *Toms, Coons, Mulattoes, Mammies & Bucks: An Interpretive History of Blacks in American Films* (New York: Continuum, 1989), 4–6.

17. Booker T. Washington, *Up From Slavery* in *Three Negro Classics* (New York: Avon, 1965), 148.

18. Moses, *Black Messiahs and Uncle Toms*, 62.

19. W.E.B. DuBois, *The Souls of Black Folks* in *Three Negro Classics*, 209.

20. Ida B. Wells, *Crusade for Justice: The Autobiography of Ida B. Wells* (Chicago: University of Chicago Press, 1970), 376.

21. Leab, *From Sambo to Superspade*, 19. Leab acknowledges that other forces may have contributed to this ban, but states that Congress acted only after a black man beat a white one.

22. Thomas P. Riggio, "Uncle Tom Reconstructed: A Neglected Chapter in the History of a Book," in Elizabeth Ammons, ed., *Critical Essays on Harriet Beecher Stowe* (Boston: G.K. Hall, 1980), 143.

23. For an extended discussion of the resurgence of interest in the Ku Klux Klan following *The Birth of a Nation*, see Wyn Craig Wade, *The Fiery Cross: The Ku Klux Klan in America* (New York: Touchstone, 1987), 119–139.

24. Bogle, *Toms, Coons, Mulattoes, Mammies & Bucks*, 47.

25. Peter Noble, *The Negro in Films* (London: British Yearbooks, Ltd., n.d.), 32.

26. Ralph Ellison, *Invisible Man* (New York: Vintage Books, 1989), xvi.

27. Robert Alexander, "I Ain't Yo' Uncle: The New Jack Revisionist 'Uncle Tom's Cabin,' " ms. copyright 1990, 1991, S.F. Mime Troupe Touring Version, 3.

28. Ibid., 59.

Chapter 5: Jacksonalia

1. I hope I'm not aggravating too many readers by incorporating sports under the umbrella of entertainment.

2. J. Randy Taraborrelli, *Michael Jackson: The Magic and the Madness* (New York: Birch Lane Press, 1991), 322.

3. Reggie Jackson with Mike Lupica, *Reggie* (New York: Ballantine Books, 1985), 125.

4. Jan Harold Brunvand, *The Choking Doberman and Other "New" Urban Legends* (New York: W.W. Norton, 1984), 20.

5. Brunvand's data confirms my own.

6. One account of Jackson's behavior is contained in Ralph David Abernathy, *And the Walls Came Tumbling Down* (New York: Harper & Row, 1989), 477.

7. Alan Dundes, "Six Inches From the Presidency: The Gary Hart Jokes as Public Opinion," *Western Folklore* 48 (1989): 43–51.

8. Fred Barnes, "The Jackson Tour," *New Republic*, 30 July 1984, 18–21.

Chapter 6: Everything Is Not Satisfactual

1. Toni Morrison, *Playing in the Dark: Whiteness and the Literary Imagination* (New York: Vintage Books, 1993), xi.

2. Ibid., 14–15.

3. For a discussion of Disney decision making following Walt's death, see John Taylor, *Storming the Magic Kingdom: Wall Street, the Raiders, and the Battle for Disney* (London: Viking, 1988).

4. The Brothers Grimm did not write these fairy tales. Their collections contain *versions* collected from the folk. The Grimm versions are often tamer than versions in other collections. Folklorists recognize Snow White as AT (Aarne-Thompson) 709. Folklorist Stith Thompson translated Anti Aarne's folktale type index into English. The volume contains an exhaustive list of folktale plots. Snow White is found in the "ordinary folktale" section of the index.

5. Marc Elliot, *Walt Disney: Hollywood's Dark Prince* (New York: Birch Lane Press, 1993), 102.

6. The racially charged content of Helen Bannerman's story of a black child with neglectful parents is self-evident. Both the Mary Poppins and Doctor Doolittle book series were replete with derogatory racial references, most of which have been removed during the past couple of decades. For a discussion of these books, see Jan Nederveen Pietrese, *White on Black: Images of Africa and Blacks in Western Popular Culture* (New Haven, CT: Yale University Press, 1992), 166–167.

7. Donald Bogle, *Toms, Coons, Mulattoes, Mammies & Bucks: An Interpretive History of Blacks in American Films* (New York: Continuum, 1989), 39–44.

8. Ibid., 43.

Chapter 7: In Search of the Young, Gifted, and Black

1. Lorraine Hansberry, *To Be Young, Gifted and Black: Lorraine Hansberry in Her Own Words*, adapted by Robert Nemiroff (Englewood Cliffs, NJ: Prentice-Hall, 1969), 217.

2. Storylines on these themes can be seen in other situation comedies and several short-lived series also fall into these categories. The series that will be discussed are those that by virtue of their relative longevity on network prime-time television can be described as "popular." I am also using the concept of family in a narrow way to include only those television families in which a child is in school. Consequently, the popular program *Sanford and Son* is not considered here because the "son" is an adult.

3. Melvin Patrick Ely, *The Adventures of Amos 'n' Andy: A Social History of an American Phenomenon* (New York: Macmillan, 1991), 215–216.

4. Much to the dismay of the NAACP, the *Amos 'n' Andy* show did have a following among some black viewers. By the same token, some Northern as well as many Southern NBC affiliates refused to carry *The Nat "King" Cole Show.*

5. Interview with Kanter in *Color Adjustment* produced by Marlon Riggs and Vivian Kleiman, 1991.

6. "Julia," *Ebony*, November 1968, 59.

7. Interview with Diahann Carroll in *Color Adjustment*.

8. Ibid.

9. Todd Gitlin, *Inside Prime Time* (New York: Pantheon Books, 1985), 125.

10. Herman Gray, "Television and the New Black Man: Black Images in Prime-time Situation Comedy," *Media, Culture and Society* 8 (1986): 223–242.

11. F.O. Shyllon, *Black Slaves in Britain* (London: Oxford University Press, 1974), 12.

12. It could be argued that the inability of Todd Bridges, Gary Coleman, and Emmanuel Lewis to maintain their popularity into adulthood is not much different from the problem faced by so many child actors, white and black. However, while some white child actors, such as Ron Howard, manage to escape the fate of the majority, as yet no blacks have done so. The only possible example is Sammy Davis, Jr., who appeared in some movies as a child and enjoyed enormous success as an adult. He was, however, short.

13. Interview with Norman Lear in *Color Adjustment*.

Chapter 8: Ethnic Aliens

1. Alan Dundes and Roger D. Abrahams, "Of Elephantasy and Elephanticide," in Alan Dundes, ed., *Analytic Essays in Folklore* (The Hague: Mouton and Co., 1975), 192–205. Readers are encouraged to consult this remarkable study in order to fully understand the breadth of the elephant joke cycle and the depth of the authors' analysis of it. In a similar vein see Alan Dundes, "The Curious Case of the Wide-Mouth Frog," in Alan Dundes, ed., *Interpreting Folklore* (Bloomington: Indiana University Press, 1980), 62–68.

2. Ibid, p. 200.

Chapter 10: From Real Blacks to Reel Blacks

1. See Seth Cagin and Philip Dray, *We Are Not Afraid: The Story of Goodman, Schwerner, and Chaney and the Civil Rights Campaign for Mississippi* (New York: Macmillan, 1988) and Kenneth O'Reilly, *Racial Matters: The FBI's Secret File on Black America 1960–1972* (New York: Free Press, 1989).

2. J. E. White, "Just Another Mississippi Whitewash," *Time*, 9 January 1989, 61.

3. Pauline Kael, "The Current Cinema," *The New Yorker*, 26 December 1988, 73–75.

4. Brent Staples, "Cinematic Segregation in a Story about Civil Rights," *New York Times*, 8 January 1989, 13.

5. Mike Royko, "Deep-thinking Film Critics Miss Point," *The Brockton Enterprise*, 19 January 1989, 18.

6. Ibid., 18.

7. Vincent Canby, "Mississippi Burning: A Painful Time," *New York Times*, 8 January 1989, 13.

8. Ibid., 13.

9. Ibid., 13.

10. See Corporal James Henry Gooding, *On the Altar of Freedom: A Black Soldier's Civil War Letters From the Front* (Amherst: University of Massachusetts Press, 1991).

11. Carl J. Cruz, "Sergeant William H. Carney, Civil War Hero" in Eleanor Wachs, ed., *It Wasn't in Her Lifetime But It Was Handed Down: Four Black Oral Histories of Massachusetts* (Boston: Office of the Massachusetts Secretary of State, 1989), 8, 9.

12. Clyde Taylor, "Discursive Violence: The Dialectical Irony of the Relations of Domination," 1988 unpublished manuscript.

Chapter 11: Of Primates, Porters, and Potables: Images of Africa on Screen

1. Donna Haraway, *Primate Visions: Gender, Race, and Nature in the World of Modern Science* (New York: Routledge, 1989).

2. James R. Nesteby, *Black Images in American Films 1896–1954: The Interplay Between Civil Rights and Film Culture* (Lanham, MD: University Press of America, 1982), 145.

3. Roger Ebert, *Roger Ebert's Movie Home Companion 1991 Edition* (Kansas City: Andrews and McMeel, 1991), 228.

4. Shawn Slovo, *A World Apart* (London: Faber and Faber, 1988), ix.

5. Ebert, *Roger Ebert's Movie Home Companion 1991 Edition*, 656.

6. For interesting behind-the-scenes looks at the making of this movie, see Katherine Hepburn, *The Making of the African Queen: Or How I Went to Africa with Bogart, Bacall and Huston and Almost Lost My Mind* (New York: New American Library, 1987).

7. Ibid., 68.

8. Haraway, *Primate Visions*, 155.

9. Fossey gives few clues about the source of her attachment to animals. She does, however, quote from *The Yearling* and draw an analogy between the antics of pets in her campsite and those in "a Walt Disney movie." Dian Fossey, *Gorillas in the Mist* (Boston: Houghton Mifflin and Company, 1983), 132.

10. Ibid., 19.

11. Peter Viertel, *White Hunter, Black Heart* (New York: Bantam Books, 1954), 42.

Chapter 12: From Homer to Hoke: A Small Step for African-American Mankind

1. William Hoffman, *Sidney* (New York: Lyle Stuart, 1971), 89.

2. Gary Null, *Black Hollywood: The Black Performer in Motion Pictures.* (Secaucus, NJ: Citadel Press, 1975), 185–186.

3. Edward Mapp, *Blacks in American Films: Today and Yesterday* (Metuchen, NJ: Scarecrow Press, 1972), 68.

4. Murray Schumach, "Hollywood Wary on Charges by the N.A.A.C.P.," *New York Times*, 27 June 1963, 10.

5. Larry Glenn, "Hollywood Change: Negroes Gain in a New Movie and Elsewhere," *New York Times*, 22 September 1963.

6. Mapp, *Blacks in American Films*, 69.

7. Ralph Nelson, "Considering 'Lilies of the Field,' " *New York Times*, 29 September 1963.

8. Patricia A. Turner, "Tainted Glory: Truth and Fiction in Contemporary Hollywood," *Trotter Institute Review* 4 (Summer 1990): 5–9.

9. Paul Chutkow, "He's Got an Eye for the Prize," *New York Times*, 8 April 1990, 15.

10. Bob Greene, "Audience Will Find the Right Movie," *Chicago Tribune*, 21 January 1990, 1.

11. Bosley Crowther, "Lilies of the Field" movie review, *New York Times*, 2 October 1963, 51.

12. Roger Ebert, *Roger Ebert's Movie Home Companion 1991 Edition* (Kansas City: Andrews and McMeel, 1991), 158.

13. Donald Bogle, *Toms, Coons, Mulattoes, Mammies & Bucks* (New York: Continuum, 1989), 216.

14. Calvin C. Hernton, *White Papers for White Americans* (Garden City, NY: Doubleday, 1966), 65.

15. Hoffman, *Sidney*, 147.

16. Ebert, *Roger Ebert's Movie Home Companion*, 656.

Index

About the Author

PATRICIA A. TURNER is Associate Professor of African-American and African Studies and of American Studies at the University of California, Davis. She served as consulting scholar on the documentaries *Ethnic Notions* and *Color Adjustment*. She is the author of *I Heard It Through the Grapevine: Rumor in African-American Culture*.